Phil Tufnell was born in Barnet in 1966 and played cricket for Middlesex and England between 1986 and 2002, winning 42 Test caps and taking 121 wickets. Since retiring from the game, he has become a hugely popular summariser on *Test Match Special*, a team captain on *A Question of Sport* since 2008 and in 2003 he won *I'm a Celebrity . . . Get Me out of Here!*

John Woodhouse, who worked with Phil Tufnell on the writing of the book, is a journalist, broadcaster and sports writer. He has also worked with Graeme Fowler, Steve Harmison, Rob Key and James Taylor on their autobiographies.

How Not to Be a Cricketer

Phil Tufnell

**SIMON &
SCHUSTER**

London · New York · Sydney · Toronto · New Delhi

First published in Great Britain by Simon & Schuster UK Ltd, 2021
This edition published in Great Britain by Simon & Schuster UK Ltd, 2022

1 3 5 7 9 10 8 6 4 2

Simon & Schuster UK Ltd
1st Floor
222 Gray's Inn Road
London WC1X 8HB

www.simonandschuster.co.uk
www.simonandschuster.com.au
www.simonandschuster.co.in

Simon & Schuster Australia, Sydney
Simon & Schuster India, New Delhi

A CIP catalogue record for this book
is available from the British Library

Paperback ISBN: 978-1-4711-9457-3
eBook ISBN: 978-1-4711-9456-6

Typeset in Bembo by M Rules
Printed and bound by CPI Group (UK) Ltd, Croydon, CR0 4YY

MIX
Paper from
responsible sources
FSC® C171272

To Mum and Dad for pointing me in the right direction, and to my lovely wife Dawn for being always by my side

CONTENTS

INTRODUCTION

I'm cleaning out the sheds (that's sheds plural – Phil Tufnell is very much a two-sheds man). Amazing how lockdown makes you do things you would run a million miles from in normal times. As I venture into the darkness, the sheer horror of the abandoned junk before me, illuminated only by the few specks of sunlight able to penetrate the parts of the window that aren't encrusted in cobwebs, and my eyes become better accustomed to the light, I see a looming bulk before me. It's either that big round rock from the start of *Raiders of the Lost Ark* or it's – no, it can't be – a stack of coffins. I'm waiting to hear the door slam behind me and the dulcet tones of Peter Cushing when I spot some words on the side of one of them – 'Philip Tufnell – Australia tour 1990'. Cricket coffins. I force my way past some loppers, a dead lawnmower and a befuddled vole, and there before me are the relics of my previous life. Fifteen of them.

I drag them out one by one, set them out on the lawn, take a deep breath and tentatively begin peering inside. Laid out before me is my cricket career – kit, caps, bats (not heavily used), all sorts of stuff. Lid after creaking lid, zip after stubborn zip release not only several large moths but a host of memories – Christ, that was the tour when ... Bloody hell, that was the bat ... Wow, that was the ball from ...

And then, hang on! It can't be! That's the willow the rest of the England boys signed for me on my debut. That squiggle says David Gower. Who else have we got? Robin Smith, Goochy, Alec Stewart. Even Jack Russell put his Weetabix down for five seconds to scribble something. And what's this? No way! My cricket shirt, the light blue one, from the World Cup in 1992. I wonder if I still fit in it.

Hang on, Dawn's shouting – 'Phil, why are you stripping off in the shed?'

There is just so much of this stuff. And as I rummage through it, piling it up, separating it out, one question occupies my mind above all others. How the hell did I survive in cricket so long that I managed to accrue all this? I was the model cricketer – if anyone wanted to know how not to be one. And yet here was undeniable proof of my longevity.

Truth is, I was a professional for nearly two decades. That time included more ups and downs than the big dipper at Margate and more bumps than the dodgems next door. And yet somehow I climbed off the ride unblemished. I survived to walk away on my own terms.

Not only that, but I played 42 Tests for England, on some of the biggest stages in world sport, met incredible people, made amazing friends and travelled the globe. For someone who never quite fitted the mould, I was actually pretty good at not being a cricketer.

Makes sense, then, to provide my own blueprint for a life, sporting or otherwise, for those who somehow always seem to end up doing things differently, for those who never read the rules, for those who wake up at half past nine wondering where the hell they are and realising they should have been somewhere very important at half past eight.

Of course, there's another way of describing this venture – a book full of hellish and terrible mistakes. Phil Tufnell's a cricketer? Come off it. Get him out of here!

CHAPTER 1

How Not to Keep Your Head Down

I was always being blamed. 'Come off it, Athers. I wasn't even there. I was at the hotel having a shower. That might look like my leopard-print thong, but I think you'll find it's lacking the crushed velvet lining and is a size too small.'

I'm still expecting it now. A minor dispute will kick off in the dressing room at Melbourne, they'll CSI the area and they'll find a fingerprint from 25 years ago. Honestly, I'm surprised I didn't get done for Sandpapergate.

My problem was I was always 'in the vicinity'. *Phil Tufnell – In the Vicinity* is the Netflix show begging to be made. A sort of *X-Files* for a new generation. 'But it can't be true – how can he possibly have been in so many places at once?'

It really did feel sometimes as if every disaster, on and off the pitch, could be traced back to me. It was like I was a blame magnet. One Middlesex game we were skittled for next to nothing. The entire batting line-up had failed and Gatt blamed it on me for being run out for two. Everyone else had come trudging back in and he hadn't said a word. As soon as

I appeared, he launched into the kind of bollocking usually reserved for new recruits on the army parade ground. Maybe he was right. For me, a double hundred was always just around the corner.

Off the pitch it would be exactly the same. I'd go into a bar after a game. Some chap would offer to buy me a drink. I'd have a quick half and be on my way. I'd go to the same place two days later and no sooner had I stepped over the threshold than someone would shout, 'Oi! Tuffers! Dave saw you in here two days ago and you were dancing on the tables at midnight.' I was always said to have been doing a whole lot more than I actually did. Honest.

Whenever there was a bit of a rumpus, a bit of controversy, an odd or much-mentioned moment in the cricketing firmament, so often I seemed to be there or thereabouts. It was as if I was in *Quantum Leap*, only instead of our bemused hero finding himself in one episode at JFK's assassination and the next at the California Gold Rush, I would find myself in Australia watching David Gower buzzing an England match in a Tiger Moth or in South Africa hearing Hansie Cronje make his infamous declaration offer to get a result at Centurion. I don't know what it was. I always just seemed to be there, like a little meerkat, peeping out of its burrow seeing what was going on. And I'm not just talking about cricket. Even now, I'm the sort of chap who could be happily queuing up at the bank only for some bloke to run in with a mask and a sawn-off shotgun, see the police screeching up outside and chuck me the gun. I'd end up with 15 police-issue rifles being pointed at me while being told 'not to try any funny business' and to get on the floor.

'No, it wasn't me! I was just withdrawing twenty quid when this bloke threw me the gun.'

'Come on, sonny. Don't be a fool.' And there I'd be, staring at 25 years in the Scrubs.

Okay, I know what you're saying. 'Yes, but, Phil, quite a lot of the time it was your fault.' And okay, I agree, sometimes those vicinities were of my own making. But I'll tell you this: at least 2 per cent of them weren't.

You have to believe me, I just had an uncanny knack of being in the wrong place at the wrong time. When, at Adelaide, just days after the Tiger Moth incident, Gower flicked a legside ball from Craig McDermott lazily down the throat of a grateful Merv Hughes, not only was it a terrible shot but he'd given his wicket away right on the stroke of lunch, one of the game's greatest cardinal sins. Accompanying him on the plod back to the dressing room was his irate captain, Graham Gooch.

Fearing the imminent explosion, everyone stayed well clear of the dressing room. Except me – because I happened to be having a kip on the physio's bench when they both walked in. While I'd missed the incident, at that moment dreaming about being chased by a jacket potato, it wasn't hard to tell something was amiss. The 20° drop in temperature was a giveaway. I knew I was screwed. If I got up and walked out it would look like I wasn't bothered. If I stayed it would look like I was earwigging. All I could do, as I slowly dragged a towel over my head, was desperately hope they hadn't seen me. It could have been worse. Had I been on my feet, I would have had to pretend to be a hatstand. My frozen form convinced no one. When the storm simmered slightly, Gooch looked towards me – 'And as for you, Tufnell . . .'

'No,' I was thinking, 'leave me alone. I was just in the vicinity.'

A similar thing happened on the next Ashes tour when Athers

declared at Sydney with Graeme Hick 98 not out. Myself and the other players were sitting on the balcony waiting for him to reach the landmark, so when Athers called him in two runs short, most of the boys, knowing there was likely to be a scene of some unpleasantness in the dressing room, stayed out there to let the dust settle. Me being me, I just blithely wandered back inside and started getting ready to field. I was sat there putting my socks on in the midst of this terrible friction. There I was, once again, in the vicinity.

Even retirement was no shield against it happening. After the 2005 Ashes, I was asked to make a light-hearted video about the mess the Aussies had made of the summer. It included all the big-hitters – Ricky Ponting's disastrous decision to insert the home side in the second Test, Shane Warne's dropping of Kevin Pietersen at The Oval and Adam Gilchrist's sudden inability to hit the ball. I thought the clip, done off-the-cuff down my local, was going to be used in-house by some company or other.

What happens next? I'm lying in bed and my phone starts going mad. The video I'd assumed would be watched by about 15 people had in fact come up on the big screen at the Allan Border Medal, the biggest night of the Australian cricket year. Among those sat open-mouthed and deeply unimpressed was Australian captain Ricky Ponting. Within seconds it had become the talk of the night and was all over the media. Between switching off the telly and slipping under the duvet, I'd somehow become Australia's public enemy number one. I had visions of Qantas taking multiple bookings from irate Aussies wanting to fly over to strangle me. I tried to brazen it out, asking what had happened to the famous Aussie sense of humour, but I think I was only truly forgiven when, for the Allan Border Medal the following year, I ate a massive dose of humble pie in a video laughing at England's own failings in our 5-0 defeat.

I can trace my relationship with trouble back to one day 47 years ago. I had been selected to swim for my school at a competition. In my infancy, I had mastered the crawl, but to me it seemed a bit of a workaday stroke, the sort of thing anyone can do, just up from the true tedium of breaststroke. In my eyes, the glamour boys of the chlorine were the ones who did butterfly. That great revolution of arms between gulps of air. Plus, there was some epic splashing. It was the occasion of this competition that I chose to switch to my new favourite stroke. In hindsight, I can see it wasn't a great idea. By the time I reached halfway, at least half the pool's contents were in my stomach and three PE teachers from various north London schools had jumped in to save me. On the plus side, it was a memorable day out.

Dad was picking me up. A fit young lad had departed his vehicle two hours earlier; now crawling back in was a half-drowned rat. Understandably, he wanted an explanation, the problem being he didn't like the one he got. Fair to say there was a bit of a 'debate', which resulted in him stopping the car and ordering me to take the Tube. His thought process was that he would pick me up a little way down the line; that putting a bit of distance between us was a good cooling-down move. He hadn't quite reckoned on the extent of the distance. I ended up not a couple of stations along, but in police custody.

A minor contretemps had arisen over my ticket. I had one but, as kids are prone to do, had chewed and generally mutilated it to the point where, when the inspector asked to see it, I was able only to produce what looked like a small pigeon dropping. The bloke could have listened to sense, but 1970s ticket inspectors had a reputation for being a little shirty and this one was no different. He insisted on the full weight of the law being brought crashing down on me. I believe he cruised the Northern Line basing himself loosely on 'Hanging' Judge Jeffreys. The noose being seen as a little OTT for juvenile ticketing offences, I was issued a stiff talking to and a small fine. But the entire episode had confirmed something in me from an early age – trouble can often come looking for you even if you don't go looking for it.

Five decades on and I can give little Phil a pat on the head – 'Well done, mate, you certainly got that one right.'

CHAPTER 2

How Not to Make a First Impression

I was sat in the chair at 'Slasher' Harry's, your friendly community barber. As he squeezed the life out of me, attaching the nylon hair cover to my neck, and pinged a small globule of saliva into his spittoon, I reflected that this wasn't a position I particularly wished to be in.

Dad hadn't been hugely impressed with my latest transformation. It had started with getting my ear pierced. Well, I say 'pierced' – that actually makes it sound quite professional – it was more like an act of mutilation performed by a mate. Only 14, we were too young to have the deed done properly and so applied ice cubes to the relevant lobe, heated a knitting needle to furnace temperature, and whacked it straight through. I had eight holes, so haphazard that there were safety pins and studs sticking out at all angles. And only in one ear. It was like having a chandelier on the side of my head. It weighed me down on one side. I did initially use plasters to cover my adornments when

Dad was around, but eventually I gave up. Even if he hadn't spotted them, the smell of pus would have given them away.

As expected, Dad gave me a bit of stick. 'What do you think you're doing? Only girls have earrings.'

But what really annoyed him was my Mohican. The same mate had razored both sides, left a strip of long hair down the middle, slapped on the sugar water (with added green food colouring), and created this enormous half-wheel of spiked hair.

I opened the front door and Dad was stood there. He stared at me for 15 seconds before regaining the power of speech – 'What the f***?' He gave me a clip round the ear, his mood not lightening when he ripped a fingernail on a stud.

'The tartan bondage trousers and the earrings are one thing,' he told me, 'but I ain't having that.' With which he marched me straight down to Slasher's.

'Harry!' he barked. 'Get rid of it!' I was a Mohican on Monday and a skinhead on Tuesday.

I could be – shall we say 'different'? – on the cricket pitch, too. I reached the first team at Southgate Cricket Club quite quickly, which meant I was playing in the Middlesex League, a high standard, at a very young age. These were hardened campaigners, blokes often in their thirties and forties who'd been doing this stuff for years. No wonder they looked at this scrawny little kid with the ball in his hand and thought, 'I've been playing this game for twenty-five years. I'll soon show him who's boss.'

But I wasn't going to run up and meekly be their patsy. From the off, I'd give them a bit of jip, trying to put them off their stroke. 'Come on then, you silly old bastard. Why don't you have a go?' And it worked. Down the wicket they'd charge and be stumped.

Club cricket has changed, thankfully, but at that point there were definitely players around who felt the need to flex their muscles. There was a lot of 'Who do you think you are, young man?' Such a funny attitude. 'What, I'm supposed to be in awe of you because you're older than me? Sorry, mate, but that's not actually how life works.' If I could make monkeys out of them by holding one back or pitching one on leg stump and hitting off then I was going to do it.

Often in league cricket it felt as if there was an established network of characters who shouldn't be unduly rattled. 'If you're playing at X club, then don't upset Y.' That was a red rag to a bull. I made it my business to make sure they were the first people I pissed off. I didn't quite understand why they had this protective screen around them.

'Listen, pal,' I'd say, 'you shouldn't even be here.' Only when I got older did I realise some people were respected because of their overall immersion in the club. Maybe it wouldn't even exist without that person. Those things can go unseen when you're young.

At that stage, I was also quite a singular character in a team environment. At Southgate we had a very hard captain in the Yorkshireman Micky Dunn. I had a few run-ins with Micky and there were times when Dad had to come down to smooth things over. Micky's main bugbear was that he reckoned I lost concentration in the field. He was always accusing me of having a fag and a lie-down at third man. Micky's ire was also reserved for Teddington Cricket Club. They used to have a few young Surrey boys, while Southgate always had the Middlesex lads, like myself, and I think a bit of niggle stemmed from there.

We had a cup match against Teddington and batting was Micky's nemesis, the man who riled him more than any other, well on the way to seeing his team home. I'd not had a bad day, but I'd had a bit of a set-to with Micky over a shoddy bit of fielding. He'd lost his rag at me and I'd lost mine back. I was just mulling this over when I saw the ball coming my way. In a seamless flowing movement, almost balletic in its execution, I picked it up and shied at the stumps. Micky's arch-enemy was left floundering halfway down the track as the bails went flying. 'Go on then!' I shouted. 'F***ing have some of that!', causing at least half a dozen spectators to choke on their sandwiches. Next thing I knew, this big, gruff Yorkshireman was lifting me off my feet and embracing me like a baby. And then the rest of the boys were all over me, too. Instead of me being this separate figure, it became an all-for-one moment. The penny dropped that it wasn't all about me, or at least it began its long and sometimes circuitous journey.

It was Jack Robertson, ex of Middlesex and England, who had shown me how to bowl spin.

'Phil,' the Middlesex Colts coach told the 11-year-old me, 'hold the ball like this and then pretend you're turning a door handle.' I did exactly as described, the ball spun and it felt pretty good. Up to that point, I was more interested in being one of the fast men, whistling the ball past batsmen's noses, sending them flat on their arses. I'd seen that on TV and it looked particularly good fun. Jack, however, gave me something to consider. 'There's lots of quick bowlers out there,' he said, 'but there aren't too many left-arm spinners.'

But while Jack basically set me a course for the rest of my life, I'd have never lifted anchor if it wasn't for my family. Without them, I would never have been a sportsman. They were the ones driving me miles to matches, dropping me off, picking me up, making sure I had the kit I needed. When I played football, Dad loved to be involved. He'd get his tracksuit on for games and become part of the set-up, helping to put up the nets, sorting out the half-time oranges and taxiing players around. At the same time he was very good at walking that fine line between encouraging me and – which you see a lot of dads do – battering me over the head with 'do this, do that'. That's not to say he wouldn't get fired up. He'd hear the opposition dads having a bit of a pop at some of our boys and that would be it. 'Oi! Don't you say that about our lads.' There'd be the occasional car-park contretemps. It made me laugh. He wouldn't have weighed ten stone wet through.

Dad loved his sport. He'd played football and cricket in the army and supported the Arsenal. His Saturday routine was to work in his silversmiths in the morning and then head down to Highbury for the game in the afternoon, something he'd been doing since he was a kid, his own dad lifting him up so dozens of other fans could help to pass him and the other kids down to the front. Over the heads of these blokes, all in caps, wearing suits and ties they'd go. It must have been an incredible feeling. No wonder it stayed with him so long.

Dad would also recall getting the 298 bus to Highbury on a Saturday only to find Denis Compton sat on the back seat with his boots over his shoulder, hair slicked back in a manner familiar to so many who worshipped him as a dashing left-winger for the Gunners and equally extravagant batsman for Middlesex. Often he'd tell the story of how he was there in the crowd, one of 63,578, when Manchester United came to Highbury in 1958 and beat the Gunners 5-4 in an all-time classic. Five days later, many of those Busby Babes were taken away so cruelly in the Munich air disaster. The brutality of that event, the injustice, always shocked him.

Dad would take me down to Highbury with him until it got too lively at the back end of the '70s. It went from being a fun afternoon out to police horses tearing around chasing nutcases chucking bottles at one another. Understandably, he thought a place where there might be a bloke wandering round with half a Corona lemonade bottle sticking out of his head wasn't particularly great for a young lad. Even when people did watch the game, chance was it would be marred by a bloke with long hair, no shirt, and flared high-waisted jeans running on the pitch and mucking around.

It was my dream to play for the Arsenal. There are pictures of me in the garden in my Gunners kit.

From the age of 10 to 14 I was a very good player, a left-half assassin, and played at a decent level alongside Des Walker, who went on to play for England, and Gus Caesar, who, unlike me, actually did make it with the Gunners. In that short heyday, I could see a pass and was good in the air. I also saw myself a bit in the mould of the Leeds United hardman Johnny Giles, not averse to leaving a foot in from time to time. In fact, the more I've thought about it, the more I've concluded I was a bit of a thug. No VAR, so I could get away with it!

At that time, my dad said, I had the speed of a gazelle and the constitution of a cart horse. Two years later, he was saying the same thing but the other way round. It broke his heart when I switched to goalkeeper.

'You don't want to go there,' he said. 'That's where the guys who can't play go.'

He was right in that it wasn't exactly the glory position. But then again, my laziness was kicking in and so having a little stand around in goal seemed a decent option. When it got cold, I could wear tracksuit bottoms and a lovely thick roll-collar jumper under my top. People were cracking the ice in the goal-mouth while I was stood there nice and toasty.

When it came to cricket, chances are I'd never have played if I hadn't gone to Highgate School. As a family, we always played cricket in the summer in the back garden, but really I was a football boy. The highlight of my school day was the lunchtime game of football, a proper good match with your jumper off. These weren't mere kickabouts. They were tough games – Leeds vs Arsenal standard.

It was only because the football stopped in summer and I was sitting around looking for something to do that I played cricket. Standing around in a field all day didn't have the same appeal. At Highgate, though, it was clear from a young age that I had a bit of a talent for the game, although I wouldn't be showing it off up there forever because a few years down the line I was expelled.

Highgate was a posh school. I started there when I was seven, and for the first few years I liked it. All I ever seemed to do was play sport. In the senior school, on the other hand, we played sport at the weekend and everything else was geography, maths and bloody physics. It all came as a bit of a shock. 'Hang on, what's all this? Sitting at desks doing work? What happened to messing about?'

Then there were the teachers. So often they seemed distant, wandering round in gowns. The teachers I got on with were the ones who took the time and could see something in me, like John Emburey did later when I turned up at Middlesex. Chief among them was Mr Kelland, a geography and PE teacher who had played a bit of first-class cricket with Sussex. You didn't mess with Mr Kelland. He had been a decent fast bowler in his day and was clearly built for power. But he saw enough in me as both a footballer and a cricketer to really push me on. He was one of those teachers who somehow clicks with you, who you actually want to work for, to impress. Through his encouragement, I found myself in the first teams for both cricket and football while still a couple of years the junior of my teammates. Several years later, when I was selected for my debut tour, I was touched when Mr Kelland wrote me a letter. Typically honest, while congratulating me on my call-up, he told me I should have been a footballer, that a header I'd scored was the best he'd ever seen.

Teachers like Mr Kelland made life interesting, gave me a little leeway, rather than just wanting to whack me over the head all the time. I switched off very, very quickly to those kinds of teachers. There's more to teaching than just banging on. As soon as the banging on started, I stopped listening. Simple as that.

Okay, there was a rebellious streak in there as well. While my brother Greg, much harder-working than me, became head boy at Highgate, from the age of 12 I was behind the bike sheds with a fag. I always had the haircut, the skinhead or the quiff, as well as Doc Martens, and leather jacket rather than school blazer. Anything to kick back, to make a point. And actually, in a funny sort of way, my mum and dad quite liked that. Their attitude was, 'Well, you've got to have something about you.'

It's very similar to being a spinner. At the end of the day, you're out there bowling slowly against some of the best players in the world. You've got to have a little bit of the unexpected up your sleeve otherwise you're sending it down at 50 mph rather than 90 mph and the bloke at the other end is just going to smack you about. My dad always encouraged me to have a bit of character, to do things differently. Obviously, there was a limit. I think we both understood it wouldn't be a great idea to burn the gym down or set fire to the headmaster's car, but definitely he was the same as me in that he would back me up if he felt someone was being pedantic or if I'd broken an entirely pointless rule. When I grew my hair long and the school insisted I cut it, my attitude was 'Why? What difference does it make to anything I do if I do it with long hair or short? You don't need short hair to play sport any more than you need short hair to sit through double maths.' Later, I'd see Dad's own line over hair was the Mohican, but when it came to a bit of hair down to the shoulders he was straight on the phone.

'What's the point', he asked, 'of alienating pupils and putting their backs up over such senseless things?' Hard to argue with that. Only by connecting and communicating with people do you get the best out of them. 'You've got the wrong trousers on.' It means nothing.

Him and Mum wanted me to be in the top sets and do my homework, but after a while they understood there was no point pushing me to be a mathematician or a scientist because I was just no good at that stuff. They tried with me but in the end they thought, 'Well, there's only so much you can do.' They could lead the horse to water but they couldn't make it drink. Well, not water anyway.

I was never in serious trouble as a kid. There was a lot of hanging around on street corners and a bit of 'Come on, lads – on your way!' from the local bobbies, but that was as far as it went. My criminal career went no further than nicking a couple of Mum's fags before heading off to school. She smoked Rothmans King Size, posh fags, in a blue packet. Other times we might chip in together and get an older kid to get us ten Player's No. 6 from the shop.

Each morning, all I'd think about was lunchtime when me and my mates would walk down Highgate Hill. At the same time, the girls from Channing, a private school nearby, would be walking up and we'd all meet in a little square, a classic courtship scene by the municipal toilets. We felt so cool.

When, by mutual agreement, as they say on the sports bulletins, it was decided I should leave Highgate, cricket went on the backburner. Unfortunately, at Southgate Comp., like a lot of state schools, cricket just wasn't a thing. Sport was all a bit jumpers for goalposts, nothing massively organised. Me and a couple of mates actually got cricket started. We spoke to a teacher about it, and while initially he was a bit, 'Come off it, lads – what the f*** do you know about playing f***ing cricket?' (teachers really could be quite sweary in those days), once he watched me bowl he could see there might be something in the proposition. From that point on, we did actually play a little bit, although I expect the minute we left everything returned to how it was previously.

At Southgate, I pretty much did nothing. I was still all set to sit my O levels and would have done – had they let me in. When I turned up in the bondage trousers with brothel creepers and black leather biker's jacket, they were having none of it. They insisted I go home and change into school uniform. I went home as requested but didn't bother going back. The fact of the matter is I was never very good at being told what to do or what not to do. I was the kid who ignored advice on principle, even if I suspected the advice might actually be pretty good. There was part of me always convinced I knew better. In the end, I only did one O level, art, under supervision in the headmaster's office. I like to paint now, so maybe it stood me in good stead.

Before I left my last place of learning, a careers adviser offered me the helpful assessment that I'd 'never amount to anything'. What a boost to the self-esteem that bloke was. I mean, it wasn't like I had no ambition. Head of the Bank of England or MI5 had their appeal. Actually, quite often these days, when I'm doing question and answer sessions, people ask if there was something I really wanted to be when I was growing up, like a train driver, spaceman or UN peacekeeper, and, always wishing to give value for money on these occasions, I reply, 'No, not really.' If I'm feeling a little more conversational, I'll say 'bumbling about' because – impressionable youths, avert your gaze now – the real answer was bumbling about.

Certainly take no notice of my Wikipedia entry, which will seek to persuade you that on leaving school I 'trained in quantity surveying and was faced with the tough decision of whether to play cricket professionally or to work as a quantity surveyor'. I can only think there must be another Philip Clive Roderick Tufnell out there somewhere because I have no idea what a quantity surveyor is or does. Surveys quantities? Quantities of what? And why? There's a quantity. Take it or leave it.

I did experience a number of other work environments, though. Before I found what can loosely be described as my 'calling', I tried labouring, mini-cabbing, all kinds of things. But most of my time was spent apologising for cocking things up, like the time I helped a mate plaster the side wall of an office block and then stepped back to watch it all peel off like someone pulling at a gigantic patchwork quilt. Another time we were painting a new flat on the Thames waterfront when the sun streaming through the plate-glass windows caused a state of deep tortoise-like inertia. Next thing we knew, a couple of potential buyers were being shown around only to find two 'workmen' asleep in the bedrooms.

'This is the better one,' I told them. 'It's en-suite.'

The mini-cabbing wasn't much better. I was liable to get confused. One time I picked up an old dear. Fifty minutes later we pulled up at Royal Ascot. 'This isn't my optician's,' she pointed out.

The army was mentioned at one point, but I concluded it was probably not the place for me if it involved being told what to do. 'Could you ask the enemy to hold fire until 10:30? I had a bit of a big night.'

I'd have been better at surveillance work, something which suited my well-honed ability to lurk unnoticed in various north London greasy spoons keeping my nut down trying to avoid work of any kind. Had there been such a thing in the early '80s, professional gamer too would have fitted like a glove, recognition of the hours I spent perfecting my *Space Invaders* technique in the kebab shop.

Thing is, who needs O levels when you've got a doctorate? Middlesex University awarded me the honorary title in recognition of my 'achievements in sport and the media'. Never having been overloaded with gongs, I was shocked when it was announced, but there I was on the day in my gown, my dad and wife Dawn watching, with a certificate in my hand. I don't insist on being called 'Dr Tufnell', but if ever the call comes over the PA – 'Is there a doctor in the house?' – I'll be first up there. I've watched *Casualty*. I know how it all works.

The day after the ceremony, I was commentating on the England vs India Test match at Lord's alongside the India batting legend that is Sunil Gavaskar.

'You'll never guess what happened to me yesterday,' I told him. 'I received a doctorate from Middlesex University.'

'Oh, right,' replied Sunny. He couldn't have sounded more uninterested if I'd described my favourite washing peg. 'I've got about thirty of those.' He's a doctor of every Indian university going.

To put any lingering debate to bed, I didn't wear the bondage trousers under my gown. It had been 30 years since they were my signature garment. Gaining popularity during punk, they were not so much a fashion statement as the ultimate two-fingered salute to authority. I enjoyed punk and the way it attracted people who just didn't seem quite to fit in. I went to a few punk gigs around that time including UK Subs, Angelic Upstarts and The Damned. However, I soon realised that one thing tartan bondage trousers weren't great for was getting you into many places and so I moved on. If there was a fad out there, I'd be on it. I drew the line at the New Romantics, though – as punks we always had fights with them.

More than anything I just wanted to be part of something exciting, part of a radical movement, something that wasn't going to end up with me being a clerk for Barclays. Not that there's anything wrong with being a clerk for Barclays, I just didn't want it to be me. I didn't want to be part of the mainstream and if that meant I was anti-establishment then so be it. Where I did want to be part of something was sport. I liked the idea of being part of a team – and, of course, the sporty boys tended to get the girls. Unfair as it is, it's rare that girls are falling over themselves to go out with the bloke who comes top in maths.

Slowly I was piecing together the world that would come to dominate the next couple of decades. Cricket – tick. Women – tick. Hang on, there's something missing. Oh yes, booze.

Like a lot of families back then we had a little bar, shaped in a semi-circle, made from wrought iron, in the posh room for when people came round. Also like many, we had an ice bucket shaped like a pineapple. Mum and Dad were very sociable people. They were quite funky, had a few quid and went out to dos. They were in the silver trade after all and so it wasn't unusual for them to host gatherings at the house. There'd be friends from Garrard, the Mayfair jeweller, and Mappin & Webb, all these people turning up in lovely cars, including once, I have never forgotten, a beautiful Triumph Stag. We'd be watching *Match of the Day* and they'd all be in the other room having a drink. The first time alcohol passed my lips was when I nipped in there during one of these Saturday night dos and helped myself to a Dubonnet and lemonade. I still remember the way the bottle had become crystallised round the top, but I'm not sure I remember much else.

From then on, it was the usual kind of thing. You'd be out having a fag with mates and then someone would produce a couple of cans or we'd all get a bottle of Strongbow from somewhere and go over to the woods. As soon as we turned 15, we'd head to the White Hart in Southgate. At first older kids we knew would go in and get us a couple of pints and from there it was just a natural progression to going into the pub ourselves.

I was enjoying life, having a grand old time at home and with my friends, until Mum was taken from us by leukaemia. Initially, Dad, wanting to protect us from this devastating diagnosis, didn't tell me and my older brother Greg what was happening. But as the months passed and she became progressively more tired and weaker, it was clear that something was very wrong. She'd be in hospital for lengths of time and Dad had no choice but to tell us what was going on. The treatments didn't work and we had to watch her fade away before our eyes until finally she disappeared.

I don't think the loss of someone so close is something anyone ever truly gets over, but as a family we had no choice but to soldier on. It was a very upsetting time, a changing time. We had a very nice house, but it felt like the whole light of our family had gone out. I can still remember my dad sitting down with us boys and saying, 'Listen, I'll always be here for you, but, you know, there ain't going to be cups of tea waiting for you when you come home from school. You won't be able to shout, "Mum, can I have a cheese sandwich?" and it magically appear.' There was a massive empty hole where Mum used to be and, with my dad and brother out all the time, working or doing their own thing, I found myself increasingly on my own. In search of company and a bit of an escape, I'd get a few mates round. I say 'a few', but next thing I knew there'd be about 20 of us there, all with a few cans, and so we'd sit around, get pissed and smoke fags.

The hope was that a load of people who weren't invited wouldn't turn up. I'd seen that happen at other people's houses, mainly because I tended to be one of the ones who arrived on spec. Most weekends between the ages of 14 and 17 were the same. Bus down to Southgate, meet some mates, go to the kebab house, play *Space Invaders*, hang around (for hours) and then all of a sudden someone would say the magic words – 'I've heard there's a party up Winchmore Hill.' The source of this information tended to be along the lines of someone's sister's older brother's mate's cousin – twice removed. Whatever, we'd head off down there, clumsily gate-crash, and I'd spend the next few hours drinking, smoking and maybe snogging some poor unfortunate girl in the bog. That was it – for three years. Compared to the emptiness at home, it was fun.

I saw more of Dad when I started working for his firm of sil-versmiths. I liked being with him. He was a similar personality to me, always looking at life slightly humorously, and a sociable character with it. A bit of a cheeky chappie, he'd tell me how in his army days he'd be chased round the mess hall by the sergeant for mucking about.

Whatever sport I was playing, he was always one for having half a lager and a chat in the bar after a game. He saw life as something to go out and be involved in. To him, there was no point in sitting back and being a wallflower. But never did Dad live out his sporting ambitions through me – although he was very, very key to my success.

While Middlesex had shown an interest in the adolescent me, cricket had slipped way off my priority list after Mum died. Eventually, one day while I was metal-banging, Dad said to me, 'Boy, you don't want to be down here. I could give you this business, and you'd have a good standard of life, food on the table, but try and have a go at the cricket. I'll give you a day's wages to go back and trial with Middlesex.' Well, that was it. Turn up at Middlesex for two hours in exchange for a whole day's pay. What wasn't to like?

Off I toddled, trialled for Middlesex, and got in, playing club cricket with Southgate along the way. When a few years later I rang and told him, 'Dad, I'm off to the Caribbean for three months,' he laughed. 'See, I told you, didn't I? And you wanted to sit there hammering pots and pans!' He felt very happy that a better path was opening up for me than the one he had. Dad enjoyed a very nice life, but it was all earned through hard physical labour in the dirt, dust and heat of industry. He was very proud that I made it in sport. It was just very sad that my mum didn't get to see it as well. That would have been lovely, but I know also that her reaction would have been very similar – outwardly unassuming but deep down very proud.

Occasionally, when he was getting old, Dad would phone me

up. He'd tell me how someone had delivered something to the house and had seen a photo of me in action on his wall.

'Oh, Phil Tufnell! How do you know him?'

'Well, actually . . .'

I'd have got precisely nowhere without him.

CHAPTER 3

How Not to Get Caught

It might have been better if I'd stayed bashing pots and pans. Well, from the point of view of those who had to deal with the version of me that arrived on the doorstep of the professional game.

My first touring experience was with the England Under-19s to Barbados. It seemed the only people who didn't realise the abject foolishness of such an enterprise were those who organised it. A bunch of lads barely out of school set free on a sun-lashed, rum-sodden island with hundreds of bars and miles of beaches. What did they think was going to happen?

Former England captain and bowling legend Bob Willis was in charge, which only added to the otherworldliness of the experience. This was a bloke I'd routinely watched perform heroics for England, not least in skinning the Aussies alive with his bowling in the legendary 1981 Headingley Ashes Test. Now he was sat with a clipboard checking whether we were back at the digs before curfew. Well, he was the first night. After that he gave up. Bob, who I would forever call 'Manager' from that moment on, was himself too free a spirit to be bogged down with all that nonsense.

I recall one evening we were invited to a do at the British High Commissioner's mansion. None of the lads was particularly enamoured by the thought of such an event. When you're 17, saying hello to civic dignitaries can be deathly dull. But, actually, I found it quite good fun. I didn't see much not to like about being given lots of free drink and nibbles to the backdrop of a steel band. And I think for their part, our hosts, traditional types, garters, ironed underwear, quite enjoyed having a few little scallywags running round the place for two or three hours. Bob, though, seemed to want to liven things up. I heard him before I saw him, singing a Bob Dylan (he wasn't called Robert George Dylan Willis for nothing) track by the pool, at the conclusion of which he flashed past a window and, fully clothed, leapt into the deep end.

I concluded at that point that there was a lot more to Bob than met the eye. How he'd ended up looking after us lot I do not know, but I was glad he gave up on the curfew-checking business early on. He could see he was on a hiding to nothing from the moment we got off the plane, dumped our bags and went down to Harbour Lights for a 12-hour session on the rum. I can still picture Bob sat out on the hotel veranda at 4:30 a.m. awaiting our return. It was the first time any of us had drunk a serious amount of the spirit and we were absolutely hammered, bouncing off the walls. There was a good deal of being sick and, as I recall, some concern for our health. It could be argued a tour hasn't got off to the best of starts when half the squad spend the first night in the recovery position.

Barely had our heads touched the pillow than we were being called down to breakfast. In wandered a team not of vibrant young sportsmen, the promising future of English cricket, but a sorry shower of ashen-faced zombies. Fellow former England Test bowler Bob Cottam had the misfortune to be co-piloting the trip with Bob. While the teenagers before him tried, in one or two cases in vain, not to throw up at the sight of a tray of fried eggs, he felt a little chat was in order.

'This is not a Club 18–30 holiday,' he informed us. 'This is important. Now you've blown a few cobwebs away, you need to understand that there is hard work to be done. You will be training and you will be playing. You cannot be caught coming in at a ridiculous hour and still be drunk in the morning.' I took Bob Cottam's wise words on board. From that moment on, I vowed not to get caught.

It was a plan that, throughout my cricketing life, didn't always work, something I reflected on one night in the early hours as I absolutely pegged it round the back streets of Limehouse. Many questions were going through my mind at that point, but two in particular were dominating. One, how is the WPC behind me still hot on my heels? And two, will it be the end of a very short-lived first-class career if she catches me?

To explain, I need to remind you of Britain's great tradition of double acts – Morecambe and Wise, salt 'n' vinegar, the Krays. At Middlesex, for a while at least, there was Tufnell & Sykes. Ah, Jamie Sykes, aka my partner in crime, occasionally quite literally. Jamie, an off-spinner to my slow left-arm, was a proper cockney. A no-nonsense character, if he'd gone on to be Phil Mitchell's sidekick in *EastEnders*, no one in the Middlesex dressing room would have batted an eyelid. Alex Barnett, another young Middlesex spinner of the time, once described Jamie as 'the guy you would call if someone owed you money and you wanted to speed things up a little'.

Sykesy, like me, enjoyed a beer, but unlike me, who retained the profile of a stickman, he would accrue weight. His solution was to sweat off the pounds by mummifying himself in bin liners before training. Not a great look, but at least it diverted attention away from me as I dealt with my own hangover. We both shared the same sort of anti-establishment view of life and became a crew, with our own slightly unorthodox way of going about things. To the entertainment, or annoyance, of everyone around us, Jamie and I would keep ourselves amused by bickering and bantering in the dressing room. Barely out of short trousers, we were like an old married couple, joined at the hip, which extended for a while to off-the-pitch activities.

While Jamie did drive, he preferred to be in the passenger seat, as he was prone to get a little, er, displeased with the antics of other road users. He was in just that position when, after we'd been out for a couple of drinks, I noticed a police car in the rear-view mirror. When it stuck on the blue lights, I knew the chances were I was over the limit. I was about to pull over when Jamie suggested it would be an altogether better idea to try to lose it. I was making a very weak attempt to do so, much removed from the car chase scenes in *Starsky & Hutch*, when I turned straight into a dead end. 'It's no good,' said Jamie, 'stop the car.' I was just admiring his newfound moral code, wondering perhaps if he'd found God, when he added, 'Leg it!' I'd gone from county cricket to a bit part in *The Bill*.

I abandoned the vehicle and proceeded in a northerly direction on foot. At that point, I was in the absolute prime of my physical capacity. For a good three minutes I was absolutely haring round the backstreets. Over 3,000 metres I'd have beaten Steve Cram hands down. I was just coming off the gas a little, thinking I'd surely left my pursuant gasping in my wake, when

I heard a jingling. I looked back and there was this same police officer, right on my heels, handcuffs clanking against her belt. I couldn't believe it. I'd been going like the absolute clappers and she'd stayed with me every inch of the way. Even with me in my civvies and her weighed down with her jacket, truncheon, cuffs and everything, she'd managed to keep up. I tried to escape once and for all over a wall, but in classic *Juliet Bravo* style she grabbed hold of my legs and started hitting me with her truncheon. Within seconds back-up arrived. 'All right, all right,' I was saying. 'It's a fair cop. Just keep the dogs off my trousers.'

And then a load of armed CID appeared. Her fervour for justice, I soon found out, came from the fact there'd been an armed robbery in the vicinity (there's that phrase again) and the police thought we'd done it. Talk about wrong place, wrong time. 'Please, just put the guns down,' I was pleading. 'I'm a cricketer who's had two pints of lager. Ring Mike Gatting!'

In the long term, no county could tolerate Tufnell & Sykes. In a sad day for British buffoonery, Middlesex disbanded the duo by not offering Jamie a contract. Remarkably, considering his aversion to the driver's seat, he now runs a black cab. I was crossing the road outside Lord's recently when I heard a shout. 'Oi, Tufnell, you f***ing useless c***.' It had been at least three hours since someone had bellowed that at me and so I turned round – and there he was leaning out of his cab window.

For my part in an incident that no doubt is still talked about in the corridors of Scotland Yard – 'Tufnell & Sykes? I was there when they were nicked!' – I received a totally deserved fine and year's ban for being over the limit. The inconvenience of having no car was, as it is meant to be, incredible. It was like losing my right arm, one of many reasons I never did it again. As a cricketer, I had all sorts of kit – predominantly a shedload of pads, guards, shields and boxes – to lug around. I'd be drag-ging great cricket coffins on and off trains, clambering on buses and spending a fortune on taxis. On a three-day match, I felt like I'd played the first two before I even arrived. I was ruined.

Thankfully, Gatt didn't live a million miles away and came to the rescue. 'I'm not diverting to your house to get you,' he said, a little brusquely I thought, 'but I pass near you on the North Circular about a quarter to nine.' So there I'd be, a bedraggled figure stood at the edge of this seething mass of traffic every morning waiting for my lift. Occasionally, a lorry would stop.

'Where are you heading, mate?'

'Lord's.'

'You f***ing what?'

Then Gatt would appear, screech to a halt, I'd clamber in quick smart, and he'd nip back out into the traffic.

Middlesex could justifiably have thrown the book at me for this and other misdemeanours, but while, of course, there were bollockings, and the threat of the sack was ever-present, they tended to look after me. They knew I had something in me and wanted to help me find it. I appreciated that.

My own family had gone from strong and secure to pretty much non-existent. Dad's way of dealing with Mum's loss was to immerse himself in work, while Greg was busy with his own burgeoning business career. In many ways, Middlesex were a second family to me. They provided structure, protection and a sense of belonging, which was exactly what I needed, and a massive reason I always loved playing for them. I could never have played for another county. That sounds strange when play-ers nowadays flit about all over the place, but I just couldn't have pulled on another jumper. So welded to the club was I that, had I been shown the door, I most likely would have walked away from the game for good. I really wasn't interested in starting again somewhere else. What was I going to do? Pack a bag and live in digs in Derby?

Okay, I did try it once. Briefly, very early on, when my prospects were unclear, I had a look at playing for Sussex. Dermot Reeve invited me down to Hove, and fearing I was about to be bombed out by Middlesex because of my attitude, I accepted. I played, went to McDonald's, went back to the B&B, watched telly and went to bed. I did that for three days and went home. I know it was one match and I'd hardly met these blokes properly, but it just wasn't the same. Sounds daft, but one incident above all others made up my mind to get back to Lord's and do my best to stay there. Sat next to me in the Sussex dressing room was a player whose underwear should, for the good of the nation, have been incinerated. Then and there I thought to myself, 'I can't do this. I can't play cricket for the next twenty years with a bloke who does this.' I can remember that moment as clear as day. Just imagine, if it hadn't been for him I might have been playing with Garth Le Roux and Imran Khan for the rest of my career. Gatt's hair would never have been ripped out.

The nearest I came to having that same decision to leave Lord's made for me came during a match against Yorkshire at Abbeydale Park, Sheffield, the ground where Michael Vaughan and Joe Root took their early steps in the game. I was actually sent off. Something I have never heard of happening on a cricket field before or since. Especially when the marching orders come not from the umpires but a player's own team.

Things had not been going well. Wherever we played, there always seemed to be one or two batsmen determined to come down the track and whack me around the park. It was nothing personal. Whenever a new spinner came into the game it was understood that senior batsmen would go after them and try to hit them out of the equation. Professional sport is brutal. We did it at Middlesex on a regular basis. We'd look at the opposition and say, 'Right, who's their spinner?' Occasionally it would be a second-team lad who'd just graduated to the first XI. One of the senior boys would say, 'Right, leave him to me. I'll destroy him.' It happens at every level, like when the Australian all-rounder Shane Watson went after the Lancashire left-armer Simon Kerrigan on his England debut at The Oval.

At that stage, I really didn't have the bowling tools to counter-attack. I also found the balance between standing up for myself and allowing other people to help me very tricky. As a young spin bowler, I knew there would always be big grown men queuing up, bat in hand, to f*** me up. I knew also that to counter that I needed to walk out there with a bit of something about me. But this time my attempt at self-confident aggression mixed with my frustration and general surliness to cause a perfect storm.

I was being hammered by a couple of canny Yorkshire batsmen and getting crosser and crosser. Gatt and Embers, captain and vice-captain, decided they needed to intervene and I did not react well. Their suggestion of a change of approach, getting rid of the man saving the single in the covers in favour of a more attacking option close in at silly point, was the last straw. They were only trying to be constructive, but I took it as criticism of my bowling and tactics. In my mind they were basically saying I was shit and didn't know what I was doing. To be fair, at that moment, they probably had a point. But I wouldn't have it.

Despite my protestations, they duly brought the man in at silly point to try to turn the tables and put the pressure back on the batsman. When it came to the final ball of the over, I conjured up a brilliant plan to prove their actions wrong. At this point I didn't care about the state of the game. I wasn't thinking about getting the batsman out, and the safety of the close-in fielder never entered my head. Gatt and Embers were wrong and I was going to rub their noses in it. I dropped that sixth delivery short on purpose. I was issuing an open invite for the batsman to rock back and cut it through the covers for four. That way I could say to them, 'See! Told you I should have had the man in the covers.' And that's exactly what happened. I bawled them both out in front of the team, making a complete idiot of myself in the process.

With everyone on the field looking on in disbelief, I snatched my cap and hissy-fitted down to my fielding position at third man, at which point Gatt ran down to me.

'What the f*** is going on?'

'I don't know,' I replied. 'You're the captain, you tell me.'

'Okay, then,' he said, 'f*** off. If you don't want to take any advice and if you're not going to calm down you'd better go off for a few overs and have a think about it.'

I couldn't believe what I was hearing. 'You can't do that. You can't send me off.'

Gatt stared me in the eye. 'I think you'll find I can do what the f*** I like.'

Red-carded by my own captain, after a few overs feeling sorry for myself I walked back on to the field, kept my mouth shut, and got on with it.

After such a public show of dissent, many within the club urged the axe. I was too much trouble, they said, and not actually a good enough player to be worth the effort. My future was well and truly in the balance and, with a record as long as my arm, had the club torn up my contract I would have had few grounds for complaint. In the end, however, Gatt and Embers stood by me and reinforced to the hierarchy that I was an asset as a cricketer. One of the reasons teammates called me 'the Cat' was my ability to drift off to sleep any place, any time. The other was the number of lives I appeared to have. I had just used another.

A lot of my problems stemmed from the fact that when I graduated to first-class cricket I didn't really change. I was still that kid playing for Southgate more than happy to give people a volley. And, to be blunt, I enjoyed it. Early in my career, I encountered Graham Gooch, about to take over the England captaincy, at Chelmsford. There was always an edge to Essex vs Middlesex games, two big sides vying for championships, and I really wanted to nail one of their star names. When Gooch came out to open, you could see our players physically and mentally sharpen in the field. Nothing needed to be said. We all knew what had to happen – Gooch back in the pavilion and as soon as possible. We seemed to have missed that chance when he cruised unfussed to 29. But then he mistimed a sweep off me and was caught. To say I was fired up by that dismissal would be like saying Red Rum was a reasonable racehorse. 'Go on then!' I sent Gooch on his way. 'Have some of that. Who do you f***ing think you are anyway?'

That's a book I've yet to write – *How to Win Friends and Influence People*.

I didn't quite know how to act as a youngster new on the scene. Some people who feel like that shrink into their shell. Others go the other way. I was one of the latter and on the pitch that manifested itself in a bit of 'I don't care about you – you mean nothing to me.' I would shout and scream at these legendary names. I knew neither how to interact with them nor get the best out of myself, but I did have an idea that I bowled better when I was angry. In the absence of a hammer to smash against my thumb, getting in the faces of batsmen was a way to flick that switch. I had to operate at the extreme. The middle ground was useless. Sometimes I'd feel like I needed to punch myself in the head to perform at my best.

As a fast bowler, aggression comes with the territory. The very nature of what you do means you are tearing in, while a ball travelling at 85–90 mph carries its own message. A spinner doesn't have that. It's not as easy to express yourself, to find your demeanour, the version of yourself you want to portray on the cricket field. What I'm saying is, it's not easy to have a presence – and I really felt I needed a presence. Often I'd manufacture something, a little set-to with a batsman or an umpire, to liven things up a little, get my blood pumping, create a spark that might set fire to the game. My teammates knew the value of getting me ticking. Our wicketkeeper Keith Brown would often say to me, 'Come on, Phil, get angry!' Inevitably this sudden change in tempo wouldn't go unnoticed by the crowd. People who a few minutes earlier had been half-asleep would suddenly be looking up thinking, 'I wonder what's going on?'

Important to remember also that I did actually have a lot of anger in me at that time, pent-up from the injustice of Mum dying at such a young age. I had seen in the clearest, starkest terms that life was unfair and no one was going to tell me different.

Like anything, it's important to be true to yourself in life, and sport is no different. I had long resisted others' attempts to dominate or control me, be it at school or in a cricket environment, and once I knew anger and emotion were there for me to access at any time then I started to feel much more comfortable in my own skin. Maybe needing that spark was a sign of being mentally weak, but whatever the psychology I knew it brought me to life. Before I worked that out, I wasn't bowling aggressively. In fact, I was more like a second XI bowler. I was a timid person bowling spin rather than a good spin bowler exercising his right to be on the pitch. Now I started attacking the crease, following through, and really working my action. My mindset was a focused 'F*** you. I'll get you out.' And it worked – I was bowling well. At the same time, for better or worse, I was also building a reputation – 'Tantrum Tufnell', that kind of thing. For me, though, my detractors could keep having a go all they wanted. I knew the truth about myself. You've got to find your place in the world and I was pretty damned sure mine didn't involve pandering to what other people thought I should be. I was coming for the batsmen and I wanted them to know it.

Gatt and Embers could see I had desire and aggression which, if harnessed, could only add to my arsenal as a spin bowler. They also knew that to knock the rough edges off would take time. Thing was, on occasions I'm not quite sure they appreciated just how rough those edges could be. On one occasion, we had a bit of media training, which actually came without warning. As the players pulled up one by one at Lord's, some bloke with a microphone jumped out and asked for a quote on a pertinent cricket issue of the day, the idea being to illustrate how easy it is to be caught off guard and say something you shouldn't. I told him to f*** off, which was later used as an example of how not to deal with a reporter. We then had a sit-down over coffee and biscuits with Radio 4's John Humphrys, who gave us a few tips, none of which stayed with me any longer than my custard cream.

Thankfully for all concerned, I did start to realise that it's okay to take advice from others. Not listening to people of vast experience with great careers could only be self-destructive. Yes, you have to own your decisions and can't keep passing the buck, but taking heed of others is not a sign of weakness. It took time and luck and patience and support – more than I acknowledged at the time – and slowly but surely I got into my craft. I started to understand that a bowler doesn't have to try to take a wicket with every ball, that you can build pressure, get a batsman playing where you want him to, and spot little pointers to help work them out such as watching the way they set up or open their hands. In due course, batsmen started getting out to me – good ones, too, and more often.

When it came to guidance, I was particularly lucky to have John Emburey on my side. Embers, a fellow spinner, was a good-looking man. He held himself well and had an excellent telephone voice. These characteristics would occasionally lead people to think he was upper crust, but in fact he's a Peckham lad. He might have had a good telephone voice, but the rest of the time he was as down-to-earth as they come, which explains why, when once asked why he was rubbing his shoulder, he came out with the all-time classic response, 'the facking facker's facking facked'. Very versatile word, 'fack'.

For me, Embers was the complete mentor. As a lively lad fighting against the world, he saw a bit of his younger self in me. He taught me that entering every battle really wasn't worth it. The only person I was likely to damage was myself. He showed me that it didn't hurt every now and again to give a little bit.

'Look,' he'd say to me, 'this is a good old screw here. Get your nut down and you'll get yourself a nice house and maybe even play for England. Otherwise, what are you going to do?'

He saw a path and then tried to point me down it. If it looked like I was about to wander off-road, he wasn't slow in letting me know. He had some right pops at me, but it was only because he didn't want to see me throw it all away. Gatt was the same. Their overriding ethos was always the same – 'We're not here to have a go at you. We're trying to get the best out of you. You're playing for one of the best counties in the country. You're good and we want the best. That's why we've picked you. We're trying to create something here and we want you to buy into it.'

It helped that Gatt was a very unselfish captain. He could give you a bollocking, but it was only because he really wanted to get the best out of you as a cricketer, for you to do yourself justice. 'Stop being a twat,' he'd tell me. 'You're talented and if you apply yourself properly you're going to give yourself a better chance of achieving your potential.'

He also never bore a grudge. We could have a bit of argy-bargy, but I knew that when I came in the next day everything would have been forgotten. 'All right, Tuffers?' 'All right, Gatt?' It was never false. Never done just for the sake of it. You knew it was done and dusted. You were mates. With me, Gatt was prepared for the long haul. Always trying to make me better. Always a second chance. In doing so, he was another who saved my life.

Even so, I really don't know how I survived at Middlesex in those early years. I was so close to being bombed out. Earrings, ponytails, run-ins with umpires – I was always offering reasons for someone on the committee to put their foot down – 'Right, we've had enough – he's more trouble than he's worth.'

It perhaps wouldn't have been so bad if I'd been a better liar, but all I ever seemed to do was dig myself into a deeper and deeper hole until one more bucketful and I'd have been popping my head out on the beach at Melbourne. My behaviour wasn't malicious. I just thought, after all my family had gone through, none of it mattered. And so, at the end of every season, the same story unfolded. The coaches would tell me they liked my aggression on the field, that they thought I could bowl, and they wanted to back me, but to earn that investment I'd have to mend my ways. Every year I'd nod and the cycle would start all over again.

CHAPTER 4

How Not to Be a County Cricketer

For the first few years at Middlesex I flitted between first team and second XI. With the second team boys, I felt a bit more in my element, sharing the same views on life, fashion and the universe with blokes my own age, but going from there to the first XI dressing room was utterly overwhelming. When I pushed open the door for the first time, it was a bit like that scene in *An American Werewolf in London* when the two lost backpackers burst gratefully into the Slaughtered Lamb pub high on the moors only to be greeted by a deeply unwelcoming silence. Instead of a backpack and an American accent, I had winklepickers, an earring and a dodgy haircut. As several gnarled old pros eyed me up and down, I knew exactly what they were thinking – 'What the f*** is that?' Then, as I stood there lost as to what to do next, they turned their backs. There'd have been a better reception for the werewolf.

'Jesus,' I thought, 'it's bad enough worrying about going out and bowling for the first team, perhaps – please God forbid – having to bat and field, without all this.' Genuinely, I could have cried. Only Angus Fraser, who I knew from grade cricket, saved me – 'Oi! Tuffers! Over here!'

I'd like to think that, in later years, when it came to me being the gnarled old pro and other young players tentatively opening that dressing-room door, my own experience taught me to be a bit more welcoming. It may have been tradition, or considered a rite of passage, but frankly it was shit. It's hard enough trying to get used to a totally alien environment, to bowl people out, avoid being hit by a quick bowler who likes nothing more than the smell of fear, without all that nonsense. Perhaps some of those older boys had been through the mill a bit and so were jealous of a newcomer's age. But I could hardly be blamed for how long I'd been on the planet. When I retired, I had a lovely silver-shaded Persian called Oscar, later introducing a little black cat, Souki, from the local rescue. The idea was they'd be mates. Truth was they never said a word to each other for 15 years. When faced with this perceived interloper, Oscar's look was always the same – utter disdain. Instantly I would be taken back to those senior players' faces when a new player arrived in the dressing room.

I'd first experienced this hangover of player hierarchy in the second XI. Stuck in a different room well away from the 'big boys', we were treated like servants. 'Boy! Take my jockstrap and put it in the drying room!' But more and more there were people in the seconds who weren't going to take that. We started telling them where to go. 'Don't ask me to pick up your sweaty old jockstrap. I'll get you a drink if you get a hundred. I'll bring your lunch if it's one of my duties. But don't treat me like a f***ing fag.'

It was only when five or six of that old guard retired and Gatt and Embers became bigger voices, along with the likes of Wilf

Slack and Roland Butcher, that things started to change. They started to break those walls down. They understood that it helps no one for a dressing room to be daunting. Why not make it a place where young players are made to feel welcome? Getting rid of that old public-school nonsense had to be good for team spirit. It was so archaic – 'I've done my hard yards and so now I'm going to put my feet up, treat people like servants, and do what the hell I want.'

No, sorry, I'll respect you for what you've done, but don't take the piss. Don't treat me like crap.

Their buttoned-upness would make me laugh sometimes. But then occasionally they'd open up and tell you stories of what they'd got up to when they were younger. 'Hang on a minute,' I'd say. 'You were worse than us!' I didn't understand why they couldn't lighten up a bit more often and felt the need to be on such a down about people just because they were young and wanted to have a bit of fun.

Middlesex wasn't the only county to be stuck in the past. Lancashire was similar, with its 'no women in the pavilion' rule and expectation that second XI players should knock on the first-team door to seek admittance. Yorkshire was another for stuffy nonsensical regulations. Hot days at Headingley always used to make me laugh. Yorkshire would be toiling away in the field, bright red and sweaty, and then come the break they'd have to put their blazers on to go to lunch. They'd be sat there enviously watching us relaxing in T-shirts and shorts.

Yorkshire also had a reputation for overly officious gatemen. On occasion, England players had been refused entry when turning up for a Test. 'I don't care who you are, you haven't got a pass so you're not coming in.' I'd laugh – until I had the same experience at Lord's. As tended to happen quite regularly, I'd arrived at the ground without my Middlesex tie. Usually, the gateman would turn a blind eye, but this time a chap was stood guard who I didn't recognise – and he clearly didn't know who I was either.

'I'm sorry, sir, you can't come in here with no tie.'

'But . . .'

'Sorry, sir. They're the rules.'

This couldn't be happening. 'Look, I'm very sorry about the tie and everything, but I am actually playing. You know that big green thing on the other side of the stand, I'm going to be required on it quite soon.'

We went back and forth like this a few times, me becoming increasingly desperate. I wondered what it might say on the scorecard – 'Phil Tufnell – did not bat (left on the pavement)'.

In the end, when it became clear I wasn't going away, he rang up to the dressing room. Gatt had to come down.

'Listen,' he said, 'I know he hasn't got a tie, but you've got to let him in because he's actually in the team.'

After no small amount of harumphing, he finally let me in.

While the gateman incident was utterly ridiculous, in a funny sort of way over time I came to embrace the tradition of Lord's. Once I began to play regularly, I saw how privileged I was to play there compared to one or two other places on the circuit. Derby was the away trip that generally produced the most groans. Before the more recent renovations, the pavilion at the Racecourse Ground had a feeling of a slightly well-to-do prefab. The dressing room in particular was a sight to behold, basically a changing area with a couple of really old showers and a toilet with a flimsy door. I could imagine it being used as a set location for *Porridge*.

The key was to get there early. That way you could avoid the seat next to the khazi. As being early wasn't really my forte, my preparation for a day's play was ten blokes standing a few feet away having a shower and then one by one settling themselves on the pan, because in cricket everyone makes sure to go before the start. Same would happen at lunch. A succession of male organs trailing past my seat as people had a shower, and then just a thin partition wall shielding me from whatever was happening in the toilet. How was a fitness fanatic like me supposed to carb-load in those circumstances?

Everything wasn't so much tired as deep in a Rip Van Winkle-type sleep. The showers were that shade of baby-poo brown, possibly to hide the array of nasties that lurked in there, that was unaccountably popular in the '70s. If health and safety had looked in that plughole in the drain, heaven only knows what they'd have found.

It wasn't Derby's fault, but having been used to changing at Lord's, a few days there could come as a bit of a shock. The players' toilets at Lord's were luxurious, always spotless and in a room lit by a beautiful big sash window which alone must have cost a fortune. I used to sit on those toilets with pleasure. I'd then hang out of that window and luxuriate in a fag.

We had four lovely baths in individual cubicles. Big things, like mini swimming pools. Even Angus Fraser could stretch out. Bath use, though, wasn't something to be assumed. It tended to depend on seniority. For a new kid to walk into that dressing room and start running a bath would have been a massive faux pas, like a pot-washer parading round a kitchen in Gordon Ramsay's hat. You had to gauge carefully whether you had bath status. When you became slightly more senior, and the day was coming towards the end, and you felt brave enough, and had performed well, then, and only then, did you feel it might possibly be acceptable to look up to the dressing room and make the international sign for 'run me a bath' – two hands turning imaginary taps at the same time. Depending on who was twelfth man, the request would be greeted with either two fingers or a thumbs-up. Whatever the situation, being first to use the bath was vital. You really didn't want to be next in after some sweating, dirt-encrusted heap had been soaping themselves for 30 minutes. I've seen less significant tidemarks on the Thames.

At the County Ground, Hove, they actually had a team bath. But don't go picturing a scene comparable to those old FA Cup finals at Wembley where the winning team would be up to their necks in suds while swilling champagne and tossing the trophy around. Sussex's was a tiny dressing room with a much less sizeable bath at one end, again in baby-poo brown. Not only that, but it only ever filled up about six inches. Basically, it was 11 dirty blokes sat in a puddle.

By now I was well used to seeing the state that fast bowlers get in. When they took a wicket you'd run up and slap them on the back and the sweat would fly everywhere. On closer inspection you'd see they had snot in their moustache and were foaming slightly at the mouth. Then there were the feet. Pacemen would take their boots off at the end of the day's play and there'd be great chunks of hard skin and toenails hanging off. Fast bowlers' feet are horrible, toes all funny shapes, like sharing a dressing room with ostriches. No way did I want to be bathing with that. What with them and the wicketkeeper with fingers all mangled and pointing every which way, dressing rooms were like a Hammer horror film. You can always tell a wicketkeeper in a pub – they're the one holding their pint between the palms of their hands.

I never quite got used to the business of communal de-robing. Putting on your whites is not too traumatic because a long shirt can hide a multitude of unpleasantries. But people whipping the stuff off at the end of the day's play in order to take a shower was something else. Frankly, I saw some shocking sights, some of which I've managed to blot out over time, some of which I'll take with me to the grave, and some of which still occasionally cause me to sit bolt upright in bed screaming. A full frontal of Mike Gatting was one thing. If he bent over to pick up a sock it could be far worse.

It didn't take me long to work out a strategy to avoid this cricketing catwalk of naked shame. I'd delay the moment of truth as long as possible – make another cup of tea, go outside for a fag, sit in my underpants making inane conversation and await my chance. When things quietened down, I'd slip a towel round my waist and strip off. At such moments I was instantly transported to getting changed on a beach as a kid. I wondered for a while if I should bring in a windbreak.

I think actually most players were more shocked at the sight of me clothed than unclothed. I compare it to my dad – he never wore a pair of jeans in his life. He donned a suit and a pair of brogues and then put his work overalls on over the top. So traditional was he that I never once saw him in a T-shirt, and yet every day he watched me bend the school uniform rules to breaking point in a pair of drainpipe trousers and brothel creepers. Thing is, I didn't care what setting I was in, I wasn't going to give up my individuality. When I turned up at Lord's in winklepickers, ponytail, earring and leopard-print G-string, it was because I liked winklepickers, ponytails, earrings and leopard-print G-strings. That was just me. In fact, I miss that thong. I wish I could remember where I got it from. I don't think it was M&S. I don't recall the label being St Michael. 'Leopard-print thongs, sir? Yes, just over there on the right, in front of the peephole bras.'

Of course, now I've gone full circle. I see kids wandering round with their arses hanging out of their trousers and I'm thinking, 'Really? Do you have to? No one wants to see that.'

Whatever its condition, whatever the cast of characters, put a bunch of hairy-arsed blokes together in a room for a length of time and it will soon start to look and smell like a pigsty. Dressing rooms could be pungent places full-stop. By the time day four of a match came round, you'd walk in and be knocked off your feet by the smell of rotting kit. Add in a dozen or so grown men who have spent three days drinking lager and eating curry and it was a surprise the plaster wasn't peeling off the walls. Any self-respecting woodlouse would have long moved out.

I've seen it suggested that I was quite a messy person in the dressing room, but I think you'll find it was always the posh boys, the ones who had been to university, who had their gear spread out all over the floor. Maybe they were used to someone cleaning up after them.

At Lord's, Simon Hughes' changing spot would be over the other side of the room. Even so, his shoes, socks and all sorts would somehow find their way over to mine. I was having none of that. 'Oi! Get your stinking boots out of my corner!' I'd say, flinging them back in his direction. I was quite picky about things like that – my corner was my corner. There was a lot of room in that dressing room, a great old place, massive windows made by, I don't know, Christopher Wren or somebody, so there was no need for anyone to encroach on anyone else's area. Gus Fraser and I sat next to each other for the best part of 20 years and there was very little encroachment by either party, although irritatingly his string vests used to appear in my space from time to time. I mean, who wears vests? Gus used to say they soaked up sweat. I don't care if they soak up London Gin. I've never worn a vest in my life and I intend to keep it that way.

While I was very keen on tidiness, my kit was rarely the cleanest. I'd get told off sometimes because I'd be rolling around in the field all day, maybe do a couple of sliding stops, and would have all mud and green up one side of my trousers, and then the next morning I'd put them straight back on again. I used to walk down the steps very quickly and trip over when I hit the grass to make it look like it had just happened, but the other players were having none of it. 'You can't walk out looking like that. You've got to make sure you've got a fresh pair of trousers. You look like you've been dragged through a hedge backwards.'

In my defence, it's worth remembering that in those early days at Middlesex I was pretty much operating on my own. Mum had passed away, Dad wasn't around so much, and so, yes, there were times when I'd get to a game, open my coffin and everything would still be scrunched up from the last time I'd played. I was trying to survive. Getting through the day was more important than ironing. One of the reasons I got married very young was to sort out that side of my life. I know it's a very old-school reason to tie the knot, but I really did need someone who could put the basics of my life in some kind of order.

While the Lord's dressing room did eventually become a sanctuary, its corridors were a place where I'd keep my head down. There were always committee men around, and when I heard them coming I'd dive into the physio's room, a cleaning store, or hide under the floorboards. I preferred saying hello to the people just beneath the surface. I'd go down to see Mick

Hunt, the groundsman, and have a poke around in the big sheds where all the mowers were kept. Ground staff are always good lads. Working boys, having a fag, nipping off for a cup of tea, giving the wicket a brush. Obviously, the captain would be trying to stay sweet with the groundsman all the time, but as players we never did. But then as I got older I'd say to Mick, 'Look, mate, sort me out. Don't worry about the seamers.' It started off as a bit of a joke, but over time I reckon it had an effect. 'Oh, Phil's playing today, maybe I'll take a bit of grass off.' It was subtle brainwashing – I'd have been good at leading a cult.

I liked having a chat with Middlesex scorer Harry Sharp, too. They're very knowledgeable, these guys. They don't just jot things down, they watch the game. Harry was a mine of information. He could tell you if you'd dismissed batsmen a certain way – 'You've had him caught at slip twice, Phil.' It meant I could devise a plan based on knowhow not guesswork.

Harry was also handy when it came to choosing which end to bowl from, something I'd always had difficulty with. It was a commonly held opinion that spinners should bowl into the wind, because it would hold the ball up in flight. But I hated bowling into the wind. I didn't want to be offering up nice floaty deliveries that sat up and asked to be smacked for six. I wanted the ball to be coming on to the batsmen, deceiving them, hurrying them. If I wanted to then hold one back a little, I could make the decision myself.

At Lord's, it was simple – I'd bowl from the Nursery End and Embers would bowl from the Pavilion End – it suited our styles. At other grounds, it all seemed so complex.

'Which end do you want to bowl?' a teammate would enquire.

'Why are you asking?' I'd wonder. 'What's the catch? Is

there something you're not telling me? Is one end shorter than the other?'

Other times, I wouldn't get a choice. The other bowler would be adamant. He'd grab the ball – 'I'm bowling that end.' And again I'd think, 'Why? Is there a sniper on the pavilion roof whose range doesn't extend that far?'

Some bowlers would memorise which ends had worked for them at which grounds. I could never remember, which is where Harry came in again. 'You bowled at the Radcliffe Road End last time out at Nottingham, Phil, and got a few wickets.' And that would make me more comfortable in my choice.

The opposition groundsman was always worth an ask, too. 'Well, Tuffers, that end's a little bit drier than this one. Last week I saw a bloke pitch one outside leg and hit first slip on the head.'

What I wanted more than anything was the ground to be flat. While Lord's had its own quirk with its infamous slope, at least that went side to side. Amazing how many grounds, like Chelmsford and Headingley, had the bowler either clambering up a mountain or tumbling down a hill. It could lead to arguments. Seamers always preferred to fall forwards, but then so did I, and I didn't see why, just because they were a seamer, they should have first choice. I wasn't going to shoot myself in the foot. Occasionally, I'd be accused of being selfish. How does that compute? Feeling comfortable in my approach could only help my action, which meant a greater chance of taking wickets, which in itself helped the side. If I was bowling well and thought I could get wickets at the end that 'belonged' to the faster men, so be it. I was there to win matches.

Harry and Mick were great boys, but my liking for the behind-the-scenes crowd didn't stop there. It seemed in my nature to gravitate towards the waiters, the waitresses, the attendants who looked after the dressing room. Having Lord's as your home ground was basically like living in Downton Abbey. Someone would open a cupboard and I'd be having a fag in there with one of the porters. I always liked to keep out of sight.

Occasionally, however, there'd be no avoiding the committee. Generally, it would go something like this.

Me: 'We've won the league, any chance of a bit more money?'

Them (looking sombrely at their notes): 'No.'

Me: 'Oh, right. Okay then. Bye.'

Occasionally the cheeses would come into the dressing room and wander about. We had our whites and they had their uniform of pinstripe suits and massive ties. 'Hello, everyone, lovely to see you', they'd say, and then head off back down to have their lunch and gin and tonics while watching the cricket from the beautiful Writing Room with its antique furniture and oil paintings.

I don't know why but these old boys seemed to enjoy scaring the life out of newcomers. They'd be very stiff and austere but then once you'd been there a while they'd be okay. I'd always say to them, 'Hang on a minute, why were you such a twat?' I could only think it was a rite of passage, again like *Downton Abbey*, where after 20 years a scullery boy makes his way to head butler and is occasionally allowed upstairs to see the family. At Christmas they might even call him by his first name.

'Would you like a sherry, Philip?'

'Oh I say, Your Lordship. Don't mind if I do. Actually, leave the bottle, would you?'

Starting out on the MCC ground staff, basically a training academy for promising young players, I'd sometimes liven these old boys up a little. As well as selling scorecards and generally helping round the ground, occasionally we'd be asked to bowl at those MCC members who fancied a net. The MCC member-ship is a broad church, but it is also fairly aged, mainly because the waiting list is about as long as the M1. You could push a ping-pong ball to the North Pole with your nose and still come back to find you'd only moved two places up the list.

As a result, on such occasions a small formation of chaps with sticks and ancient leather cricket bags would approach. You'd hear them in the distance discussing campaigns in the Boer War or reminiscing about the rationing of gobstoppers and pow-dered egg. Most had spent their working lives in the City and had memories of turning out for the Harrow first XI 60 years previously and sticking a half-volley from 'Piggy' Davison into the duckpond at Eton. Fair play, and good luck to them – I hope I'm sat on a shooting stick in the nets at Lord's at 75 – but for us young lads it meant we had to stay an extra hour. Perhaps it was this mild irritation that made us go at the old chaps a little harder than was strictly necessary. I don't think they saw much spin, let's put it that way. I resorted to my schoolboy penchant for fast bowling, whistling a few past the monocle. Eventually, we all got a bit fed up with this extra requirement, so we'd either hide in the dressing room or go to the pub. The poor old devils would be left standing there in their pads made out of sticks and gloves padded with goat wool.

Some people find county cricket and all that goes with it a bit slow, a bit of a toil, especially if they've played for England, but I never saw it like that. To me, it was a place to relax away from the focus of the microscope, a chance to break out of that shell. What I really loved was festival cricket, playing on outgrounds. By sheer virtue of these being once-a-year occasions, sometimes even less, there was always a great atmosphere – marquees, nice little clubhouse, crowd tightly packed in, many having brought their own deckchair. Uxbridge, Dartford, Folkestone, Guildford, that big noisy bowl at Scarborough, it didn't seem to matter where we played, people always seemed to come out in numbers. What more lovely way can there be to spend a day than playing cricket to the clink of wine glasses, laughter among friends, kids throwing up on the bouncy castle? I loved those occasions, even Colwyn Bay in North Wales, rumoured to be the shortest straight boundary in first-class cricket (not great for a spinner) and where occasionally you'd have to retrieve the ball from a graveyard.

The trips into the wilds of the minor counties, however, could be a little hairier, an occasion that particularly springs to mind being a Cheltenham and Gloucester Trophy first-round game against Herefordshire in the tiny village of Kingsland, population 986.

Of course, the big city boys of Middlesex rocking up in the shire was a big deal. Everyone packed into that little ground that day wanted to see us get our arses kicked, and when, in a grandstand finish, Herefordshire inched past our total with a ball to spare, all hell broke loose. As we trooped off, the local boys, big lads, of farming build, thronged around us. All we wanted was to get into the dressing room, grab our stuff and get out of there, but some of these lads clearly had other ideas. Things – how shall I put this? – started to get a little bit boisterous. Before I knew it, a pint of bitter had gone over my back.

A scene rarely pictured in the many watercolours of English village cricket grounds, suddenly things began to get a bit tasty. There were scuffles. To them we might have been the la-di-da boys up from London, but we weren't short of a few people capable of handling themselves. Mark Ramprakash could be a fiery character, and that's before you threw the likes of big

Angus into the mix. There was pushing and shoving until finally we managed to get ourselves into our tiny dressing room – someone needs to tell the people of Herefordshire there's 11 players in a cricket team. This shoebox was about as far from the esteem and majesty of Lord's as could ever be imagined. When I asked if they had any pegs to hang my clothes from, I was given a nail and a hammer.

In the manner of all good war films, we regrouped. But even then there were people kicking the door and banging on the walls. There was chanting – 'Hereford! Hereford! Hereford!' – like a football crowd. I was hoping that someone might give the SAS, based in the county town, a ring to help us out. In the meantime, we were all getting our bats out, selecting our weapons of choice, fighting among ourselves for the heaviest ones, to defend ourselves against the imminent storming of our sanctuary.

Thankfully, the security then turned up. Bert, I think his name was. Aged, at a conservative estimate, about 85, and decked out in a Herefordshire tie and pin-striped suit, he took stock of the situation. 'Don't worry,' he said, tapping his pipe out, 'I know these lads. I know their mothers. I'll have a word with them. There won't be any funny business.' When he said 'funny business', my mind immediately turned to the final scene in *The Wicker Man*, where Edward Woodward slowly burns to death in a giant effigy filled with pigs, sheep and the odd unfortunate goose. Thankfully, we were never sacrificed to the gods, although I still tend to skirt around Herefordshire if I find myself in the area.

We didn't actually need irate young farmers to raise the temperature in our dressing room. There were members of the team quite capable of filling that role internally. We all used to run off when Ramps got out because we knew it would be absolute carnage, bats getting smashed, mugs of tea flying across the room.

With most batsmen, you'd give them half an hour to stop steaming. Then slowly they'd inch their way into the conversation. 'It swung,' they'd say, to nobody in particular. And nobody in particular might reply, 'Well, he's a swing bowler. He's supposed to swing it. What did you think he was going to do, not swing it?'

Or the batter would say, 'It nipped back a bit.' And someone would reply, 'He always does that. He nips it back. He bowls the nip-backer.'

Gatt, for one, was never out. Even if his middle pole was knocked back, his response would be, 'Sure that was a no-ball. Must have been. No other explanation.'

Then there were the dressing-room batting and bowling spats that occasionally happened when one considered the other not to be pulling its weight. 'We won the toss, it's a green wicket, and they're a hundred for one at lunch. What the f***'s going on?'

The seamers, expected to have weighed in with a few wickets, would come back with something along the lines of, 'Well, how come you didn't bat like that?' It was a verbal boxing match, with the spinners becoming embroiled in the rumble if it was a turning pitch. No chance of someone taking you to one side – 'Perhaps you should try a bit more of an offside field, Phil' – it was always, 'Embers, Tuffers, its turning – why the f*** haven't you got them out?'

Mostly these things were done in jest, and actually it was healthy – rather than cause a rift it actually confirmed that the team had to work as a unit if it was to perform to its best – but if things got a bit fruity I'd use it to get me going. 'Right,' I'd think, 'I'll f***ing show you. Give me the ball after lunch and I'll sort this out.' And then, of course, the captain would chuck it to the seamers and I'd be stood there at third man, absolutely seething. 'You bastard. You know it's turning and you've given it to them.' Nine times out of ten when I did finally get the ball I'd get on a roll.

Inevitably, tempers fray. Desmond Haynes had a go at me in a curry house once. We were having a five-minute to and fro over tactics. I'd had a couple of drinks and was giving him a bit of chirp – 'You don't know what you're talking about' – when all of a sudden he slammed his fist on the table, the poppadoms flew three feet in the air, and it all kicked off.

'Come on, man! You've wound me up now. I'll show you what I'm talking about. Come on! Outside!'

Even in my inebriated state, taking on Dessie, a man of great strength and physical fitness, didn't strike me as a particularly great idea. 'Sorry, Dessie. I've thought about your point of view and on reflection I think you might be right. Anyone for a chapati?'

Threats of physical violence did come my way once or twice. Certainly in my early years there were a couple of occasions where I was talked to – how shall I put this? – very firmly, and every time for the right reason. At the time, I might have thought, 'The world's against me – how dare you do that?', but when I sat and thought about it, I'd realise, 'Yes, actually, I was being an awkward shit.' And that comes from inexperience and youth. Senior players are like village elders: they teach you the way of the world and how to go about your business. They would give me a bit of rope because they knew I was talented, but it was clear that if I pissed anyone off for the sake of it I would see another side to them. 'Don't make me angry. You won't like me when I'm angry.' Five minutes later, there Gatt would be, looking round the wrecked dressing room wondering why the whites he had on were shredded to ribbons.

In that domain, where you're playing a game over several days, you're all feeling it in different ways, maybe you've got something going on in your private life that no one else knows about, and you're living in very close quarters, it's hardly surprising that people snap occasionally. 'You what? You got something to say? Come on then!'

Generally, players get on okay, but even the most mild-mannered have their snapping point. Devon Malcolm was a lovely, gentle man. The only time I saw him angry was after an England XI vs Rest of the World XI one-day match in Jesmond. Devon, famously short-sighted, was in the shower with his glasses off. Taking advantage of this situation, Chris Lewis kept putting more and more shampoo in his hair. Devon hadn't noticed and so was lathering and lathering and lathering. No matter how much he rinsed, it didn't make a blind bit of difference. Eventually, he got wise to Chris's little game and that was it, he went for him, chasing him round the changing room and then (with the addition of a towel, I should add) out of the changing room. Chris was a strong bloke but he knew he was in big trouble if Devon got hold of him. For the rest of the day he skulked out of the way, disappointingly for the casual observer.

In most dressing rooms there is someone whose one-liners – intentional or otherwise – will always collapse the tension. Darren Gough generally assumed that role for England. 'All these sheep here in New Zealand,' he told the dressing room once, 'and you can't get a bacon sandwich anywhere.'

I tended to rely on actions rather than words. In the West Indies, for instance, my Shivnarine Chanderpaul batting impression did occasionally raise a small titter among my fellow tourists. His bizarre face-on stance was something I'd perfected playing French cricket as a kid in the garden. However, there were occasions when I too sent the teacups flying. Later in my career, when Middlesex were threatened with relegation to the second division, I felt some of the newer players weren't pulling their weight.

'Come on, boys! What do you think you're doing? You're just cruising. You're playing for Middlesex here. This is a club that wins championships. You're not doing it, boys. You're not doing it! Stop worrying about where your next Red Bull's coming from and get on with it.' We were in transition at that point. A lot of those great championship-winning players had gone. There was only really me and Angus left and we were knocking ourselves out just to try to keep us in the game. While it takes time for new players to bed in, it did feel sometimes like the effort wasn't good enough. Sometimes a bit of a rage is a good way to make a quick and justifiable point.

To be consumed by anger and disappointment as a professional cricketer in the long-term is a waste of a career. You should always realise how fortunate you are, and I knew that to play at Lord's alongside some great players was something pretty special. To be there at lunchtime on the last day of a championship game, glorious summer's day, lamb chops on the menu with ice cream for afters, and you've just got a five-for to bundle out Yorkshire, there's nothing better. To sit in that famous old dressing room, sun beating down outside, gentle breeze blowing through the balcony door, chatting with friends, patting one another on the back, is something else.

And then, when you're all sorted, pop the blazer on and go down to the Tavern for a quick drink before heading home, windows down, through Hampstead, the buzz of winning a game of cricket for your county still in your head. There's not a lot to dislike about that.

Sometimes as I was driving that familiar route, I would think of my dad's working life, so different from mine, in his silversmiths, and the time I had spent down there with him in the heat and dust, the boys covered in soot and polishing grease, and me – Bang! Bang! Bang! – smashing dents out of pieces of hotel silver.

A toenail in the shower at Sussex wasn't really that bad.

CHAPTER 5

How Not to Tour

Many dressing rooms become bogged down in superstition. I was never hugely bothered about stuff like that. The only thing I really felt strongly about was being first to touch the ball at the start of a game.

'Over here ump, please,' I'd say. He'd throw me the cherry – and Jack Russell would dive in and intercept it. He had exactly the same inexplicable quirk as me. Oh well, his need was greater than mine. He'd be holding it and catching it long before I was bowling with it. And anyway, there was a decent chance I'd drop it on the concrete steps and be bollocked by the rest of the team.

Embers was the same as me in being scathing of spiritual forces. I don't suppose he saw too much evidence of them in Peckham. And yet one day while having a bit of a wander round Calcutta we spotted a fortune-teller in a little courtyard. Well, even our cynicism was tested. So long as it's not an out-of-control double-decker bus, who doesn't want to know what's round the corner? This being 1993 and with Russell Grant yet to be added to the England coaching staff, we thought we'd sit down with the chap and see what he had to say. Whatever it was, it couldn't be any worse than the hellishly unsuccessful tour we were experiencing.

He alone didn't predict the future. He had a partner in soothsaying – a blue parrot. Whether it was a Norwegian Blue I couldn't say, but whatever its lineage it was barely more alive than the one in the *Monty Python* sketch. It was missing various parts of its anatomy, notably an eye, a wing and a leg. Its single foot had just one claw. I'm fairly sure its beak was held on with Pritt.

'Facking hell,' whispered Embers, 'what the fack are we doing here?' It's why he's never had his own travel show.

At that point the chap produced the tarot cards. He laid them out so they were overlapping. The parrot then hobbled from its cage. He spoke to it in parrot and it set off walking up and down the line of cards. By now a crowd had gathered, transfixed. A small boy was crying.

Occasionally, we'd hear our names mentioned and a burst of laughter. I knew what they were saying – 'That's Emburey and Tufnell, the two spinners supposed to come over here and bowl us out. They're so desperate they've come to see the nutcase with the blue parrot for a bit of divine intervention.'

The parrot took its time, mainly because it kept falling over, but eventually picked a card, holding it in its beak for several seconds. It really did know how to build up suspense. The guru read it out to the Indian army officer who had accompanied us as security. He listened and then gave us the translation.

'Mr Emburey, Mr Tufnell,' he said, 'good news. The parrot says your fortunes will improve.'

'Excellent!' Me and Embers exchanged smiles.

'The change will come on 21 March.'

I had a think. Why did 21 March ring a bell?

'Embers, what's happening on 21 March?'

Embers looked at me. 'Tuffers,' he said, 'that's the day the tour ends.'

The parrot, looking a little sheepish, if that makes sense, hobbled back into its cage. He'd pulled a terrible trick on us but even so I did feel sorry for him. He needed a little crutch.

As well as the man with the bird, we visited a palm reader in Madras, a trip organised by the management to provide a photo opportunity for the press. Me and Embers considered the request – 'Facking hell, Tuffers. I knew it wasn't coming out the hand too well, but is this really the answer?'

Embers had a point. Nowadays, they have analysts, laptops, bowling plans for every batsman. In 1993, the answer was 'Get 'em down the palm reader.' I'm not quite sure what nuggets they were expecting – 'I think, my friend, you need to bowl a little bit more outside off stump to Tendulkar.'

Two tuk-tuks were arranged to collect us. Had we already seen the palm reader, I'm pretty sure he would have identified a journey through the thronging traffic of Madras in one of these rickety affairs as a life-threatening experience in itself. It was absolute chaos, people everywhere, noise coming from every angle, dogs running around. Eventually we stopped outside a small wooden shack. Inside was a chap sat on a metal bed with his legs crossed. For a second I thought he was levitating.

We all shuffled in and joined him cross-legged while he embarked on the reading and the press boys took a few photos. There was a slight communication issue in that he didn't speak English and I didn't speak Gujarati, but, as he inspected my hand, I could tell by his face that things weren't looking good.

He gestured over to our fixer, the local man who had sorted the visit, and mumbled something in his ear.

'What did he say?' By now I'd become consumed by the proceedings. I genuinely felt my future lay in this man's hands.

'He says he doesn't think you're going to be getting any wickets.'

'Come on,' I said, 'there must be more to it than that.'

'No,' replied the fixer. 'The reading is clear. You're f***ed.'

As a tourist, I liked the occasional jaunt off the beaten path. The thing I loved most about Australia, for example, was going up-country; little one-horse towns that didn't have much more than a few houses dotted around and a main street with a pub. It was like being transported to the Wild West. I wouldn't have been the least bit surprised to see a gunslinger ride into town for a showdown with the sheriff.

The sudden arrival of the England cricket team in town was more often than not the cue for chaos. On one notable occasion we were in Geraldton, Western Australia. Myself, Allan Lamb, Robin Smith ('the Judge' – he had a barnet like a horsehair wig) and Devon went for a night out and found ourselves in a little bar where they seemed to have a penchant for line-dancing. 'Turn to the right, one-two. Turn to the left, one-two' – all this kind of stuff. Within minutes, I was in the middle of it, going the wrong way, bouncing into the locals. Next thing I knew someone had chinned me and I was wondering, firstly, whether this was such a good idea, and, secondly, where was big Devon. Thankfully, the next words I heard were those of Judgey and Lamby. 'Oi! You can't be doing that!' Someone at the pub also pointed out that this wasn't any way to welcome the England cricket team and it all calmed down. I was only on soup for three days.

A similar thing happened when I got trapped in another bar with the former Aussie paceman Mike Whitney, quite a tough character, a bit of a lad. Aside from the Aussie physio, a man known to me only as the Smiling Melon – don't ask – we were the only people out that night and my presence was soon noted. It was a young crowd and soon they were all shouting over at me – nothing too tasty, but Mike was trying to calm them down. It didn't work. All of a sudden these pots of lager started coming over, with Mike and the Smiling Melon standing in front to protect me.

More often than not, the Aussies just wanted a bit of banter, which was fine by me because I loved all that, especially its capacity to come from unexpected places, such as the doorman at the Hyatt Regency guiding us into the hotel – 'Welcome to Brisbane, you Pommie bastards. You're going to get a dicking off us. Steve Waugh's going to f***ing murder you. Where would you like your bags?'

It was the same with the team bus drivers in the Caribbean. 'Yeah, man! Brian's going to get you today! Curtly and Courtney are coming for you!' This was on the way to the ground!

I became very adept at embracing that attitude and having good fun with it. And if we did do well that day, if we survived the bowling onslaught or got Brian out for only a few, I'd be giving it straight back to the driver on the return leg. But generally, climbing those steps onto the bus would bring only a further torrent of gloating – 'I told you Brian was going to get you, Tuffers. You wouldn't listen, but I told you.'

I loved how the reality of each country we visited was so different from the stiff and formal description we'd be given as part of a 'cultural chat' before we travelled, the idea being to make us more comfortable as a team, less prone to shock.

'Now,' the speaker would say before we headed to Australia, 'if you see someone with a hat with corks hanging off, don't be alarmed, it's just to keep the flies away. And remember, although it might seem that way, not all the women are actually called Sheila.'

It really was that basic. You'd walk into a room before a tour to India and be told, 'Now, for anyone who doesn't know what curry is . . .' They'd be stood at a whiteboard pointing at a bhuna with a baton.

Prior to the South Africa tour, we had a health and safety briefing which succeeded only in scaring the living daylights out of us. Bombarded with crime figures and murder rates, we sat there thinking, 'Bloody hell! Where on earth are they sending us?'

For India, crime was replaced with food poisoning – 'Don't drink the water, don't eat salad, don't eat red meat, don't eat chicken.'

'Hang on!' I'd think. 'I'm going for three months. How am I going to survive?' There wasn't a lot of meat on me to start with. I was reminded of that trip ten years later when I was on *I'm a Celebrity, Get Me Out Of Here!* Both were ventures that sparked a serious amount of weight loss.

After the briefing, in would come the doctor. 'Roll up your sleeve, Mr Tufnell.' For the next 15 minutes I was a human pin cushion. Malaria, yellow fever, dengue fever, tetanus, Dutch Elm disease – on and on it went. I'd be thinking, 'Hang on! Don't eat the food. Don't drink the water. Now a load of jabs. I thought we were just having a game of cricket!'

That's not to say things couldn't get a bit tasty. Cricket is, after all, played in some of the less stable political environments. There were times when I looked at a sniper riding shotgun on the team bus and thought, 'I really would have been better putting a bit more into my tennis.'

On the Zimbabwe tour of 1996, we were introduced to then President Robert Mugabe when he came down to a game at the Harare Sports Club to meet the teams. Athers, captain at the time, was running around gathering everyone together and so when Mugabe walked into our dressing room before the team handshake on the pitch, the only one there was me. Luckily, I recognised him and didn't ask him to get me a cup of tea.

Mugabe had a palace not far from the ground, which was handy for him but difficult for us – anyone seen in the vicinity after 6:30 p.m. was in danger of being shot. If nothing else it was an incentive to keep up with the over rate. On the first day I was not out overnight. When I got back to the dressing room, everyone was already changed, showered and ready to go. In fact, some of the boys were outside on the coach.

'Out, now!' I was told by a security man.

'Hang on,' I said. 'What about my pint of lager? I like to relax after a long innings.'

'Well,' he replied, 'you can relax, but you'll have to stay in the dressing room overnight or we can't guarantee your safety.'

I whipped my gear off, chucked it in a corner, stuck my tracksuit on and threw myself onto the coach as it wheel-spun out of the car park.

Again my batting heroics had gone unappreciated. 'I mean, of all times, Phil,' groaned the boys, 'why did you have to hang in there?'

In Jamaica, meanwhile, for the first Test against West Indies, the nets at Kingston's Sabina Park weren't ready and so we were taken off to use the facilities at a ground in nearby Trenchtown. When we arrived, we were a little surprised to see the two local blokes who made up our armed security detail embark on a full scan of the perimeter before we were ushered in. It wasn't the most salubrious of grounds – the windowless breezeblock changing rooms were nothing if not original – there was rubble all over the place, and we had to shoo a load of goats away before we could get started. But it was okay and we had a good net before packing up to head back to the hotel. I had a chat with one of the security boys while one or two players had a last couple of throwdowns.

'Not a bad little spot, this,' I said.

'You're joking,' he replied. 'This is where all the local gangs have firefights. This is where they all come and shoot each other. If one gang has a beef with another they all meet at the cricket club and sort it out.'

And as I started to look round, it all became clear. In the long grass, there were baseball bats with barbed wire and nails sticking out. That ball I'd bowled that had turned sideways had done so because it had hit a bullet casing. We'd been totally oblivious to all of it, but these two security guys were basically on hand in case we were centre stage in a shootout.

Naivety has occasionally been my forte. When we played West Indies in an exhibition game in New York, myself and Gus Fraser were just walking out of the hotel as West Indies wicketkeeper Jeffrey Dujon was coming in.

'Where are you going?' he asked.

'Oh, just for a little wander,' we replied.

'Well, don't turn left whatever you do.'

'Oh no, Jeff, don't worry about it. We're only going for a stroll. We'll head left. It's all right.'

At this point, Jeff became quite stern and fatherly.

'Boys, listen to me,' he said. 'You can't go left here.'

He was blocking our way. 'Jeff, come on, let us past.'

'No, I'm not letting you go.'

He was absolutely adamant and so in the end we opted for the easy life and turned right. Jeff was correct, of course. Turn left and we'd have been in the gun crime epicentre of the Big Apple. Turn right and within five minutes we were gawping at the billboards in Times Square.

Security was more necessary, and apparent, on some tours more than others, our India tour in 1993 being a case in point. An England team finding itself in India during a period of high volatility was nothing new. The previous visit, in 1984–85, had coincided with the assassination of Mrs Gandhi, and later, the morning after he'd entertained the team at his residence, the British Deputy High Commissioner Percy Norris was shot dead on the way to his office. Before we arrived, a temple had been razed to the ground, sparking disturbances in which hundreds had died. Our first match, in Ahmedabad, was subsequently called off as, the authorities claimed, our safety could not be guaranteed. Another game, in Cuttack, was played in an empty stadium – aside from the 400 army officers on duty to protect us.

One officer had been assigned to travel with us to and from the ground. His 'uniform' consisted of a pair of black plimsoles like you might have worn at school in 1973, a pair of multi-pocketed green trousers such as you might find in a surplus store, a diamond-patterned Pringle jumper and a beret. He was equipped with a Sten gun, held round his neck with an Olympus Trip camera strap. I got chatting to the bloke and told him it was reassuring he had the old Sten gun in case of assailants.

'Well,' he said, 'what I'll have to do if anyone attacks is take it off and hit them round the head with it because I've got no bullets.'

We might as well have just been sat there with a cricket bat in our hands. 'Stay clear! We've got Gunn & Moores!'

To be fair, the general at the ground had a proper uniform. It was just everyone else who looked like they'd come along in any old odds and sods they could find. I mean, if I was in the army – and fear not, Defence Secretary, I have flat feet – I'd like to think there'd be some sort of ensemble upstairs in the spare room which I could sling on and roughly look like I was playing the part.

It was all a little odd to start with playing to a crowd of soldiers, but after a while they all sat down, had a cup of tea and watched the game. However, seeing soldiers on patrol in the hotel corridor outside your room never felt right, or even that secure. On one occasion, myself, Neil Fairbrother and Judge were together when three gun-toting men walked in. They didn't look like the other army blokes and initially we feared the worst. I was just about to say my last when one of them spoke up – 'Excuse me, could we please have an autograph?'

In the end, it no longer became a surprise to be having a chat only for a bloke with a Lee–Enfield to walk round the corner. 'All right?'

'Yes, thank you.'

'Normal' life as an England cricketer abroad would then carry on.

Issues in India weren't confined to the field of play. There were plenty up in the air, too. An Indian Airlines pilots' strike meant replacements from Uzbekistan were brought in, many of whom didn't speak the language, not great in terms of air traffic control. Other holes in the schedule were filled by hastily bringing pilots back from retirement.

There were several flights on that tour where I thought my

time was up. On one occasion, the plane carrying the England team suffered complete hydraulic failure. As it circled above the airport, there was a massive bang, the plane lurched to one side and everyone thought the end had come. The captain managed to bring it under control, the aircraft screaming down the runway and stopping a matter of feet from the barrier at the end. The captain came over the intercom – 'Praise be to Allah!' On disembarking, there was revealed to be a gaping hole in the bottom of the fuselage the size of a cricket coffin. Divine intervention, it seemed, had saved the team from unscheduled retirement.

Thankfully, this was a flight I wasn't on. The plane, chartered to carry the team from Bangalore to Jamshedpur for the fifth of seven one-day internationals, wasn't big enough for everyone. Me and Athers were deemed least likely to play and so were left behind. It's barely comprehensible in these days of ultra-professionalism, itineraries worked out to the second, but back then with me and Athers it was basically, 'Okay, lads, wait on the corner outside the sultan's palace at half past eight next Thursday and we'll be back to pick you up.' No one phoned to check on us or anything. Marooned, all we could do was have a bit of a holiday. Each morning we'd meet up for breakfast and then spend the rest of the day sat round the pool. He'd read *War and Peace* and I'd get pissed. Occasionally, he'd take me to some sort of educational place, show me a bit of culture and then we'd go out for a bit of dinner. By the end of the week we were like an old couple. I could see people whispering in the hotel, 'Are they ever going to leave?'

Reunited with our colleagues, as a team we were becoming more and more concerned as to our safety. We were touring a country in turmoil, everywhere we looked there were guns, people were being killed on the streets daily and the transport was both decrepit and dire. The last straw came when one of the key individuals in India who had assured our safety resigned after two plane crashes claimed multiple victims. To allay our fears, the management gathered us all in a hotel room for a chat with a chap from the British High Commission. We waited a while and then this big posh bloke, sweating heavily in a suit and tie, arrived. He couldn't have looked more 'British High Commission' if he'd tried. All he was lacking was a helmet with a feather sticking out the top. This man's upper lip was so stiff that a flick of the finger and it would have snapped like a twig. Initially I thought I recognised him as an extra in *Brideshead Revisited*.

'Now come on, you chaps,' he said, pouring himself a brandy, 'don't worry yourselves. It's just India. I've been here thirty years and we've never had any serious trouble. You're the England cricket team, it'll be fine.' Considering what was happening daily on the streets, I couldn't help wondering what exactly constituted 'serious'.

And then he walked off. 'Right,' said one of the management, 'I'm glad that's put your minds at rest.'

Why, yes, of course. A drunk bloke from the High Commission has wandered in for five minutes and told us not to worry – that's covered everything pretty much.

As far as we were concerned, we'd just been told, 'Chin up, everyone! Queen and country, that's what matters. You just need to knuckle down and get on with it. If the worst does happen and the plane does crash, you can all rest happy that we'll give you a good send-off.'

There was such an arrogance about it. It was as if just being the England cricket team was enough to negotiate a war zone. 'I say, chaps. Would you mind awfully not shooting at us? We've got a one-day international in Calcutta in two days. Be jolly inconvenient to have to play it with only one eye.'

The message just didn't compute and so we said no. Flying in India just wasn't safe, the concession being that we then travelled by train, which took a long time but, the odd rat aside, was actually quite fun. We could mix on a train and have a bit of a laugh, whereas on a plane we were strapped in, petrified.

Railway stations in India were a massive eye-opener. On one occasion, we arrived in Calcutta at four in the morning. We were getting off, all in our white England tracksuits with snazzy red flashes, clutching multiple bags and coffins, and all we could see were hundreds of people asleep on the platform. Others were cooking; a few kids were running around playing.

I had only one thought – 'What is this place?'

We tiptoed over people and gathered at the front of the station awaiting our transport to the hotel, and as we did so the city came to life around us. This sea of humanity came from nowhere – people living on the streets, others making their way somewhere, some just looking lost and hopeless – and surrounded us. It was as unnerving as it was moving.

This early morning scene in Calcutta was my first experience of true culture shock. I had been abroad and seen a different way of life, but this was off-the-scale different. I might as well have been on another planet. The noise, the movement, the smells, the poverty. I'd close my eyes wondering if it was real. And then I'd open them and it would still all be there.

The coach pulled up. Far from the luxury travel you might get in England or Australia, this was an old rickety bus, dirty inside and out. A little bloke with a pair of sandals and a loincloth took our bags and began stacking the coach – and then he walked over to the gutter and went to the toilet.

'What is this place?' I said out loud to no one in particular. And then I said it again, and again. I knew only one thing for sure – it was very different from Hertfordshire.

Nowadays, the England team has a permanent security adviser, compared to the old way – arrive and find the hardest bloke in the area. To be honest, though, while having motorcycle outriders on the way to and from grounds did make you worry sometimes, and blokes with shooters knocking around the hotel was a little disturbing, I always felt I had more chance of being killed by neon-green prawns than anything else.

CHAPTER 6

How Not to Die

Home and abroad, as a cricketer you are so reliant on other people for your food that the law of averages says there's bound to be times when contamination occurs. There was a constant threat of dysentery at even the poshest places. When Middlesex were invited to Buckingham Palace I thought about taking a bucket. Travelling up to Lancashire, meanwhile, a London lad like me would often find himself in the cubicle just because they eat such different stuff up there. The sheer volume of gravy played havoc with my insides. But it could happen anywhere – bound to when you spend your days cooped up in dressing rooms with a bunch of sweat-encrusted blokes. All it takes is a couple of them not to have washed their hands and there's germs all over the place.

Having said that, the warning signs are occasionally right in front of your eyes. When Gooch and Gatt were laid low by a prawn curry before the second Test in Madras in 1993, no one who had seen the dish arrive at the table was in the least bit surprised. It's shade of green immediately reminded me of a customised Ford Fiesta a mate had back in my teens. The entire dish was glowing, pulsing. It really should have been served to the theme tune from *Doctor Who*. If I'd been Gatt and Gooch I'd have asked for a Geiger counter. Gatt's stomach lining had been well hardened over the years, but this particular dish took even the big man down.

I was a bit more circumspect in India. I would have a masala omelette for breakfast and then hopefully nip down to the High Commission later for some beans on toast. Occasionally, we'd get a food parcel sent over by a UK supermarket as a promotional thing. It was a bit like being in the trenches – dry biscuits, all that sort of stuff. The only surprise was it wasn't airdropped. During the up-country games, at lunch and tea tour manager Bob Bennett would set out tables of offerings for those who didn't fancy a local dish. It was like a little farmers' market. Bob was quite a well-to-do chap who generally wore his England blazer and a tie, and now here he was in civvies and a chef's hat serving up grub to the boys.

In India one time, I was feeling familiarly dicky – the usual business, stomach cramps, sweats – topping up at one end, constantly coming out the other – and my time to bat was coming nearer and nearer. Hovering over a hole is no way to prepare for a Test innings. Eventually, there comes a point where you have to get the gear on – pads, box, thigh pad, arm guard and all the rest of it – and it becomes completely impractical to go to the toilet. If a wicket falls you've got three minutes max to be out there ready. There's no point waving from the toilet window and shouting, 'Do you mind waiting? I'm going to be another five minutes here.'

On this occasion, the old sweats came on again and I was feeling delicate in the extreme. I considered making one last dash but Phil DeFreitas was having a bit of a slog and so I knew

I could be required at any time. When Daffy survived to the end of the over, I saw it as a chance, but the rest of the boys were having none of it. 'You're next in, Phil – you won't have time.' It was all right for them. Any other position in the order and if needs must you can swap with the next man in. As number 11, I didn't have the option. I was just about to go anyway when I heard 'Howzat?' from outside. The next over had started and Daffy had missed a straight one and got out LBW. Out I went, the heat hitting me like a mallet in the face. Right-arm off-break Rajesh Chauhan was bowling with men all around the bat. First up, he bowled me one full length outside off stump, ripe to be hit through extra cover.

'Right,' I thought, 'foot to the pitch, high elbow, swing of the bat, follow through.' It was absolute textbook – except for the follow through, which wasn't quite what I'd been expecting. There was a gasp from short leg. 'Oh, Tuffers!'

A cricket pitch is no place for a stomach upset. Aggers (Jonathan Agnew) tells a lovely (well, maybe not lovely) story about a game he played in. The bloke opening the bowling at the start of a day reached the top of his mark, tore in and carried straight on into the pavilion. But any illness could spread like wildfire. When Joey Benjamin and Devon came down with chickenpox at the start of the Ashes tour in 1994–95, they were whisked off and I didn't see them for a month.

'Where's Joey and Dev?' I'd ask.

'They've gone on,' I'd be told. It was like a dark presence had taken them away in the night.

If illness didn't get me, then the natural world seemed hell-bent on sorting me out. Playing international cricket, you tend to tour some fairly hot and exotic places. And with that heat and exotica come some seriously unpleasant beasts.

During lockdown in 2020, commentating on England's trip to Sri Lanka from the safety of The Oval, I was intrigued to see on camera a giant lizard fielding down at fine leg. Aggers had clocked it, too, and immediately recalled a similarly grotesque creature giving me some serious grief on the same ground three decades earlier. On that occasion, disturbed from his slumber in the journalists' tent by a sharp shriek, he looked up to see me being pursued at third man by what looked like a mid-sized dinosaur. Until Aggers mentioned it, I'd banished it from my mind, but now the terror came flooding back. This thing had appeared behind me totally unannounced. Only a hissing noise alerted me to its presence. Looking round, I saw this huge forked tongue darting in and out. It seemed we'd gone from playing Sri Lanka to a Jurassic Park invitational XI. Oh look, there's Jeff Goldblum at silly mid-on.

Instinct took hold and I pegged it towards the wicket. I was about to grab a stump and shout, 'Arm yourselves!' when I saw it had given up its pursuit. I think it had spotted an ice-cream vendor with more meat on him. You never quite knew what you'd encounter touring the world with England, but Sri Lanka could be particularly hairy as a lot of the country is jungle and so it didn't need a beast to wander too far off track to find itself being commentated on by Jonathan Agnew.

In Australia, I voluntarily put myself in the presence of monsters. A few of us went to see some crocodiles on a farm. It was a place where they bred them to make them into handbags. Bit rough really. No animal was put on this earth to end up carrying round a lipstick, vanity mirror, and packet of extra strong mints.

The place absolutely stank. No café, or visitor centre, or bit of crazy golf for the kids. To be fair, there was a gift shop. It sold dead chickens you could throw into the enclosures.

My immediate thought was, 'I'm not sure I really like this. It smells to high heaven. I can't see too many fences. What are we doing here? Who organised this trip?'

This old Aussie bloke gave us a tour. 'This is Mabel,' he said, 'the biggest saltwater croc in ninety-seven years.' I followed his gaze and was met with the sight of a gnarled beast the size of a small battleship enclosed behind a tiny bit of chicken wire. Forget a crocodile: a stick insect could have breached that barrier.

'Why don't you go up to her?' he invited. 'She's very nice. She's not attacked anyone for two years.' And to be fair she did look fairly placid. No worse than Ramps after a run of low scores.

Producing a chicken on the end of a fishing rod, the old chap decided to get her going a bit, dangling the morsel in front of her nose. She clocked it, stared at it for a few seconds, and then all of a sudden – wham! – she ripped it to pieces.

'Well, so nice to have met you. If it's all the same to you we'll be off now.'

All the time I was there I was looking for his helper with one arm.

Australia was also the worst for snakes and spiders. England always played a few games up-country and the first thing you did when you walked into those little old dusty dressing rooms was bash under your seat with your bat, same in the lockers. At the hotel the next morning, someone would pipe up that they'd gone out on their hotel balcony and found a python sunbathing – 'I phoned reception, and they said not to worry.'

Not all beasties are land-based. One time I was fielding in Australia, out on the boundary, when I was mildly concerned to see both umpires and the batsmen hit the deck. I was wondering what the hell was going on – I hadn't heard a rifle crack – and was just about to wander in and ask a couple of questions when my fellow fielders started to do the same. Someone shouted to me, really quite forcefully, 'Get down on the floor!' It was like being in a very odd episode of *Kojak*. It was then I heard a terrible noise, a huge buzz, getting nearer and nearer. Peering through my fingers, I saw a vast swarm of bees passing in a wave across the ground. I couldn't help cursing my luck that these things had never appeared when I was batting and become entangled in Merv Hughes' facial hair.

In India, too, I had faced nature's air force when an immense squadron of dragonflies nosedived the field of play. Giant things they were, like pterodactyls. You could hear their wings going right next to your head and I really wouldn't have been at all surprised if three or four had latched onto me and carried me away.

Of course, the old classic is the wasp up the trousers. Edgbaston endured a minor invasion one time – and again I was the last to find out. The first I knew was when people began tucking their trousers into their socks. I looked down and there were hundreds of wasps on the ground, woozy and a bit half-arsed, like England's one-day side in the late '90s. At that point I reached for my own socks, but not before one errant insect had found its way up there and, as I danced around, attached itself to a testicle. That was its final view. Even through the agony I pitied it.

If the wildlife didn't get you then chances were either the weather or geography would. In Perth there was me, Devon, John Morris and David Lloyd, who I think was out there doing a bit of commentating. John had this posh mate who'd just had a new fishing boat. It was a substantial vessel and for the first

20 minutes I was imagining myself pulling up in it in Cannes, draping a jumper over my shoulders and casually disembarking to the admiring glances of the international film glitterati – Nicole Kidman perhaps, or at the very least Pauline Fowler from *EastEnders*.

We were heading over to the island of Rottnest, a 45-minute chug across the sea, for the afternoon. Rottnest is famous for its native quokka (a rare short-tailed wallaby), as well as the southern blind snake, legless lizard and moaning frog. That lot was for David Attenborough. Our idea was to have a couple of drinks in a bar, chuck a towel on the beach and get back.

It was a beautiful sunny morning when we set off. We loaded the beer and wine aboard and were looking forward to a little spank across the briny. 'No problem,' said our captain, 'we'll be there in a jiffy.'

It was just at that very last moment before we set off that even a confirmed landlubber like myself detected a slight change in the wind. 'Ooh!' I thought. 'I wish I'd brought my jumper.'

The bloke who owned the boat wasn't hugely experienced – I don't know whether he'd been trained in this sort of thing, or had even read the instructions – and we'd just chugged out of the harbour when this huge 'Boom!' went off.

'Blimey! That was a bit loud,' said Bumble (David Lloyd), always an observant man. 'I wonder what that means.'

Only later – much later – after one of the most hellish experiences of our lives – did we discover that the 'Boom!' means 'Do not, whatever you do, leave this harbour. There's a hurricane on the way. Leave the harbour now and you are doomed. Only one fate awaits you.'

Instead of a jaunty 45-minute trip, we finally limped into Rottnest harbour five hours later. The seas we faced on that journey – and why this has never been turned into a Hollywood survivor movie is beyond me – were towering. Time and again they reared above the boat. And each time they did so Devon, John, Bumble and I had only one thought, 'Oh my God – this is it! We've gone.' Even if we did survive the rough sea, there was no way we could see off the great white sharks circling below.

We were all half-pissed, none of us knew what we were doing, how to radio for help, where the flares were, the life dinghy: nothing. I'd watched the first series of *Howards' Way*, but I didn't feel it qualified me for a situation like this.

Hour after hour we clung on for dear life. I swear even now thinking about it my knuckles are white. Eventually we pulled into Rottnest, headed for the nearest bar, waited for it to calm down and made it back without any further drama. A simple little tootle out to the island and back had taken the entire day.

Safely back on dry land, I switched the TV on in my hotel room and saw just how lucky we'd been. It had been carnage out there. Boats had capsized, people clinging onto upturned hulls while shark fins circled in the water. Helicopter rescues had been launched. I couldn't believe what we'd found ourselves caught up in.

Talk about the cruel sea – although in my experience the land isn't much better. I fell down a pothole before a match in Grenada. Someone had given me and Judgey – the usual suspects looking for a rum punch at half past ten at night – directions to a nice little beach bar. 'Go along the sand, up over the headland, and down to the beach – you can't miss it.'

All we had was the light of the moon. We'd done the sand bit and were now, inevitably, roaming lost on the cliffs.

'Judgey,' I said, 'are you sure this is the way?' It would have been nice to have an idea, what with there being a 40-foot drop onto the rocks below.

Eventually we made it down to another beach and found ourselves on a bashed-up old jetty. It was concrete, mangled and the sea was smashing against it. And then I disappeared – 'Aaaghh!' – like in *The Vicar of Dibley* when she falls in that puddle. I'd plunged about 15 feet when I became snagged by my shirt. Good job, because where the pit bottomed out was anyone's guess. Well, good job until I realised what had broken my fall was a razor-sharp strengthening rod. If I'd fallen at a different angle it would have gone straight through me. Skewered. There'd be a little memorial there to this day. 'Here lies the spot where reasonably successful England spinner Phil Tufnell was turned into a kebab.'

Up above I could hear Judgey's familiar Durban accent.

'Tuffers! Tuffers! Where the fick have you gone?'

'I'm down here!' I ripped my T-shirt off the rod and managed to clamber out.

Next day I went back to have a better look. As I peered into the depths, peppered with spikes, it reminded me of one of those pits people used to dig to trap wild animals. I was covered in scratches and bruises but knew I'd been incredibly lucky, just an inch or two away from certain death.

Thankfully, I do have a self-preservatory streak (some would call it cowardice) which prevents me from getting into precarious situations more than once a fortnight. Heights I tend to avoid. I have a slight reflux reaction to them. All the more amazing, then, that when I filmed the travelogue *This Could Go Anywhere* with the former New Zealand captain and batting legend Brendon McCullum, I agreed to do a freefall skydive. I should point out I was strapped to a burly character who'd done thousands of jumps before. Even so, when he casually chucked 'I always check I've packed my emergency parachute' into the conversation as we hauled on our jumpsuits, I couldn't help but feel a little twitchy, turning to mild panic when he said he'd 'only' deployed it about 20 times. I was about to ask what happens if the emergency 'chute fails when I thought better of it. I could only assume there was a big haystack out there somewhere.

The plane itself was reassuringly beefy and although the pilot looked about 19 she knew what she was doing, taking us up at what felt almost like the vertical to the required altitude. I was just about to ask what was for the in-flight meal when the door opened. Now, I don't care how blasé you are about flying, everyone knows it's not a good idea to go round opening doors on planes. I've flown on dozens of Jumbos and never did the flight attendant open the main exit to empty my ashtray. Immediately, I was enveloped by intense wind and cold, momentarily taken back to an early season county championship clash at Leeds. I was straddling a big, soft, yellow banana-type bench which at any other time I would have found quite pleasing, but now I was being edged towards the door until I found myself with my legs dangling out of the door. And then, just as we plopped out into the void, my co-plummeter flipped me round so I could see the bottom of the plane speeding away. Left behind in mid-air strapped to a vast plunging New Zealander really was quite a disturbing feeling.

Forget jumping out of one, even sitting in a plane has never sat that easily with me, especially since an experience on my first Ashes tour. We were heading to a place up-country, near Adelaide, called Port Pirie. It was only a little plane and from the word go I didn't like the look of it. As I boarded I couldn't get Glenn Miller out of my head. Perhaps my nerves would have been better settled had I not asked the captain, 'Which way are we heading?' To which he pointed towards a vast bubbling black cloud full of lightning. I looked at my boarding pass to check it didn't say 'Armageddon'. I took my seat at the back of the aircraft. I had heard the old joke about planes never reversing into mountains and at this moment in time it rang true.

Once in the air, rain battering the windows, the stewardess appeared. On the verge of tears, she served us our drinks. She appeared again a short time later to top us up, by which time the sky outside was jet-black and a measure of turbulence had started. Her tears were a more than adequate mixer for the neat vodka we demanded. Within minutes we found ourselves not so much in an aircraft as a washing machine. The turbulence was so violent that, even strapped in, our heads were banging on the ceiling. For me, this was confirmation of what I'd been saying since the minute I'd joined the England squad at Heathrow – flying is a sure-fire way of speeding your entry to the grave. I was sat in a pool of sweat.

'I told you lot,' I wept. 'I warned you but no one believed me. And now you'll pay.' I was like a soothsayer. Or the Grim Reaper. One or the other.

'You all made fun of me,' I continued (I think I was snarling now). 'You were blind and now you can see. You never took any notice of me, you bastards, and now we're all going down because you didn't listen to the Cat.'

I was the one who knew everything. Before we hit the ground, I fully intended letting Gooch know I should have been bowling with a slip and four on the offside.

By now, the stewardess was crying her eyes out, deep sobs of loss and despair. I swear if Laurie Brown, the physio, hadn't produced a bottle of Drambuie from somewhere, the airport staff at Port Pirie would have pulled back the door of that flight and found the cream of English cricket turned to stone by fright. I never have been, and never will be, more glad to set foot on the ground. Look carefully and you can still see the mark where my lips were welded for several hours to the tarmac. Some years later, this flight would form the basis of the first film in the *Final Destination* franchise.

I really should have left my relationship with small aircraft there. Instead, five years later, I found myself sat in a crop-sprayer heading for the Victoria Falls in Zimbabwe. It had seemed a good idea until we'd arrived at the airstrip and it was revealed there wouldn't be enough room for all of us in the altogether sturdier-looking Cessna. Drawing the short straw, I got myself inside the crop-sprayer with a few others.

'Excuse me, captain, there's no seats . . . Oh, we're off.'

'Run to the front!' ordered the aviator. 'It'll help us get off the ground.'

A short while later we flew over a small dribble of water – 'Drought season,' he explained – and headed home. 'Everyone to the rear!' he shouted as we came in to land. He opened the doors to find six England cricketers in a heap at the back.

Flying is a fear I've never really conquered. For me, it's like a shark attack. People are forever telling you it'll never happen and then you open up the newspaper and some poor devil's been eaten alive.

'I've been selected to play for England in Australia – great! Shit, I'm going to have to get on a plane and fly there.' We seemed to spend half our lives on planes, a bedraggled bunch of semi-drunks, wandering the world.

One time we flew straight from Zimbabwe to New Zealand.

The plane was like a National Express coach; it seemed to stop everywhere, and by the time we landed in Auckland at 11 p.m., having travelled all day through a dozen time zones, there wasn't one of us who didn't feel in need of a drink. We asked a random bloke where might still be open and were directed to this tiny dive where I proceeded to have one of the best nights I've ever had on tour. There was just something about us all being there, in our tracksuits, getting absolutely smashed, totally unplanned, that was so enjoyable. It was seven hours later when Athers suddenly had a thought – 'Shit! I've got to give a press conference.' And so, finally, we all started drifting away. I was last seen surfing on physio Wayne Morton's back while singing the *Hawaii Five-O* theme as he lay flat on the pavement and the rush-hour traffic streamed by. People were winding down their car windows for a better look as this stream of zombified cricketers weaved its way to the hotel. 'Oh, England have arrived. Jolly good.'

An Australia tour would involve flights every couple of days. Perth to Melbourne, Melbourne to Adelaide, Adelaide to Cairns, Cairns to Sydney, Sydney to Perth. Sometimes I would genuinely wake up in the night and have no idea which city I was in, let alone which hotel. Even now I'm petitioning *The Guinness Book of Records* to admit me between its covers for 'most wardrobes walked into thinking they were the toilet'.

My flying phobia did have its positives. It was, after all, a great excuse to order a few nerve-calming beverages once aboard. 'Look, everyone, I'm sorry about this, but I'm going to have to have three Bloody Marys here. I don't want to, but this is for everybody's benefit not just mine. I'd disturb everyone with my screaming otherwise.'

I should really have got a doctor's note – 'Must have three

vodkas and half a lager before boarding.' I could have worn it round my neck like Paddington Bear.

Actually, what I did carry was my mum's St Christopher. My dad gave it me after she died, the only keepsake I have. In times of stress I always reach for the old patron saint of travellers and he's done a wonderful job of keeping me safe. But then I was doing some work with the art historian Sister Wendy for *The One Show* and she told me he never existed. I was astonished.

'Hang on, Your Holiness,' I said, 'I've Googled it. It's got the day of his birth, day of his death and what he got up to in between. It's Wikipedia; it doesn't get this stuff wrong.'

I'll tell you now, Google holds no sway with the sisterhood. Wendy explained that the saint was made up in an attempt to make travellers feel safe in dangerous times. Otherwise people would be too scared to undertake pilgrimages. It was a little deflating. I'd long relied on the saint to protect me. But I took on board what Sister Wendy said. You had to, she was only a couple of rungs down from the CEO. I still, though, have a lot of faith in my mum's old St Christopher. If I'm ever going on a plane or somewhere a little bit dodgy, he always comes with me. After all, few would consider my own level of saintliness enough to fall back on.

CHAPTER 7

How Not to Impress the Leader

Aside from the spectre of death, touring, for the most part, is a wonderful experience, especially when you think what everyone else is doing, ploughing through another English winter while we're living in T-shirts and Speedos.

It is also incredibly odd. I mean, in what other circumstances would you spend Christmas Day in a Zimbabwe hotel room the size of a hamster cage sat on your bed eating a KFC bucket in your underpants while your roommate John 'Creepy' Crawley plays The Smiths' greatest hits on his guitar and the rain batters against the window? For some reason it's an image you just never see on a Christmas card.

On that occasion, the hotel bar wasn't even open. They'd shut it for Christmas Day. We were all stuck there thinking, 'Well, what the hell are we going to do?' Athers had caused no small measure of discontent by laying down a three-line whip banning wives and girlfriends from the tour, so there was just us in this completely empty hotel. It was basically the African version of *The Shining*. We didn't dare leave our rooms for fear of encountering kids bombing round corners on tricycles and blood pouring out of the lift shafts. It gave Bumble's cry of 'We bloody murdered 'em!' a whole new meaning.

Wherever we ended up, we had no choice who we roomed with. They tried to mix it up, I think in an attempt to guard against cliques and engender team spirit. I could understand their thinking – 'Change it around and everyone gets to know everyone else.' But it's an ethos that's deeply flawed. Inevitably, you're putting chalk and cheese together. I was happy with whoever, but I'm not so sure that was the case the other way round. For a start, I really did like a fag or two. And then there was my habit of stumbling in at all hours, shouting and swearing as I stubbed my toe on a chair.

I wasn't the only one whose habits might be described as 'testing'. Jack Russell used to wash his underpants and hang them on the lights to dry. That's without all the other stuff he used to take on tour being strewn around. Boxes of Weetabix and tins of baked beans were the least of it. Jack would have paintings on the go, sneaking out occasionally to capture a snake charmer or remarkable landscape on canvas, and so the room would stink of oil paint and turps. Then there were his tea bags strung up over the sink. Used properly, Jack stated, a tea bag provided five cups. His penchant for shaving his bats also meant there'd be big curls of wood everywhere. No wonder when the ultra-organised Alec Stewart shared with him he put white tape down the middle of the bedroom floor and told Jack not to cross the line. On Alec's side was all his kit, numbered and ironed in rows. On the other, Jack's jockstrap would be hanging from the nozzle of the radiator.

I roomed with Jack, too, but there were similar lifestyle issues. I'd be sneaking in at 2 a.m. and Jack would have already been in bed for seven hours.

Judgey, on the other hand, would be up half the night dodging 90 mph bouncers in front of the mirror. It was as if he really believed whatever imagined foe was bowling at him was really there. I'd be half convinced myself, never quite daring to look in the mirror in case Craig McDermott was in there in an unpleasant take on the a-ha 'Take On Me' video.

Because of his lack of a sense of smell, Athers was often dumped with me or Wayne 'Ned' Larkins. The fact we both smoked like chimneys, it was reasoned, wouldn't bother him. Even if that was true – and even those who can't smell are unlikely to enjoy an environment where you can't see the other side of the room through the haze – myself and the gnarled Northamptonshire opener had enough alternative peccadillos to send even the most placid character round the bend. I might have woken Athers more than a few times bumbling into the room at some godforsaken hour, but at least Athers was in there. Wayne's habit of making marathon calls home meant Athers, sensitive to his roommate's privacy, would spend half his free time in the corridor. Paying hotel rates, Wayne blew his entire fee for the 1990–91 Ashes tour on phone calls to Blighty. Only natural, then, that people eventually started asking, 'Hang on, if we're all going to be together for months, any chance I could be put with the kind of guys who keep the same hours, have the same lifestyle?'

By the end of my career everyone had a single room. Even so, while definitely a step forward into the modern world, I had mixed feelings about this progression. I quite liked having a roommate. It was someone who had your back a bit. Certainly there were times when I had issues in my private life when I appreciated someone else just being there. Although again, maybe the reverse didn't always apply. I recall Phil

DeFreitas once complaining, 'Hold on a minute. I've got to bowl tomorrow and Tuffers is having a row with his missus about the washing machine.' His point being that it was four in the morning.

Thanks to his rapid elevation through the ranks, Athers reached the privileged level of having his own room early on, a status reserved in pre-enlightenment days only for captain, vice-captain and one or two senior players. However, if he thought this would provide him with an out from my nocturnal escapades, he had another thing coming. The first time he felt the need to have a word I'd happened to bring a lady back to my room for a drink. Athers was next door with his own bedtime companion, the latest from Stephen Hawking, and was finding it difficult to concentrate on theoretical cosmology due to the sounds coming through the walls. To be fair, he left it a while before he came knocking.

'Phil, er . . .'

'Oh, hello, Athers. Want to come in?'

'Well, no, not really, thanks all the same. I just wondered if, you know, you minded getting on with it. Only, there's a decent chance I'll be batting tomorrow morning.'

A similar occurrence happened before a Test match in Jamaica. Again – and I'd hate anyone to think this was a particular feature of my international career – I was having a little bit of a shindig in my room with a couple of ladies, sharing a few drinks, listening to (very loud) reggae music and jumping up and down on the beds. You know, the usual pre-match preparations of an international sportsperson. Unfortunately – and I have to say this was very bad planning on behalf of the hotel management – Athers again found himself in the unfortunate position of being in the next room along.

There was a knock on the door. I opened up and once more there was Athers. I'm sure he was in boxer shorts and T-shirt but in my head now I'm seeing him with nightshirt, cap and candle, like Wee Willie Winkie. I was going to invite him in, but something about his body language, possibly the clenched fists, not to mention the steam coming out of his ears, suggested he hadn't come to ask about the availability of a dry martini.

'Tuffers,' he said, in the crossest yet most controlled voice he could manage, eerily reminiscent of when Eric Morecambe got André Previn by the lapels, 'I really would like to get some sleep. It's just, you know, I've got to face Curtly Ambrose and Courtney Walsh in the morning. I mean, sorry to bother you and everything, but those two boys can be incredibly fast. Perhaps you could turn it down a little – please?'

My best move at this moment would have been to apologise profusely. Instead, I said, 'I was just hoping that we would win the toss and be batting so I probably wouldn't be needed to bowl 'til the afternoon. After all, you've got to see the ball when all I've got to do is bowl it.'

I looked at Athers' face, now a colour which, if it was to be found in the household paints aisle of B&Q, would be described as 'Raging Puce'.

'You're right, Athers,' I said. 'You always are. I'll turn it off immediately.'

I shooed everyone away and was as quiet as a mouse for the remaining half-hour until sunrise. I lay on my bed and considered how Michael Atherton's patience really was quite a remarkable thing. Some people would have been banging on the door the minute the noise started up. Athers had suffered for several hours. Even when his elastic finally snapped, he didn't rant and rave. Perhaps had he seen *Reservoir Dogs* he might have taken a different approach.

Of course, a wiser, and slightly less hungover, man than me would have made damned sure not to upset Athers the next day. I mean, really I would have been well advised to get to the ground early to buff Athers' boots. Instead, when England did indeed bat first, as twelfth man I retired to the physio's room for a much-needed kip, explaining to its occupant I had been kept awake by a stomach bug.

'Really,' noted Athers when he was told. 'He must have got that bouncing off the walls at 3 a.m.' At this point the patience I had so admired appeared to desert the Lancastrian as he proceeded to give me the mother of all dressing downs. His point, that while I had been away in the land of nod, he and Stewie had been down here on planet earth battling to survive the world's two greatest fast men, was quickly, and without remonstration, taken on board.

If there had been counsel for the defence, they could have pointed out on behalf of their client that in those days it was a bit batters and bowlers. They went off and did the batting, we read the paper, had a shower, had a bite of breakfast, or caught up on 40 winks. Of course, this defence would have offered an easy win to the prosecution barrister.

'But does your client not realise that when he requires support, all ten of his teammates are out there on the field with him?'

It wasn't that I didn't want to support the batsmen, I just couldn't see how I could do so from a distance of 75 yards. Then came the idea, quickly implemented, that teammates should sit on the balcony. I'd been responsible, albeit in a rather roundabout way, for improvements in the science of team bonding.

Mind you, by the same token, when I went out to bat, everyone just stood outside laughing.

Tours back then lasted for months. Hence why we tended to be away for Christmas. Zimbabwe excepted, there was generally a big Christmas party for everyone. It was traditional on these occasions for players to get up on stage and do a little turn for the entertainment of their teammates. On my first tour – you know, the one where most players really would do their utmost to make a positive impression on the captain? – I chose to do a Keep Fit with Graham Gooch fitness class.

'Come on, lads,' I said, mimicking Gooch's high-pitched Essex twang, and playing on his stringent belief in a disciplined physical regime, 'everybody drop to the floor and give me ten.'

I went through an array of exercises, and everyone was having a bit of a giggle, although Goochy himself perhaps was not quite so fulsome as others with his laughter. He looked more like someone at the Oscars, smiling through clenched teeth after missing out on the Best Actor gong to a lifelong rival. It could be argued that this was not a great way to form an everlasting bond with a captain. And again that argument would be right. But, you know, it was Christmas. And I did get Gooch's voice just right.

My impression might have gone down a little better with the skipper had I not seriously riled him twice already that December. The first time was in Adelaide before a one-day game. I'd enjoyed a very interesting evening chatting with a couple of young women who had very generously invited me back to their place, I presumed not to watch the *Neighbours* omnibus. No sooner had we arrived than two more women arrived. If we were watching the *Neighbours* omnibus, I feared I might be a little left out.

On more than one occasion that night I looked across the room to check Wayne Larkins wasn't in an adjacent bed and that I was actually having an extremely vivid dream. Ned wasn't there, although I swear even from a distance of ten miles I could hear him snoring. When I woke the next morning, I remembered little of the previous few hours. There might have been something with a tub of Vegemite, but I couldn't swear on it.

What I did distinctly recall was asking that the alarm be set for 7:30. Since it hadn't gone off I assumed it was still early, and was just about to settle back down for a bit more kip when I caught a glance of the clock. The double take is much admired by makers of sitcoms, and I have to say had they seen the one I performed at that moment they would for certain have been deeply impressed. The clock said 8:30. 'SHIIITTTT!'

One of the women gave me a lift back to the team hotel into which I hared at breakneck speed, heading for the lift, only to find friction, or the lack of it, against me. Running in hotel lobbies is rarely advisable. The only time I ever saw a shinier surface was when I went head first down a luge run on Channel 4's ill-fated celebrity winter sports show *The Jump*, one of the few reality programmes which picks its winner on least bones broken.

If you really are wedded to the idea of running in a hotel lobby then at least don the appropriate footwear, preferably something with the tread of a tyre on a Massey Ferguson tractor. Sadly, I was still wearing my going-out shoes. At that moment in time, I was essentially a human ice-hockey puck. The rubber plant was an innocent party in the subsequent collision. As I pulled a leaf back from my face, the lift door opened. From my position on the floor I could see a pair of unblemished white trainers. They looked vaguely familiar. My eyes travelled upwards – pristine socks, hairy legs (combed), shorts and polo shirt ironed to military level, jet-black Zapata moustache. I felt for sure it wasn't Kylie Minogue. Graham Gooch looked at me. His expression reminded me of the time I stood barefoot on a rotting seagull. Beside him were team and tour managers Micky Stewart and Peter Lush. A triple crown of bad luck (tip: always go round the back of the hotel).

My absence had already been noted at breakfast when there was a gap where my full English should have been. The management had enquired about my whereabouts and in a laudable, but perhaps not brilliantly thought-through, attempt to cover my tracks, Lamby had piped up, 'I think he's run down to the ground.' I'm not saying this was an unlikely scenario, but if Lamby had said I had been kidnapped by kangaroos it would have been more believable.

Gooch was, admittedly with some justification, a tad angry. I was twelfth man for the game and, therefore, it wasn't entirely beyond the realms of possibility that I might play a part in the encounter. Along with Micky and Peter, he warned me that if anything else of that nature happened, I'd be on the next flight home. Whether that was just to scare me, I don't know, but if it was it worked. For ten days.

We had arrived at a hotel in Bowral for a game against a Don Bradman XI (Bowral is his hometown) at about 11 p.m., at which point most of the guys went straight up to their rooms. One or two of us, however, fancied some refreshment after a long journey and so headed for a drink. I got chatting to the woman behind the bar and at closing time we decided to continue the discussion back at her place. Another player tagged along in the taxi and, as tends to happen in these circumstances, time becomes an alien concept until suddenly you hear the birds singing and see the sun coming up. Not generally a concern in the team hotel, but definitely a matter for mild worry when you're umpteen miles away in the middle of nowhere, there's a game starting in the morning – and the person you're staying with doesn't have a car. 'What? You don't have a car? Oh shit!'

No worries. Everyone has a phone. We can ring a cab. What's that? Phone's not working? Hmm, now that really does put us in a bit of a spot.

Thankfully, we were in the presence of one of life's great problem-solvers. 'There's bikes,' she said. Great. Not ideal, but panic mildly allayed. 'Children's bikes.'

We looked in the garage and, after a brief fight over the Raleigh Grifter – the alternative was a pink My Little Pony machine festooned with ribbons – we were on our way. We were both actually quite proficient at bike-riding, but just in case both bicycles had stabilisers.

Travelling incognito across the Australian suburbs in an England tracksuit is never easy at the best of times. On children's bikes where each pedal stroke brings your knees up to your chin, especially so. The receptionist had given us directions – 'left, right, right, right, left at the roundabout, left, right, right, left then right and you'll be there no trouble' – but for some reason we were soon hopelessly lost. All around us Bowral was waking up. It was a big day – the England cricket team was in town. In fact, draw back the curtains and, oh look, there's two of them going past right now – on children's bicycles?

A journey we had been promised would take 25 minutes had so far taken an hour. A quick trip across town was fast turning into a stage of the Tour de France. 'When in doubt ask a postman' – that's how the saying goes, isn't it? And so when we spotted one of the Australian Postal Service's finest, we felt at last the matter was in hand. It wasn't.

'Fack me,' he spluttered, covering a utility bill in spittle, 'aren't you that Pommie spinner Phil Tufnell. What the facking hell are you doing here?'

Not for the first time in my touring life, I felt this was no place for the truth. Hesitatingly at first, but with more conviction as the idea took hold in my head, I started telling him we were out on an early morning bike ride as part of our fitness programme – 'strength and conditioning, miles in the legs'.

I saw a shadow of doubt moving across his face. 'Right, well, why are you doing it on a child's bicycle?'

In these scenarios, where your pathetic excuse has been instantly rumbled, I have always felt it best to plough on regardless. 'What? You don't honestly think we'd be out on a normal bike, do you? Do you Australians know nothing about advancements in professional training? You have to work much harder on one of these. The gears are non-existent and you're permanently out of the saddle. All the best sports teams use them. Why do you think the Harlem Globetrotters haven't lost a game since 1965? Now if you don't mind, good fellow, enough of this idle chit-chat. Tell us where the hotel is and we'll be on our way.'

We sped up to the hotel à la Mark Cavendish, parked the bikes outside for our host to collect later, threw ourselves back into our rooms, had a quick shower, put the tracksuit back on and ran out just in time to get on the team bus.

Prior to the match we all lined up on the pitch for a rendition of the celebratory anthem 'Our Don Bradman'. Lyrically, it's a huge tribute to an Australian hero, but I have to admit the words passed me by as I sheepishly tried to avoid the gaze of our captain.

Thankfully, bearing in mind I'd had no sleep and spent the first hour of the day haring around on a child's bike, I didn't bat in that game and was only called upon to bowl two overs. I was just getting back on the bus looking forward to some well-deserved shut-eye when Gooch caught my eye – 'Enjoy the bike ride, Phil?'

CHAPTER 8

How Not to Achieve Physical Perfection

Strange to think that, despite the early morning bike rides and haring up and down the back stairs of hotels, in all my years as a cricketer I was never asked to pose for the front cover of a health and fitness magazine.

Neither health nor fitness were particularly high on my agenda. At Middlesex we used to go out every night. Towards the end of my career that started to change a little. Guys would train, play, eat in their room and that was it, whereas I was used to the game being very sociable.

At the end of every day we'd go down to the bar in the pavilion or the pub across the road and the opposition would do exactly the same. You'd have a couple of pints here, couple more there, find out from the locals where the best curry house was, and have a few more pints with your dinner. It was a very old-school sport from that point of view. It would be hard to imagine the Manchester United football team wandering round

Leicester at half past nine asking passers-by if they knew a good kebab house, or all 107 members of the New England Patriots squad having a game of bar billiards at the Fatted Ox 50 yards away from the ground.

In some cases, the kind of night we'd had would dictate what kind of morning would follow. If the skipper or a few of the senior players had done a few too many red wines, then it was unlikely we'd be doing much of a warm-up. Nowadays, players are expected to be at the ground for 8:30, changed into their gear by nine, and then run their bollocks off for an hour. Why? Three sessions in the field is long enough without throwing in an extensive warm-up as well. After a night out, we'd have a little wander over to the nets. The batters would have a little bat and the bowlers might turn their arm over for 20 minutes, just to get in a bit of a rhythm. Easy-peasy.

A lot of people used to say I was lazy when it came to warm-ups, but the thing was I didn't need long. I was very lucky in that I always had a nicely chiselled action and didn't have to bowl much to get myself into a rhythm. Everyone has to do a little bit of preparation, but on the other hand if I'd sent down 18 overs the night before there was no point me coming in the next morning and bowling for an hour in the nets. For me it was a couple of high catches to get my eye in, a little bit of ground fielding to get me moving, bit of a stretch, and then back to the dressing room for a bacon sandwich and a read of the *Racing Post*. If it was a nice day I'd sit on the balcony – sun in the sky, couple of birds singing, and wait for the play to start. If it wasn't then I'd retire inside.

Embers used to complain that the Middlesex dressing room was like a lorry drivers' caff, and I think it's fair to say that comment was directed at me. I was a proper chuffer and – it seems crazy now, I know – wouldn't dream of going out the back door for a fag. It never even occurred to me. Phil DeFreitas would occasionally smoke when he played for England, but he never smoked in front of the coach because in his head he knew it didn't look good. I didn't care who was there or where I was. For England, Gooch would be padding up next to me preparing to take on the world's most terrifying fast men, and I'd be blowing smoke rings in his face.

At Lord's people did eventually start suggesting, 'Phil, if you do want a fag, perhaps you could go out on the balcony.' Even then, though, I'd be a bit belligerent about it. 'Why should I? There ain't no law against it.' In my career, I never did things for bullshit reasons. And so my attitude was: 'I'm over sixteen, what's wrong with me having a smoke? I'm not doing anything wrong.' Madness when you think about it now, but going on aeroplanes was the same. I used to sit at the back in a haze of smoke, 25,000 feet up in the air, stubbing fags out in that little metal hollow on the arm of the chair.

'Oh, hang on a minute, I've dropped my fag.' Dropped my fag! In a big tube full of aviation fuel!

It made me laugh. People in the dressing room would moan about me smoking and then, when the man from Benson & Hedges came round with his stash of fags and cigars before a game in the one-day tournament they sponsored, there'd be a massive scrap for the freebies.

'Hang on a minute,' I'd be saying, grabbing as many boxes as I could, 'why are you taking my fags?'

'Oh, my nan smokes.'

Gatt would take some Hamlets and a box of 200 fags because his brother's son's best friend's mother smoked or something.

'No, these are my Bensons. Get off!'

I'd have thousands piled up in my locker, but then all of a sudden I'd run out. I'd be scrambling around in there at ten o'clock in the morning, emerging five minutes later with an old crumpled Hamlet. Ooh lovely!

It wasn't unknown for me to walk out at the start of play with a fag. I'd lean on a fence waiting for the batsmen to emerge, stub out my snout and then off I'd go. Go round the other counties and their dressing rooms would be just the same. Kent were huge faggers. It was like the old snug in your local pub. How that pavilion never burned down, I don't know. But then again this was the era when there used to be a jug of bitter in the dressing room at lunch. Embers would have half a bitter and he was far from alone. All the old boys used to have a fag and a beer with their lunch and then off out again. Imagine that at half-time in the Premier League. 'Okay, boys, grab a can of John Smith's and a Lambert & Butler, let's sit down and have a chat.'

At Lord's and around the grounds lunches were never produced with fitness in mind. Grace Road, Leicester, was particularly odd. To drink at lunchtime they'd give you little bottles of Panda Pop, the sort of thing you hadn't seen since you were ten. At Glamorgan, meanwhile, they'd always give you a bowl of soup as a starter. It always reminded me of the old hotels I used to go to with my mum and dad where for a starter they'd give you a glass of orange juice.

'Oh, lovely. Thanks so much for that. I'll only have a little bit because I don't want to be full up when the main course comes.'

Glamorgan's soup tended to be something earthy – leek or cabbage – and would always contain two pieces of hard cubed potato. I don't know how long they thought we had for lunch in Cardiff but serving three courses was pushing it considering the clientele only had 40 minutes. Add in three or four fags and a browse of the *Racing Post* and time really was of the essence.

It took cricket catering a long time to realise that light and healthy options were the way forward. We were professional athletes – still sounds daft – and we were having cabbage soup, followed by a slice of mutton, mashed potato and processed peas, and then a bowl of spotted dick and custard, all swilled down with Panda Pop. The elite of English cricket spent six months of the year chucking down school dinners.

At Kent one year, poor old Gatt got a whole tea urn poured over him. One of those giant ones which you need two hands to pour. This old girl wrestled it off the trolley, lost her grip and slung the whole steaming lot over Gatt. He shot out of his seat screaming and ran out of the canteen doors ripping his clothes off. I'd never seen him move so fast. It was as if he was on fire. Everyone was wetting towels and throwing them over him, like they do when a whale's beached in the Thames. He spent the rest of the afternoon in the dressing room. Initially, we thought he was over-reacting to get out of fielding, but actually he was properly in a bit of discomfort. The next time I saw that shade of red was when the 'On Air' sign went on in the *A Question of Sport* studio. The good news is the tea lady came round again.

Another thing about Kent was that the players' dining area was separated from the members' seats by big glass doors. They'd all stand there eating their chips staring in at us while we were having our steak and kidney pie or whatever. It was like being an exhibit at a zoo.

Eventually, at a lot of places, to avoid the complex and unpredictable nature of the dining experience, most of the boys would have a couple of cheese rolls brought to the dressing room, aside from at Derby, of course. That was no place to be bringing dairy products.

At Middlesex we were spoilt rotten by the legendary Nancy Doyle who looked after the players' dining room, a great little escape at the top of the pavilion. Famously, Nancy, who was taught to cook by the nuns at her convent school in Ireland, and who never used a recipe book or scales to serve up endless sumptuous feasts such as roast dinners, pies and desserts, was once approached by then Middlesex captain Mike Brearley, who gently enquired whether she might consider preparing food a little more conducive to the life of the professional sportsman. Brears received short shrift. 'Don't tell me how to feckin' cook,' she told him, 'and I won't tell you how to feckin' play cricket.' Brears had invaded Nancy's domain. And no one invaded Nancy's domain. Suitably repelled, he returned to the dressing room and never broached the subject again. All he could do was shiver as he saw professional sportsmen swill down a 2,000-calorie feast with a can of frothy bitter.

Even the impeccable Nancy, though, was capable of the odd error. No professional cricketer wishes to have their whites doused in hot apple pie and custard, but this is exactly what she catapulted into Wilf Slack's lap one lunchtime. Wilf, being the ultimate gentleman, instantly reassured Nancy that she needn't apologise for the accident, tucked into another portion, changed his trousers and went on to score a century. I don't believe Wilf was overly superstitious, otherwise chances are from that point on he'd have asked Nancy to sling a pudding at his groin every time he went out to bat.

Nancy was eventually made an honorary MBE, receiving her honour where she would have wanted it, in the Long Room at Lord's rather than Buckingham Palace. I was pleased for her. In the early years especially, she was a big help to me. Often she'd arrive at Lord's to find me already there in the car park, waiting for the ground to open, and allow some normality into my life. Nancy never said a great deal, but I think she took pity on me. She'd knock on the window of my car. 'Come on, I'll make you some breakfast.' Only senior players were allowed up to Nancy's in the mornings. I was in the second XI at the time but that made no odds to her. Occasionally, the older players would come in and see me sat there eating my bacon and eggs. 'Oi! You're not allowed up here.'

Nancy was having none of it. 'Feck off,' she'd tell them. 'I'm giving the lad some breakfast. Have you not seen the state of him? The way he looks it might be his last meal on earth.'

She put her foot down for me and broke the code. 'Listen, the boy needs a fecking good meal and I'm going to do it for him whether he should be up here or not. I'm a feeder and this boy needs feeding.' Suitably rebuked, they'd let it slide.

I became very friendly with Nancy. She'd always look after me, keep something aside – 'I've saved you a couple of lovely lamp chops. Put them in your bag.' She was a great lady and while on the face of it she was just giving me the occasional bite, in reality it meant a lot more. She pretty much kept me alive during those years. I was just 18 or 19 and living on fresh air and pizza.

On the road, I'd also make the most of any fuelling opportunities. I'd wake up in Southampton, somewhere like that, and be down to breakfast, always a full English, ploughing through the bacon, beans and sausages, extra toast, mugs of tea and coffee. Why wouldn't you? You're in a hotel. Why on earth would you choose the continental? If someone's slaving away in the kitchen making a full English, it's rude to turn it down. I'd wash that plateful down with a pint of iced milk. Don't start telling me milk isn't good for you. I've often felt much more sprightly after a couple of Baileys Irish Creams.

Put simply, hotel breakfasts were my feeding time because I was never going to make any food for myself. I always saw cooking as washing up in the making. Then, if, for instance, lunch at the ground was steak and kidney pie, mash and peas, I'd have my fill of that, too. 'Excuse me, love, have you got any more gravy there by any chance?' I'd go back out for the afternoon session barely able to move. Stand still for two minutes and I'd be asleep.

After lunch, that was it. I'd never have dinner. For me, dinner was a couple of pints and a bag of crisps. And then a couple more pints. Dinner was never in the equation. At Lord's I might make an exception and have a couple of nibbles at tea. It was hard to resist because on a daily basis down from Nancy's would come this huge platter of chocolate eclairs, cream cake and Battenberg.

When, late in my career, the hard-as-nails Aussie batsman Justin Langer came over to captain Middlesex, he couldn't believe what he was seeing. In Australia at tea you didn't get anything. You were lucky if you got a bit of fruit. But here we were shovelling down half a bakery. There was only so much Langer could take and the dam finally burst one day when we headed in at tea with the opposition piling on the runs.

On a long day in the field it was inevitable that minds – well, some minds – would start turning to what might be on the platter. About ten minutes beforehand, people would have one eye on the pavilion, and in the last over before the interval would start edging a little bit over in that direction. The main reason for this deeply unprofessional behaviour was that the chocolate eclairs were generally limited. There were only four or five. Speed was of the essence if one was to be secured.

Generally, it was the younger players who indulged in this

behaviour and I would look on it with a modicum of disdain. On this particular day, however, it had been a thankless task in the field and as the overs passed and the runs piled up the only thing that kept me going was the thought of sinking my teeth into a little piece of chocolate heaven. Showing a rare turn of speed, I was one of the first up the stairs and into the dressing room. Eclair in hand, I was just about to get satisfaction when Langer burst through the door. Like a red rag to a bull, I can report that the sight of a chocolate eclair is absolutely incendiary to a deeply pissed-off Australian.

'We're never gonna win nothing by eating f***ing chocolate eclairs,' he shouted, at which point he grabbed the entire plate and hurled it against the honours boards. 'SF Barnes, 11-112 against South Africa. That's some going,' I thought before a cream horn obliterated the achievement.

'We're getting battered,' continued Langer, as bedraggled slices of cake slid down the boards and dropped to the floor, 'and all you're worried about is whether you get a chocolate f***ing eclair? No wonder you Pommie bastards never f***ing win anything.'

On that occasion, I felt it wise to put the eclair to one side. I sat down in my corner and nibbled meekly on a small square of Battenberg.

To be fair, some years earlier Middlesex had announced an overhaul of the fitness regime. It was revealed we'd be flying out to an all-weather training facility in Portugal, the first time the club had invested in such a project, allowing players to train professionally without disruption by the weather. It was all thought very revolutionary, until we turned up and discovered the place the club had booked was essentially a golf course with a couple of school-quality nets and an artificial pitch at one side.

That first day we arrived early afternoon – far too late for any training – and so settled around the pool for a chat and a few beers. Next thing I knew the alarm was going off and it was seven the next morning. I crawled out of bed, showed my face at breakfast, forcing down a glass of orange juice and a bit of scrambled eggs and bacon, and then it was outside for practice in the middle.

It was so early there was still dew on the grass and it was decided it was too slippery and dangerous for the quick men to be running in. The spinners would have to start the session off – not great news as I was hoping for a bit more recovery time hiding in the field. I took the ball and began my little run-up but skidded as I reached the wicket. I put my hand out to stop my fall only for my fingers to become wedged in the tiny gap between the grass and the false pitch as I slid a couple more feet. When I came to a stop and pulled my hand free it was like an injury you might see on *Bottom*, with Rik Mayall's fingers bent back into an impossible position while he screamed with agony. The visual image and accompanying pain combined to cause me to retch violently, a stomach-full of eggs, bacon and orange juice deposited right there on the wicket. The physio ran on, himself nearly going over in my deposit, and took a look at my fingers. He said the words no professional sportsperson ever wants to hear: 'They're dislocated. I'm going to have to put them back in.'

'Putting them back in' means gripping each one, pulling it vertically up and then pushing down to slot it back into place. It was absolute agony, as confirmed by the riot of swearing that accompanied the procedure. I had my eyes shut I was in so much pain, but when finally I did open them, who was watching but the Middlesex hierarchy, the big cheeses on the committee, who'd flown over to see this great display of modern all-weather training in which they'd so heavily invested. What did they find? One of the club's supposed great hopes sat in a puddle of his own vomit shouting and screaming. It was like a motor manufacturer doing the big unveiling of a new model, pulling the silk sheet off the bodywork, only to reveal a rust-bucket with four flat tyres.

My fingers were far too painful and sore to bowl for the next few days.

'It'll be frustrating,' said one of the coaches, 'but you're welcome to stay on.' He was right. It was frustrating – for everyone else as they trained while I rested up with a piña colada.

Before our excursion to the Algarve, pre-season training meant a trip to the somewhat less salubrious surroundings of the Barclays Bank Sports Ground in Ealing. There we'd run round for a couple of hours, throw up from exhaustion and then have a five-a-side football match. Don Bennett, ex-Arsenal and Coventry City, especially loved the football part of proceedings and delighted in smashing us mere amateurs against the walls. He once tackled our paceman Neil Williams and put him straight through a set of exit doors. Nelly was lying there in a heap when Don reached him – 'Someone said "Man on!",' he told him. 'You should have got rid of it.'

Pre-season training was basically a week of trying not to get injured. Out of condition, players would be pulling hamstrings and all sorts. We'd come in every morning so stiff as to barely be able to move. And then we'd be off again – sit-ups, shinning up ropes, pulling Jumbo jets with our teeth.

The problem was it was all done from a standing start. These were the days when you finished a season, they locked the gates behind you and then six months later you'd reappear looking like Bella Emberg. None of this keeping your fitness ticking over. I'd have spent those six months being a cabbie or a plasterer or something. And then we'd be beasted for two weeks. Push-ups, push-ups, push-ups; sit-ups, sit-ups, sit-ups; football, football, football; run, run, run. No warm-downs; just back in the car, go home and back again at 8:30 in the morning. People were dropping like flies. In fact, most people wished they could be put out of their misery and swatted like one.

I did my best to do as little as possible. I'd be in the back group during a run and would stop doing sit-ups when no one was looking. My view was your heart only has so many beats and there was no point wasting them in pre-season. Much better to keep things nice and steady.

And the thing is, while seemingly everyone else in that Middlesex side got injured, I was pretty much permanently fine. I missed one game for Middlesex because my appendix burst at lunch against Nottinghamshire at Lord's. I'd had a bad pain a couple of times which had been diagnosed at some of London's finest hospitals as probably being gallstones when actually it was a grumbling appendix. I was found lying in the toilets in absolute agony and transported away in an ambulance. I remember this incident more than anything for how pissed off other people were about me missing the rest of the match. 'It's all right for him, isn't it? Feet up being fed grapes in hospital.' I'm not quite sure what I was meant to do about that. The appendix in question is in the museum at Lord's. Well, it should be.

England, too, were trying to become a little more professional fitness-wise during my career. While, at first, players were kept going by a series of red and green pills, horse-sized, said to have anti-inflammatory properties, which would also be taken before nights out to prevent hangovers, it became obvious that something a little more long-term was required. And again this initially involved a trip to Portugal, a country which in the mid-'90s must have been wondering why so many flights from England offloaded hopelessly unfit men with blazers and beer bellies.

We met at Heathrow where we were taken into a room and given the lowdown on the trip.

'Right, boys,' we were told, 'we're taking this very seriously. There'll be no golf, no messing about. This is about training, running on the sand dunes, improving muscle strength. We'll be there for one thing and one thing only – to get fitter. The room was in dead silence. Everyone looked at each other with a classic 'Oh shit!' expression.

Worse, however, was to come. 'You won't be allowed to drink.'

The thought of ten days in the sun without a nice refreshing glass or two was unbearable. So we decided to get absolutely shitfaced on the plane instead.

It was a morning flight. And, as ever, once up in the air, the cabin crew appeared. 'Would you like a drink, sir?'

With Portugal just two hours away, speed was of the essence. 'Er, yes – thanks. Don't mind if I do. I'll start with four Bloody Marys, please.'

'Seven gin and tonics,' ordered a colleague.

Keen to make a good impression, we arrived at the training facility at midday, absolutely rotten. Straight away, that afternoon's session was cancelled. 'I don't think you've quite grasped what we're thinking here,' a disappointed instructor told us.

At least we couldn't be fined – 'Look, you said no drinking in Portugal. We consumed this lot over the Bay of Biscay.'

Next day, we started off with aerobics. If you've never seen

Angus Fraser doing Zumba then, for decency's sake, do try to keep it that way. Not that the rest of us looked much better. Without any team gear we were turned out in all kinds of odds and sods. There were a couple in England tracksuits but the rest of us were wearing any old thing we'd found tucked away in a drawer when we packed – threadbare T-shirts, shiny shorts from when tight was good, old football socks, Dunlop Green Flash.

'Right,' said the instructor, a woman whose attractiveness was in stark contrast to our own, 'let's get you loosened up.'

Well, you've seen nothing like it. She had us doing the grapevine – 'Step to the side! Step back! And point!' That poor woman. We were an absolute shambles. Embers was going one way, Goochy another, others, myself included, couldn't remember any of the actions.

After about 20 minutes we turned to face the other way and there in front of us was the cream of Great Britain's professional athletes. No two ways about it, these people were beautiful examples of the human form. Each one of them absolute perfection. Training at the same base, they were staring at us in disbelief. Suddenly, I saw us through their eyes. This shambolic collection of people, of all different shapes and sizes – big, tall chaps like Gus, little, fat fellas like Gatt, skinny ones like me – some going bald, others with greying hair, puffing and wheezing their way through a mild aerobics exercise in clothes that looked like they'd come from an abandoned skip, was the England cricket team? The words in their minds were obvious to me. 'What the hell kind of sport is it where you can compete at the top level and look like that?'

That first morning set the tone for seven days that really failed to meet the billing of those who believed the England cricket team would return rippling like stallions. Their biggest mistake was not realising that the complex included a nightclub. The clientele tended to depend on which set of athletes had the morning off the next day. The hurdlers would be in there one night, the long-jumpers the next, the shot-putters the one after that. The England cricket team were in there every night. What a fantastic week that turned out to be.

Whereas treating a team as a single entity can cause resentment if some don't do as much work in a group session as others, England would later be forward-looking in tailoring fitness training to individuals. They brought in Kiwi fitness guru Dean Riddle who worked with players according to their needs, encouraging them to police their own regime in their downtime. It made perfect sense. If you're a fast bowler you need the miles in the legs and strength in the back. Batsmen need stamina if they're going to play long innings in 90° heat. A little spinner whose run-up is a matter of a few paces was a slightly different case. Naturally light and skinny, my physicality was what kept me going on those days when I bowled long, unbroken spells in the heat. To keep me that way, Dean became my running buddy – although he might have to hunt me down if I was enjoying the fruits of the locality on a couple of days off. I'd be round the back of a bar somewhere when from nowhere I'd hear his voice – 'Tuffers, come on, it's time to go.'

He understood that I needed a little encouragement. 'Sorry, but we've got to go do it, Tuffers.' And then off we'd trot.

Dean's influence bred a culture of fitness. Players would go to the gym complex more, me included. The jacuzzi is a piece of training equipment, right?

'Lovely. I feel so much better. Now which bar are we going to?'

To be fair, I had been warned to be careful with weights and changing my body shape. As Embers once said, 'You can't bowl spin if you've got muscles.' I held onto those words tightly.

I just never enjoyed exercise. I never got that exercise high, that endorphin rush, that people talk about. The only time I felt like that was in retirement when I did a 550-mile charity walk criss-crossing England and visiting various cricket clubs along the way. For the first week I felt so sore, but then I was overcome by the strangest feeling. I wanted to get out there. I even started to jog and because of the fitness from the walking I could do so without that horrible feeling of getting out of breath. I felt like I could run forever, a bit of an existential experience. It happened that one time and never again.

Later on, some of the Middlesex boys got into carb-loading, eating pasta at breakfast, and all that kind of stuff. I once had no breakfast because I was late and got six for 64. Another time I did actually give carb-loading a try and got nought for 190. 'F*** it,' I thought, 'I'll eat what I want.'

Safe to say I'm one of those people who succeeded in sport despite rather than because of what I did. I always found ways to get through, be it via my wits or responding on the pitch when I had to. Rarely was I vehemently against an area of preparation or training. It was just that it wasn't my way, and so being made to do it put my back up.

'If you eat chicken and rice and drink kale juice, you'll be a wonderful cricketer.' Really? I just thought they were lying.

'Hang on, I'm facing Courtney Walsh in an hour's time and you're telling me I've got to have muesli for breakfast. Bollocks to that. I think I'd rather go out there with a nice full English under my belt if it's all the same to you.'

Yes, you've got to look after yourself. But at the same time I was a young man playing for Middlesex and England, having a drink with all these legends and great players. Forgive me if I forgot to pack the All-Bran.

In my early England days, the ethos of 'get stuck in and enjoy yourself' was ingrained. On my first tour I was confronted with the 'Batcave', a team-room packed full of wine, beer, chocolates and liqueurs kindly provided by the tour sponsors. The Aussies were sponsored by Castlemaine XXXX. I'd walk in and be faced with a wall of canned beer. Others weren't particularly happy with the goods on offer. Australia is, after all, one of the great wine nations.

'We can't have this,' Lamby would cry. 'We need some wine. Hold on a minute, I've got a contact in Adelaide.'

I'd then hear him on the phone. 'Hello, Dave – Lamby. We need twenty-five cases of the Sauvignon, fifteen of the Pinot Gris, and ten of the Pinot Noir. Get it here immediately!'

I'd go back to the team room a few hours later and there'd be a skyscraper of Australia's finest wines. What was a young impressionable 20-something meant to do?

It wasn't just Australia. When we toured the West Indies in 1997–98, the ECB decided in their wisdom to put us up at a very nice hotel at Jolly Harbour in Antigua for the first couple of weeks. I'd never stayed anywhere that was all-inclusive and I found the whole experience astonishing. We were given a blue wristband which essentially doubled as a key to heaven. We went to every bar in the complex, raised our wrists accordingly, and next thing we knew 25 free rum and Cokes would appear. I couldn't comprehend it. 'You've given me an armband? Which means I can have as much rum as I want? For nothing? Really? Do you know who you're messing with?'

It became a matter of honour to make the absolute most of every minute of our stay. And then to add to the joy it did nothing but piss down for a fortnight. Every day there were hundreds of really fed-up holidaymakers, and us – 18 England cricketers whooping and celebrating – 'Yessss!'

We did nothing but eat, drink and be merry. I even invented two new ways to do a tequila shot. One is to use it as an eye-wash, which I'll admit does smart a little. The other is to make a small puddle of it in your hands and snort it up your nose. Again, while this method has rewards, there is a downside. You spend the next four days numb down one side of your face. People ask you a question and then look at you as if you're mad when your reply is utterly incomprehensible. You'd think they'd put a warning on the bottle – 'Do Not Inhale'.

Such was the non-stop nature of this bodily abuse, at times I'd have to employ something at which I was always extremely good – the tactical chunder. I've done it many times and in many places – nightclubs, round people's houses, sometimes mid-conversation without anyone even realising. I did just that in the old Shearer's Bar at Newcastle United's St James' Park after a charity football match. All the old pros were there slugging back the pints and I was talking to two of my goalkeeping heroes, David Seaman and Neville Southall, when all of a sudden I just had to lean over the arm of my chair. 'Anyway, listen, it's been a brilliant day, lads' – Bleugh! – 'so glad to have met you.' So perfect was its execution, I honestly don't think they noticed.

Perhaps not surprising considering my refuelling habits, but on any England tour there always seemed to be a moment where I'd be on a drip. It was the perfect storm. A few beers the night before, not rehydrating properly, and then bowling in 95° heat and 100 per cent humidity. Then at the end of the day, instead of isotonic drinks to replace lost salts and minerals, it would be sit back with another refreshing lager. On occasion, the salts would come out in the dressing room, handed out among us. We might as well have had a salt lick hanging there like in a stable. The other thing we relished was tonic water – good for cramps. And there you have it, the high-tech cures that were around at the time. At least it meant we could enjoy a few medicinal G&Ts in the evening.

The first time I was put on a drip for dehydration was at the Adelaide Test in 1991 when we had to bat out the last day to save the game. After Athers and Gooch put on 203 for the first wicket, we were cruising, but then a mini collapse of three wickets for ten runs meant I was summoned from my deathbed. Thankfully, that was it for the panic and I was soon back with the tube of life in my arm.

A year later, and I was taken ill with dehydration again, this time while England were batting against Australia in the World Cup at Sydney. We were chasing and fortunately the team knocked off the runs without me as I listened to the game on the radio from my hospital bed. My fellow patients were full of concern. 'Bloody lazy Pom, you should be at the ground, mate.' I wished I was. Instead I was on a ward full of drug addicts barking at the moon.

Dealing with my own dehydration was bad enough, but on one occasion I was asked to deal with the aftermath of someone else's. Graham Thorpe had fainted after batting for two and a half hours in a Benson & Hedges World Series one-day international at a roasting hot Brisbane. No way was he going to be back out on the pitch for the start of the opposition innings. It was my great misfortune that myself and Gatt were sharing twelfth-man duties. Racing across the outfield to cut off a quick single wasn't exactly Gatt's forte. Not unless there was a pork pie in the vicinity.

'Tuffers,' came the shout, 'get your pyjamas on' – our kit had the look of something sold in the sleepwear section of Marks & Spencer.

'Oh, shit!' I thought. 'I'm going to have to field for fifty overs in this sweltering heat.'

I went into the physio's room and there was Thorpey flat out on the treatment table.

'Come on,' I urged him, some might say quite forcefully. 'Get yourself up. Get yourself out there, you lazy bastard. Don't make me have to go out there. Get that drip out your arm and field!'

A little unfair of me, I know. But on the other hand I really wasn't keen on standing in a blazing hot field for several hours without even having a bowl. 'Look,' I kept saying to the physio, 'he's getting better now. He's fine. Come on, help me grab his feet. Walk him round a bit. I've seen this on films. Slap his face! Don't let him slip back into unconsciousness.'

We think we have hot days in this country, but really they are few and far between compared to the extreme heat in many cricket-playing nations. The plane door would open when we landed in Barbados or Delhi and everyone would go, 'Ooh, lovely. Feel that heat.' Everyone except me, that is. Secretly, in the back of my mind, I'd be thinking, 'I've got to play cricket in this. I'm actually going to have to bowl forty overs in a day.'

Among the hottest places was Sri Lanka. You'd step out of an air-conditioned coach in tracksuit bottoms and top and by the time you sat down in the dressing room, which had no aircon, just fans to push the heat around, the sweat would be constant – drip, drip, drip, off the end of your nose.

In Perth once, meanwhile, we were absolutely baking. The Aussies have a law whereby if it reaches a certain temperature outdoor workers must down tools and head inside. The mercury has to rise to 99.5° Fahrenheit for that to happen. Underneath the scoreboard at the WACA was a thermometer. The city had been hit by a heatwave and the reading was just two degrees below the required level when we could legitimately chuck the ball on the floor and walk off. I nearly went over and stuck my cigarette lighter underneath it to get it over the line.

The strange thing with standing in extreme heat for hour after hour, potentially two days the way the Aussies dominated, is that the true awfulness only really starts when you finally get back indoors. On the pitch, adrenaline keeps you going. But then in your hotel room your head starts throbbing; your feet, too. All of a sudden you feel like you've come down with flu, a strange fuzzy effect as if your body is trying to deal with the heat it's soaked up throughout the day. At Durban, it was like being in a steamer. The ground would retain a lot of water. As the sun beat down, the field would literally steam and that warm moisture would travel straight up your trouser leg. By tea your privates were parboiled.

Not only weren't we refuelling properly, but we never used sun cream either. I used to view a day fielding in the sunshine as a tanning day. Roll the old sleeves up at fine leg. Eventually we were told to start putting on UV protection, but so many of the boys from that era have got skin problems. I myself have had skin cancers on my face that had to be burned off. We've got Allan Donald to thank for changing attitudes. Back in the '90s it was him who started wearing the warpaint. Now it's all about sunglasses because the players are prone to get sun blisters – sore, red, peeling skin – on their eyelids. That shows the ever-expanding knowledge of the dangers of raw sunlight and heat exhaustion.

When England last toured Sri Lanka, the quicks were

bowling four-over spells. When we were over there, if Angus was bowling well, he'd be left on for 15. When England played a one-off Test in Colombo in 1993, Judgey batted for seven and a half hours. Every time he came in at the end of a session, it was off with his kit and get him in the ice-cold towels, other players were fanning him, and he was being given drink after drink to rehydrate. All too soon it would be time to get back out there, at which point he'd be padded back up and sent off down the steps again.

Strange to think really that heat exhaustion was just seen as part of the game. The Australian batsman Dean Jones repeatedly vomited and wet himself at the wicket during a marathon double hundred in vicious heat at Madras in 1986. His body on the verge of shutting down. Teammate Steve Waugh reported that Jones 'looked like a corpse'. I've seen dozens of players be sick on the pitch. For some reason, as a batsman, I was never too badly affected. Perhaps it was all those five-minute innings.

Put the average county cricketer in those kinds of conditions and they'd wilt like a dandelion doused in weedkiller. As a breed, we worshipped not sun but rain. The joy that precipitation brought to professional cricketers back then is an incredible thing. One of the most fundamental changes in the English game was the culture shift which said that professional cricketers really do need to play cricket, because when I played we were always looking for a day off.

It's like any job, really. You do your best to get out of having to do it. An office worker looks out of the bedroom window and cheers when they see six inches of snow on the road, and we were the same with rain. Every morning at seven o'clock in the British summer several dozen professional cricketers were ripping their curtains open in the hope that a vast depression had moved across the country in the night. When we arrived at the ground I'd be straight out for an inspection.

'Ump, there's a slight wet patch at deep extra cover. If I'm running full tilt, slip on that and pull a hamstring, you could be threatening my career.'

If we were already out there, I'd keep looking at the sky. 'The clouds are coming up, we'd better get off before it rains.'

'But, Tuffers, we can't take the players off if it's not even raining.'

'But it will in five minutes. Look, there's a cow sitting down in a field over there. That's as good as confirmation.'

That's why I hated playing in Perth. Open the curtains there and there might be a cloud, but it would be the size of a small toaster and be 45 miles in the distance. You'd glance at the thermometer on the wall and it would already be throbbing at 90°. 'F***,' you'd think, 'I'm in for a long day here.'

The mercury erupting out of the top of the thermometer was no place for a generation of cricketers for whom boozing and bad eating went together like lager and lime, reinforced by endless days and nights on the road. With Middlesex we'd stay at all sorts of places, ranging from a Trusthouse Forte on the motorway to your classic Mrs Miggins' B&B. Occasionally, we'd find ourselves in an absolute little gem, a creaking old mansion in the middle of nowhere, the sort of place where you'd have the world's tiniest sink in the corner of your room. The main problem we always used to have in those hotels was getting the night porter up if we wanted a late drink when we got back in.

'Uh? What? What do you want?' he'd ask, peering from his duvet.

'Well, four whisky and sodas and six pints of lager for a start.'

There'd be a big sigh.

'Okay, hang on a minute. I'll have to get the keys.'

Occasionally, a big night out could effectively cost you the game. We slipped up against Ireland in Dublin, their twelfth man, a certain Mr Guinness, having more than a little say in the result. The day before the game it was absolutely torrential. The view among the Middlesex boys was that the chances of play the next day were virtually zero. To have a night out on the craic seemed only polite, but then by 1 p.m. the next day the game had begun. Hansie Cronje was playing for Ireland and made an unbeaten 94 as we were beaten handsomely by 46 runs.

Maybe if I was playing these days, things would be different. If I was being paid £1.5 million by the IPL I'd make sure I was bloody fit and practise my fielding a bit more. Well, maybe a little bit more. After all, minimal exercise and practice did seem to suit me.

Mind you, maybe I did myself more damage than I thought. I felt I needed a bit of an MOT after sitting around so much during the Covid lockdown. I went to see a chiropractor. He took one look at me and then delivered his professional opinion – 'Crikey!' The number of cracks he got out of my body was absolutely stunning. My neck was out of line, same with my ankle, my hip and my lower back. It was like a fireworks display the pops and bangs that were going off. Now, though, I can carry 12 bottles of wine around in my supermarket basket without so much as a twinge.

CHAPTER 9

How Not to Play for England

Of course, you can be as fit as you like, but it makes no difference if you don't get picked. The end of a Test match on home soil generally preceded several days' wait to see if you'd survived for the next one – Ceefax page 340 being the communication medium of choice. Either that or I'd find out from a reporter at a ground. 'You do know you've been left out, Phil, don't you?'

'Er, I didn't actually. But thanks for letting me know.' I know mobiles weren't a thing back then, but there was still this thing called the landline.

If the selectors did happen to see you in the flesh, what came out of their mouths was about as trustworthy as Arthur Daley. Selected only for the final Test of the 1997 Ashes series, I took 11 for 93 at The Oval and was awarded man of the match. Sitting in the dressing room afterwards, the selectors came in one by one. They all said the same thing – 'Well played, Phil, I said you should have been playing all summer.' And then the coach came in and said exactly the same.

'Okay,' I thought, 'so if all the selectors and the coach thought

I should have been playing all summer – why the f*** wasn't I playing all summer?' Had this come from a higher place? Was there a secret government directive that Tufnell must not play? Or were they perhaps being a little economical with the truth?

I'd made sure to turn non-selection at least a little in my favour. Once or twice I made it as far as the squad only to be told I wasn't playing on the day, in which case I had a decent chance of missing my county game.

'Well, I'd better stay on for a day, just in case. Anyway, I'm the only person who knows how Jack Russell likes his Weetabix.'

'But you'll miss playing for Middlesex at Derby.'

'Oh, really? I hadn't realised. That's a shame. But I really do think it would be wise to guard against any unforeseen developments.'

The lack of respect from above for players was clear to me before I had even pulled an England shirt on. The first time I went to Australia, we travelled economy. Fast bowlers were sat there with their knees pressed into their chin hour after hour. All the big cheeses, meanwhile, the selectors and what have you, were up the front in the lap of luxury. The actual players? Bollocks to them – shove them down the back. They'd have had us in the hold if possible.

It didn't get much better when we landed. In Zimbabwe, for example, we were stuck in shoeboxes, two to a room, while the blazers were living it up at some luxury joint. Occasionally, they'd invite the players over to get a decent bit of grub, then it was 'Off you go – back to your hovel.' Only when Lord MacLaurin took over and saw for himself what was going on were changes made. His attitude was, 'Hang on a minute, why are we here while the people who need the R&R are in some substandard place down the road?'

The disconnect between players and selectors was beautifully illustrated one time when, prior to the West Indies tour in 1994, we were invited to a reception at the House of Commons. We were there having a drink, dressed up in our England kit, while various MPs came round to say hello. Occasionally, if they fancied a bit of salmon on a water biscuit, the selectors would pitch up, too. Ramps was standing there looking immaculate when one such selector, Brian Bolus, came up to him.

'Hello, Mark,' he said, 'good luck on the tour.'

Ramps was his usual polite self. 'Thanks very much,' he said, 'what constituency do you look after?'

'No,' Brian corrected him, 'I'm the one who picked you to go.'

Ramps didn't know him from Adam.

Ramps' bemusement at this older generation of selectors had already been well cemented. In his role as chairman of selectors, former England batting great Ted Dexter had once turned up at our national training base at Lilleshall. Ramps, preparing for a summer facing the West Indies, was batting against a bowling machine set to fast and short of a length. Ted was watching him. If he wanted to remain unseen, he wasn't making a very good job of it. He was wearing a blue cravat and ultra-whitened tennis pumps. He looked like he'd just stepped off a punt on the Cam.

'Mark,' he told the young batsman, 'when I was facing fast bowlers in the West Indies I used to hit them off the back foot with a straight bat back over their heads for six.'

Ramps just looked at him. He couldn't speak. I mean, what do you say to that? He came out of that net firmly believing Ted was insane. 'He's just suggested, when I'm facing Ambrose and Walsh, to hit them back over their heads for six.'

'Ted's crazy – don't worry about that,' a couple of players told him. But I was curious, and when I did a little bit of research

I discovered that was exactly what Ted used to do. He was an amazing player of fast bowling, and all with no helmet, of course. It is often forgotten that he was also a tidy bowler. On one occasion when Middlesex were playing the West indies at Lord's, and I hadn't done too well, the dressing-room attendant came in at lunch – 'Phil, there's a phone call for you.' It was Dexter, who, apparently, was dining upstairs.

'Tufnell,' he started, 'I've been having a little watch this morning and I think you should try and bowl it a little bit slower, tease them a little outside off stump. Don't sit in the dressing room wondering what the bloody hell you're doing wrong. Give it a try.' And I did actually then go out after lunch, do as he advised and got a few wickets.

As selectors go, I quite liked Lord Ted. I thought he got a rum deal from the press who liked to portray him as a bit of a fruitcake, like when he spoke about the smog affecting the players at Eden Gardens, Calcutta, and everyone laughed at him.

'Don't be so stupid, Ted. Smog?'

But actually he was right. And with pollution so high on the agenda nowadays it would seem that he was also well ahead of his time.

Ted could be a bit mischievous. At the end of that India tour, he questioned whether our appearance, notably our stubble, might have been a factor in a pitiful series of defeats. It started a big debate about scruffiness and the whole question of facial hair. But I think, quite cleverly, he was taking the piss out of people who believe such nonsense can affect the way a team plays.

Four years earlier when, after a 4-0 home Ashes drubbing, he suggested the national team's ills could be down to the fact that the 'lines of Venus were in the wrong juxtaposition', the press wilfully misunderstood his tongue-in-cheek comment for being serious.

'Oh, my God, Ted's lost it. He's gone mad.' No, he's having a laugh.

To me, Ted was a bloke who saw things a bit differently and didn't want to fit into the traditional stiff-upper-lip image. I would always sit near him at pre-Test dinners so we could talk about motorbikes. Ted, like me, loved his bikes. He'd turn up at Lord's on this big BMW and again everyone would say he was nuts. No, he's not, he likes riding a motorbike, that's all, albeit with his leathers covering a navy sports jacket and an MCC tie. When he opened the pillion, you wouldn't have been surprised in the least to see a bottle of champagne on ice and a couple of chilled glasses. I could well imagine him being a bit of a swashbuckler in his day, a bit of a cavalier, and I didn't find it too difficult to embrace that.

The only issue with those pre-match dinners was Ted's speech. It was always the same. 'You're the eleven best cricketers in the country, now go out there and play for England.' And then the next Test would come around and there'd only be four of us left. Up Ted would get. 'You're the eleven best cricketers in the country, now go out there and play for England.' And we'd be thinking, 'Hang on, what happened to the other seven? Were they only the best in the country last Tuesday?'

He was also prone to getting names wrong, possibly because he ushered so many players in and out the door. 'Meet our new fast bowler, everybody – Malcolm Devon.'

Kent seamer Alan Igglesden once encountered Ted on his way to the Cricket Writers' Annual Dinner where the squad was about to be announced for the winter tour. Iggy thought he had a bit of a chance to be on the plane. He was walking out of the Tube station with another player when Ted approached him. 'You look like a cricketer. Do you know where the Cricket Writers' Dinner is?'

Iggy realised maybe he wasn't getting on the plane after all.

On another occasion he approached a bloke who was carrying Athers' bag up to the dressing room. 'Good luck today,' he told him. It was the dressing-room attendant.

There were times when the players did more for my selection than the selectors. Before my Test debut in Australia, we played a state game against Victoria. A couple of their players got after me a bit. When we then batted, Lamby went out and absolutely destroyed their spinner, smashing 143 at more than a run a ball. As he took his pads off, he called me over.

'Tuffers,' he said, 'you're a much better spinner than he is. You bowled well but were a bit unlucky. I couldn't let him outbowl you.' I was in a straight race with Eddie Hemmings for the spinner's spot at the MCG. Lamby making the Victoria spinner look so ordinary next to me did me a massive favour.

Even Lamby, though, couldn't save me from the chop for the World Cup final in Melbourne in 1992. I was in the team until the back end of the tournament when Richard Illingworth was preferred, playing the semi-final and final. When the big day came round, Gooch said nothing to me other than, 'Phil, you're not playing; we've decided to go with Richard.'

I was pissed off to miss out. A World Cup final comes round only every four years, so who knew if I'd have another chance? Since I'd turned 53 by the time England next reached the final, probably not. I didn't show my disappointment too much, but I did think I'd deserved my chance, especially with the way I'd bowled under pressure in the big game against the hosts at Sydney when I took the key wicket of their free-swinging opener Tom Moody. In the end, however, it wasn't to be. Shame, as I'd have liked to see the statue of me outside Lord's, holding the World Cup like Bobby Moore.

During that tournament, I looked round the England dressing room and saw all these great players and thought, 'Hold on a minute, we've got some really good people here, why can't we do this in Test match cricket?' It didn't take long to work out why.

The World Cup was a one-off competition. The players were relying on self-drive, talent and determination. In doing so, they created an incredible togetherness and strength and put themselves in the best position to succeed. In the long term, however, a team needs structure and support. We didn't have a bowling coach or a fielding coach, any more than we had a batting coach, let alone a one-day batting coach like they have today. Generally, everything came from whoever was coach at the time, who, incidentally, for a while at least, also tended to be the best mate of the captain. That, along with the endless uncertainty surrounding selection, meant that, as a newcomer, the underlying ethos of the England dressing room – self-preservation – hit you right between the eyes.

'Team' was largely an alien concept. Players were too worried about getting a five-for or hundred for themselves to ensure they were still there next time round. For me, that was a shock. Angus had been full of the joys of spring about England's West Indies jaunt the year before my debut Ashes trip. I thought Australia, commonly known as the best tour of the lot, would be even better. Team spirit would be like nothing I'd ever experienced. And then all too soon it just became guys signing deals with wine companies, looking after number one, going their own way and messing about. The senior guys never really took us newcomers under their wing. Why would they? They were all going out with the likes of Mick Jagger to some posh restaurant or banging nightclub. Great – but the rest of us were just sort of sat there thinking, 'Okay, well, what are we going to do?'

The idea of being a team disappeared and I fell into the same way of thinking. I didn't go over there to be a hooligan or to get in trouble. I went over there expecting a group experience, but there was just no feeling of being a team. It sounds daft, I know, but essentially we just wandered off into Australia for four months.

Brendon McCullum said something interesting to me once. 'International sport boils down to one thing – trying to get all the people on your team facing the same way on the coach.' When we got on the coach we were facing in all different directions. It was selfish, and it had been made that way by people forever feeling pressure over their places. There was no love or loyalty shown to anyone. Believe every game could be your last and inevitably you become more inward-looking. If you are more confident in your position, then it's natural to step out of yourself a little. Compare that to New Zealand, who didn't have nearly the base of talent as we did in England. They were decent cricketers but knew they weren't the best in the world. To counter that, they decided to work for each other, get the best out of each other. England teams had fantastic talent but rarely felt together. They were always disjointed to some degree or another.

In Australia, once the team began to do badly, that 'every man for himself' feeling was only heightened, a real knock-back to see on my first tour. Gooch understood that element of building a team and had started to do so when a younger side was assembled for that West Indies tour which had pushed the hosts all the way in a 2-1 series defeat. The ethos on that tour was 'We may be the underdogs but let's see what we can do', which was why Angus had so enjoyed it. A year on and it seemed like everything Gooch got right with that group of players fell apart with the more dyed-in-the-wool squad that had been picked for Australia.

When the team did get together for a meeting, it was seen as just something to tolerate before going out to the pub or dinner or whatever took your fancy. It was obvious what the senior players were thinking: 'Sod this. Let's get out of here; places to go, people to see.' At one team meeting, there was a lot of tutting and sighing from the management because Beefy and Lamby were late. Out of the window we saw a helicopter coming in to land. Five minutes later, they appeared in the room – 'Sorry, boys, the wind was against us.' Behind them were four members of staff pulling trolleys piled high with Cloudy Bay wine.

The chance of a positive team meeting wasn't helped by the declining relationship between Gower and Gooch. We were under the cosh for most of that tour, prone to drift a little and lose energy at crucial times. When we gathered for a meeting, Gower offered a plan.

'When I see that happening,' he said, 'I'm going to shout out "Shovel!"'

Gooch couldn't have looked more bemused if David had walked up to him and slapped him round the face with a small haddock. He wasn't a huge fan of David at the best of times. 'You what?' he squeaked. 'Shavel?'

David explained that the word could be used as a reset signal. 'Shovel' indicated a need to dig in and work hard. I thought it was a good idea. In fact, Gower had actually put it into practice with good effect as captain of Leicestershire. On this occasion, however, he was laughed out of town. Now, of course, a refocus signal is an accepted and well-used ploy. It's been psychologically proven to work in all areas of life, whether it be on the sports field or wearing an elastic band on your wrist and snapping it gently against your skin when you have a negative thought.

Looking back, I really do wish I'd had the courage to say, 'That might help me.' But at that point, very early into my international career, it seemed a much better option to keep my mouth shut. It wasn't really an environment that encouraged an ebb and flow of opinion. For the younger players especially it was down to the team room, grab a beer, sit down and listen. There was often a bit of a going-through-the-motions feel, and with Gooch and Gower not seeing eye to eye, such meetings became increasingly sporadic. In the end, if they did happen, people, myself included, tended to keep their heads down.

'Right, anyone got any ideas?'

Cue multiple mumbles – 'No, no.'

'That's it then.' And off everyone would go. For someone new to the set-up, seeking a bit of guidance on what the hell I was meant to be doing, it was a kick in the shins. Eventually, like a few others, I only attended those meetings to pick up my daily allowance.

I wish now I had been a little bit more vocal, because I did have a good cricket brain. But then I'd feel slightly awkward offering something up in front of people as experienced as Lamby and Gower. There was always the risk that by saying something you were gifting a free opportunity for others to take the piss. While players are now encouraged to speak up and formulate plans, our meetings would inevitably come up with nothing more than 'Let's try to hit the top of off stump?'

Plan B, C, and D was never discussed. Thing is, Plan A is only okay for a while. When Mark Waugh is on nought, bowling at the top of off stump is the best way to get him out. But what happens when he's on 50, 75, 130? That's when we were stuck because we never had anywhere to turn.

New ideas were all too often hastily decided on the hoof. At Middlesex we might have been relaxed in our match preparation, essentially having a chat in the pub the night before, but that was with good players in a settled team environment. England had the first, but they very definitely didn't have the second. Also, you have to take on board other people's knowledge if you are going to move forward as a cricketer. At Middlesex, I could have carried on running in, bowling and seeing what happened, but it wouldn't have got me very far in the long run. Embers was great from that point of view – a very analytical bowler, a chess player, always thinking two moves ahead. If players have knowledge then it has to be shared.

With England, communication was an issue full-stop. The key to unlocking ideas, to enthuse about different tactics and methods of playing, to refresh the 'let's go out and give it a go' approach, has to come from the coach. But all too often there was nothing, which sometimes left me floundering, a lack of certainty that made me vulnerable to the advice of those perhaps not best placed to give it. It's strange how just an odd word from somebody can affect your mindset. Instead of leaning on a plan of action, or having one or two trusted voices, my constant search for a formula meant in Australia I'd chat to the bus driver on the way to the ground. Other times I'd be on the boundary and some bloke well into his fifteenth tinny would be sat there going, 'You're never gonna get Steve Waugh out bowling over the wicket, Tufnell.' And against every instinct in my mind,

I'd start thinking, 'Maybe he's right. Maybe I should go round the wicket.'

I don't think it would have gone down well with Gooch. 'Phil, why have you suddenly gone round the wicket?'

'Well, this pissed-up bloke in the crowd said it might work.'

But it's very easy to get brain-fog in professional sport. It's a bit like the Grand National. You choose a horse in the morning but then over the next few hours as you keep hearing people making a compelling case for other runners, the less clear your own mind becomes. You end up backing half a dozen only for your original choice, which you didn't back, being 25 lengths ahead at the last fence. Flexibility in approach isn't bad, but sometimes I was a little too bendy.

That search for knowledge meant I was actually quite excited about Keith Fletcher coming in as England coach. He was regarded in the game as a bit of a genius, the fount of all wisdom, some kind of Yoda figure you could go to and be handed the secrets of the universe. Him and Gooch, because of their connections to a strong Essex team, were regarded as a sort of brains trust who knew the game inside out, how to get out there and win things. But then nothing really happened. The conversations about cricket, certainly with me, were just the usual 'Hi, Cat? Is it coming out all right?' Perhaps he thought there was nothing he could teach me. But he'd captained England in India, so then you think there must have been.

Instead, when we went to India, I saw a man prone to mistakes. For instance, he had it in his head that the Indians couldn't play fast bowling and so picked four seamers for the first Test, one of whom was the left-armer Paul Taylor, who thus created a huge omelette outside off stump for the Indian spinners to exploit. I'd not been playing long at that stage but even I could see that one coming a mile off. 'Really, Fletch? I think we might have got our tactics wrong here,' I thought. I knew better than to say it out loud.

There was no analysis of changing conditions. A tour to India was treated no differently from a tour to the Caribbean. 'Well, it'll spin a bit' was about it. Talk about a coherent approach.

Sussex leg-spinner Ian Salisbury was taken on that tour ostensibly as a net bowler to help our batsmen prepare to face Anil Kumble. And then Embers and I were left in the dressing room when he was picked for the first Test. It really did feel like we were playing club cricket for England. 'Who wants the new ball? Who wants to bat seven? Oh, hang on, we haven't got an all-rounder. Right, so we'll play seven batters. Oh, but that means one of the bowlers will miss out. I know, we'll drop the spinner.' The only surprise was that we didn't all put our subs in at the start of the day, check who had the beer money and bring our own sandwiches. Structure? Strategy? 'This is how we will dismantle India – this is how we will counterpunch – this is how we will dry this batsman up.' Forget it. There was no thinking in the box, let alone outside it. I played 21 one-day internationals, all outside England, because I happened to be there on tour. There was no concept of different squads. If you were a good player, the thinking was you could be that good player anywhere, any format, anytime.

If coaching did happen it was more orientated towards the batting, possibly because most coaches were batsmen themselves. Otherwise it was, 'Well, if they don't know what they're doing, they shouldn't be here.' I heard that a lot. Which is fair enough when things are going well. At that point, a team looks after itself, and a lack of contact with the coaches can be perceived positively as them not feeling any need to intervene. But when the shit hits the fan you need some sort of nugget, a bit of direction, wisdom, or foresight, to try to dig yourself back into a game or series. That's why if we lost the first Test match of a series it was all over. We never had any input to get ourselves back into the game.

Globally, we were always the last to find out about the latest trends and changes. When reverse swing came in, we didn't have a clue. If Athers was at the non-striker's end he would try to give his partner a chance by watching the bowler run up to the wicket, assess the ball position and then swap his bat from right to left hand to signal the reverse swinger. However, facing Wasim and Waqar sending pinpoint deliveries down at 90 mph is mentally complex enough without looking out for a last-second change of hands from a batting partner as well. This surely couldn't be how we, as an international team, dealt with a major development in the sport. It really did feel like if some bloke had wandered past Lord's and mentioned he knew how to bowl reverse swing he'd have been straight in the side. If the batters wanted to work out how to play Shane Warne, they had to sit on top of the pavilion behind the bowler's arm. At least Baldrick *had* a cunning plan.

Compared to Ray Illingworth, Keith Fletcher was a positive chatterbox. He was like Vera Duckworth to Illingworth's Trappist monk. When the Yorkshire stalwart came in, first as chairman of selectors and then coach, he spoke to me just twice. The first time I was in the nets at Headingley when he sidled past.

'If I put a hanky down where I wanted the ball to land, I'd hit it six out of six,' he muttered. It felt like a dig.

'Thanks a bunch,' I said as he walked off. What I really wanted to say was 'F*** you'.

The more senior players would say just to ignore Illingworth, but as coach and selector he had the power of life and death. He was a supremo, but instead of using that position to instigate new structures and ways of thinking, all too often it felt like he wanted to be number one just to say he was. Perhaps that was why he chose to dress as the Emperor Ming at a fancy-dress ball in Australia. That was the second time he spoke to me – and the first time I realised he was on the tour.

The early and mid-'90s was a strange period for the national team. The game was becoming much more professional and yet, in the background, as administrators, selectors, and the like, were people who'd played in a very different era.

Illingworth, for example, was really quite old, especially in comparison to Athers, a young captain trying to get some new blood into the side. He was also slightly cantankerous – 'nothing is as good as it was in my day' – a negativity which wears you down after a while. As players, it made us feel he didn't particularly like or rate us. Whatever we did could never compare. It didn't enthuse us at all to feel so isolated as a team from the people who were picking it, people who had little idea what was going on in modern cricket so wedded were they to the old-fashioned and the traditional.

Devon was a case in point. He'd just single-handedly flattened South Africa, taking nine for 57 at The Oval, bowling lightning-fast, and the immediate reaction of Illingworth and his bowling coach Peter Lever was to try to change his action. They thought his run-up was wrong; he was falling to the off-side at point of delivery and was therefore bowling too much down the legside. Okay, there might be a technical issue there to work on, but reconstruct his entire action? England had finally found a match-winning fast bowler and their answer was not to work with him, encourage him, make him feel valued, but to slowly patronise and destroy him. Their argument was, 'He does veer away so we're not wrong' – essentially, 'he does what we say or he's out'. Well, when your action is ruined you're out anyway.

Thankfully, the modern way is not to dictate; it's to understand. Coaching is much more about suggestion. When I played, if a batsman slogged one up in the air, they'd barely have sat down in the dressing room before the coach came up and demanded, 'What the f*** were you doing?' Nowadays, a week will pass and then, when that player is doing fielding practice, a coach will sidle up and say, 'Just wondered if you'd thought about that shot – maybe there's a better way of playing it.' That's a much more grown up way of doing it than blaming people, making them feel useless or like a silly schoolboy.

On the most basic level, playing for England in the first half of the '90s, you rarely felt welcome. Coaches almost went out of their way to make players feel worthless.

After the losing South Africa series of 1995–96, Illingworth named a small number of the touring side who he said had a future in Test cricket. The rest? Did he ever bother to think how that comment made them feel? I knew exactly how they felt.

Before that tour, Illingworth had reluctantly recalled me for the final Test against West Indies at The Oval. Until that final Test I'd been in the wilderness since the Ashes tour of the previous winter, but since I'd taken six for 25 in the last West Indies Test at The Oval four years earlier and was having one of my best ever seasons in the county game, presumably even he couldn't resist a compelling case for a recall. I turned up at The Oval only to be left out. Not only that but several other players told me they'd been advised not to be seen in my company if they knew what was good for them. The naughty kid at school – not that I took a blind bit of notice. When Illingworth was asked about the omission, he explained that had I performed well the selectors would have had to consider me for the winter tour. Try and work that one out if you can – they didn't pick me because I might have won the match.

That selectorial nightmare came true when I was recalled for the final Test of the Ashes series in 1997. As we celebrated the win afterwards, I knew only too well the narrative going round the selectors' minds – 'Shit! That means we'll have to take him on tour!'

You might think that creating a positive environment would be the first thing on the agenda when you've got a load of guys coming together from all over the place, some of whom have never met one another. If that isn't the job of the backroom staff then I don't know what is. And yet they never did. It was almost like they positively wanted not to make you feel welcome, that they wanted to put you under even more pressure to see if you could stand up to it. Ludicrous. When I played for Middlesex, the club had a togetherness – I felt valued. From that came commitment and positivity and a desire to work towards common goals. When England came along, I thought it would be the same but on steroids. We'd all be talking about cricket, how to develop as a team; there'd be all these amazing players, and it would be ultra-professional. I couldn't have been more wrong.

Players were asked to perform on a professional level when actually everything surrounding the team was totally shambolic. I'd look at Illingworth with his downbeat one-note approach and couldn't help thinking, 'So is this what England's all about?'

Illingworth wasn't the only one. There were other coaches in the set-up I'd look at and wonder, 'What exactly are you bringing to the party?' Their presence gave us nothing more than, 'Okay, here you are – off you go and have a game of cricket.'

Man-management in the '90s? There was none. It was just our way or the highway. Why wasn't it ever about making people better? I can understand that some of the old boys running cricket would balk at the idea of players asking for help – 'There was none of that in my day.' I can also understand that the big players of the '80s oozed so much confidence and arrogance that they pretty much ran the management rather than vice versa. But the obvious truth was that there was a new generation of players coming through who needed guidance. What use is it to any up-and-coming player to say to them, 'You should know what you should or shouldn't be doing – you're an England cricketer.' These players were no longer old-school individuals. I was probably the last of those. The final dodo.

Certainly, by the time I played my last Test in 2001, the situation around the England team was very different. Making players better was a thing. Another 20 years on and there are analysts who formulate individual plans.

Things started to change when David Graveney came in as chair of selectors. He made it his business to be a lot more involved with the players while also not trying to push his way to the front. Grav was an affable bloke who would hover around in the alleyways outside the dressing room, pop his head in, have a friendly chat – like a human being – and then go off and have a drink, the latter being a necessity of membership of the left-arm spin club.

I'm not sure Grav had the best eye for a cricketer but at least he provided a bridge between the players and the bosses – because that's what those selectors are at the end of the day. Instead of them up there like the lords of the manor and us cowering below like the serfs, Grav allowed engagement, a workable link. It felt like he was on the players' side rather than it being us and them.

There has to be association with people running and playing cricket. One lot in one corner and one lot in the other can never work. Only when you come together can you take a step forward.

The arrival of the ever-entertaining and thought-provoking Bumble in the coaching hot seat was another breath of fresh air. He was the first coach who actually stood up for his players. Before it had always been, 'Well, the players are shit – what are we supposed to do about it?' But Bumble never singled out players for criticism. Instead, like Arsène Wenger or Alex Ferguson, he took the pressure on himself. It made us feel supported. It was the first time in an England dressing room that I'd experienced any feeling of 'Right, we're here, lads, and we're together.' Before we knew it, there were pictures of the Queen on the dressing-room wall and Bumble was delivering a Shakespearean rallying cry of 'Cry "God for Harry, England, and Saint George!"' in an Accrington brogue.

Bumble's patriotic fervour manifested itself quite dramatically in the famous 'We flippin' murdered 'em!' match in Bulawayo when, on the final day of the Test, we needed a demanding 205 in 37 overs to win. We were closing in on the target when the hosts started bowling just far enough down the legside for the batters not to be able to reach the ball but not quite far enough for it to be called a wide. Not a great tactic as far as the spirit of the game was concerned, but, to be honest, one we might have used in the same circumstances.

As we strove to reach our goal, the England players were outside on the bank in front of the dressing room, shouting, calling 'Wide!', and generally voicing our disapproval. Unfortunately, a large number of inebriated locals – farming types with Popeye arms and haystack fists – started getting a bit agitated and giving us stick. We responded in kind, and what might have begun as pointed but friendly banter started to turn a bit ugly. In time, relations deteriorated to such an extent that the locals actually turned their backs on the action and started heading up the bank towards us. Their message was clear – 'This is our turf and we can do what we want.'

One or two bats were raised in preparation for battle, one of the chaps actually removing the sponsor's label to avoid any issues. Wrapping the maker's name round a spectator's head tends to invalidate the deal.

In the end it was hardly a scene of hardcore violence. One or two teacups might have been thrown before security stepped in and that was it. Bumble, of course, had been in the middle of this rumpus just before, when the game was finally drawn, he gave his infamous quote – which gives a bit of context to his highly charged state.

Possibly, the Zimbabwe cricket authorities might have reviewed the visiting team facilities after this game. Essentially, the dressing room was a big tent on a hill with all sorts of people just wandering through. You'd look up from your crossword and there'd be some bloke sat next to you telling you how shit you were. I'm not saying a flashpoint was inevitable, but a flashpoint was inevitable.

While Bumble tried to build a togetherness by putting Winston Churchill quotes on the wall and getting us to wear the same cap in the first session, there was little direct link to the cricket we played. Compare that to the team that won the 2019 World Cup, its togetherness bound by a knowledge of how to operate in every situation. Of course, Bumble was operating in pre-central contracts days. The idea we could ever be what they now call 'Team England' was farcical.

I ended my England career under Duncan Fletcher. Duncan did actually write a book about his time as England coach, but whether or not it opens I'm not sure. This was a man who clearly had great ideas but for some reason had an issue communicating with certain players. Duncan had a little game, which felt more like a punishment, where he'd hit high catches and you'd have to bag ten before it was over. 'Trial by ten' he called it. Duncan was very good at putting the catches just out of reach. You'd then have to fetch the ball and throw it back to his baseball mitt. It was a non-stop process and really hard work for the poor sod who he chose to do the exercise. People's legs would go, others would throw up. To add to the humiliation, everyone else would watch, pissing themselves.

I'd avoided this horror show until eventually, at Centurion in South Africa, Duncan decided it was my turn. Word soon got round that Tuffers was finally up for trial by ten, so much so that the rest of the boys chose seats in the stand for the best view. I tried my best to protest, but Duncan wasn't backing down – he insisted.

He did his usual trick of hitting balls just out of reach and soon I was struggling. It felt like he was taking a real pleasure in making sure I couldn't quite get to the ball before it hit the ground. In my view, he was deliberately belittling me in front of the group. 'Two can play at this game,' I thought. I worked out he had seven balls. If I threw them back out of his reach he would soon run out. With the final ball, he intentionally hit one that dropped short. I walked up to it and threw it over his head. 'Right,' I said, 'are we going in now?'

He gave me a look. He didn't need to speak. I knew what he was saying to me, and everyone else watching – 'Look – same old Tufnell.'

'If you want to get the best out of someone,' I told him, 'then talking to them isn't a bad idea instead of making them look a mug.' But Duncan seemed to enjoy distance.

The writing was on the wall in South Africa with Fletcher. I knew he didn't like me. Back in England he came to see me unannounced during a Middlesex second XI game. We were batting so I was having a relax, sat on a sofa with a fag and a bacon sandwich watching *Bargain Hunt*, when he walked through the door.

'Oh f***!' I spluttered. 'Hello, Duncan.'

He sat down opposite. 'Well, how did you think the tour went?'

'Not bad. I bowled all right in patches.'

'Well, you've got to work a little bit on your fielding.'

'Yes, I realise that, Duncan,' I said. 'But one thing that you haven't taken into consideration is that I'm actually allergic to fielding. Get me rolling around in that hard wiry grass they have in South Africa and Perth and places like that and my neck comes up in prickly heat. I have to swill down a load of antihistamines.'

He sat there staring at me – 'Allergic to fielding?'

'Yeah.'

He got up and walked out. I didn't care whether I saw or played for him again, but there was one last chapter in the story of our relationship when he picked me for the last Test of the Australia series at The Oval in 2001. Before the game he actually came out and said he'd only picked me because he'd had a look around and there wasn't anyone else. I felt a million dollars after hearing that. I mean, even if that's what you're thinking, don't say it out loud. There was just no need. It wasn't like I was expecting to come back in and cement my place for the next four years.

The end for me coincided with the lift-off for central contracts. That had to happen. The England set-up had become poisonous for both English cricket and England cricketers. There was talent but no structure to make the best of it. In fact, the existing structure acted more as a deterrent. We wanted to be cricketers, but we weren't allowed. Central contracts, the idea that the England team should be a single entity that takes precedence over everything else, the scaffolding which held the side together and provided a platform upon which to build, were a godsend.

It was that lack of a pathway that had most disappointed me about playing for England. With a central contract I could have relaxed knowing that if things didn't go well for a couple of games I'd still got a safety net. That would have meant the green light to play with confidence and freedom instead of living on the edge of every ball. The team was constantly playing on quicksand, and it took its toll. Even if you managed to find the confidence to play fluently, a wrong umpiring decision, a run-out even, could put you out of the England side for a year, two years, forever, with all that entailed – yes, cricket's a game, but it's also your livelihood. With me, if a batsman nicked one of my deliveries and was given not out, then that wasn't going to show up on the bowling analysis used at the next selection meeting. As Ramps once pointed out resignedly, one bad decision and you were gone. Consigned to the scrapheap. Who has ever performed at their best knowing that the cliff they are stood on could at any moment crumble away?

Phil DeFreitas once had two top-order batsmen dropped off his bowling. When the second one happened, he turned to me at mid-off. 'Oh well, Phil, I'll be seeing you. That'll be me done.' And he was spot on. He got two wickets instead of four and that was it – bye-bye. You could always tell when the guillotine was being sharpened. You could hear the noise from the middle. Playing for England at that time it was always about what you didn't do. The negativity could be overwhelming.

That intensity of pressure was always to our detriment. Guys who came into the side were immediately anxious, even more so than the ones who were already there. That pressure extended to the coaching staff, who, if they didn't right the ship immediately, would be sacked. There was no element of building, making ourselves awkward to beat. If we didn't get a result, that was it. Again and again we were being asked to cross crocodile-infested waters in swimming trunks and wellingtons.

Instead of taking the pressure off players, everything about the England set-up just ladled it on. How many times was I selected for an England team at The Oval with the message loud and clear – 'You've been picked to win the game for us'? When I came on in the fourth innings, I was expected to bowl a side out. Fail and it was 'on yer bike'. No calm and calculated approach to putting things in place to make us a better side. It was cricket on a razor blade.

Sport is a performance-based business, simple as that. But so much can go wrong on any particular occasion. Think of it like someone who is a brilliant student being judged on a single exam. Cross that white line, and they either sink or swim, and sometimes if it's the former it's not their fault. Now the selectors judge on coursework. They see that unplayable delivery, recognise the strength of the opposition, understand that the umpire had a bad day.

The best way to get rid of nerves is for other people to show confidence in you and the way you go about your business. That way uncertainty is buried.

Let's face it, cricket is a difficult enough game at the best of times. There are dozens of variables – pace, movement, pitches, spin, to name but a few. It's very difficult mentally to get all your ducks in a row without then worrying about factors beyond your control. If Ramps had a bad knock for Middlesex, he always knew he'd be okay. He had the backing of the club and a good one was always coming. With England, that bad knock could be a full-stop. Occasionally, I'd say to Ramps, 'Keep going, mate – everyone knows what you can do.' But it doesn't really mean anything coming from a teammate. At England level that needs to come from the selectors and the coach.

No wonder Ramps found it hard to relax at international level. He was playing in leg irons, his natural game put on the backburner for fear of being punished for getting out to an aggressive shot. He wasn't alone. So many players of that '90s era turned up and played for England differently from the way they did for their counties. In their county game they were natural. They enjoyed themselves. And then England came along and the fear factor, the lack of stability, knocked that straight out of them. Worth asking how many English cricketers played their best games for their county when they could have been playing them for England.

Thankfully, that attitude has changed in recent years. The best coaches now encourage teams to play without fear, an attitude that led directly to England winning the World Cup.

Aggressive, fast-scoring players were also allowed to play their natural game in the Test match arena without the fear of being dropped if it didn't go their way. Previously, they'd have felt compelled to drop anchor, to play long and defensive orthodox innings to impress the selectors and stay in the team. Inevitably that wouldn't work and they'd be dropped anyway.

England has essentially become an elite county side. Everyone feels settled and able to express their talent. I would have loved that. It would have meant I could relax a little bit, bowl for my country without being in the unpleasant position of always having one eye looking over my shoulder. As it was, like everyone else I had to suck it up. Make a fuss about the system? Go to the press and complain? Well, it takes a brave boy to do that. Raise your head above the parapet and you'd be gone, never selected again. All part of the vicious circle. No one said it was bad so no one believed it was bad – cricket as North Korea.

Despite everything, a lot of the boys from that era look back with an amazing amount of fondness because against all the odds we forged something out of adversity. We were all doggy-paddling around trying to keep our heads above water, not knowing where to go or what to do when we got there, and because of that, great relationships were formed.

'Athers,' I'll say, as we sit in the Tetley Bitter Home for Retired Cricketers, 'remember that time when we were abandoned in Bangalore?'

'Shut up, Tuffers,' he'll say. 'I didn't get a wink of sleep last night. You were bouncing on your bed at 3 a.m.'

CHAPTER 10

How Not to Be Suffocated

My dad taught me a very important lesson in life – deny, deny and deny again. His words came rushing back to me when an investigation was launched into an incident which occurred after a draw with New Zealand at Auckland in 1997.

It was a match made famous by their number 11, Danny Morrison, Test match cricket's ultimate bunny, a man whose ability with the bat made me look like Don Bradman, and nicknamed, for fairly obvious reasons, Danny the Duck. Waddling around, he somehow hung on for 133 balls and nearly three hours to deny us what seemed certain victory. It was awful, made worse by the fact that Danny had wisely patented his own duck-caller which, as time went on, was flying out of the stadium shop. Every ball that failed to dislodge Danny was met with a cacophony of noises more commonly heard on an episode of *Springwatch*.

It was an horrific last day, and as we sat head in hands in the Eden Park dressing room, the sound of mallards still invading our lugholes, we were all feeling more than a little emotional, me in particular – as the spinner it was my job to bowl them out in the fourth innings. Leaving behind the unopened champagne that had been put on ice at the tea interval, we headed out to the team bus – to be met by hundreds of Kiwis desperate to rub our faces in it even more. They were banging on the side of the coach, laughing and jeering – the big boys of England held at bay by the walking wicket that was Danny Morrison. There's only so much a person can take, and as we pulled off I decided to flash them a moonie.

I didn't think much else of it until it became clear that the sight of the Tufnell rear had not gone down altogether well with the assembled crowd. Someone complained – I was a bit pimply at that time – and there was the inevitable inquest. Clearly, I was the leading suspect by quite some distance. If this had been the start of an episode of *Inspector Morse*, the rest of it would have lasted about 15 seconds.

Following my dad's mantra to the letter, no way was I going to own up. The management were very disappointed by the incident and there was talk of the ICC becoming involved. My backside really had rocked cricket to its core. As the days passed and the pressure mounted, a Mafia-like *omertà* descended on those in the squad who knew mine was the offending backside. It became clear that unless there was to be a bottom-based identity parade – 'That's him, the one with the spot on his right buttock' – I was, for once, to escape the shackles of the disciplinary committee. Only now, 25 years on, do I feel safe finally to confirm it was me.

With my tenure in the team forever hanging by a thread, my attitude to playing for England was simple. 'I'm going to have a good time and enjoy it – tomorrow it could all be gone.' If certain people thought I was enjoying myself a little too much, so what? With so little chance of long-term selection anyway, I wasn't going to suddenly turn into a monk. I wasn't going to be something I wasn't. I was not going to compromise on being my true self just because I was wearing an England shirt, an attitude that very nearly led to me never even getting near one.

For the first part of my career, I had long hair tied into a ponytail. Think Francis Rossi swapping denim for cricket whites. It drove Gatt and Embers mad. 'Look,' they'd say, 'if you get your hair cut you've half a chance of playing for England.'

I'd mull this over – 'F*** off.'

'Listen, they're looking at you. Get your hair cut, sort yourself out, smarten yourself up a little bit.'

'I'm not getting it cut just to pander to them,' I'd argue. 'What difference does it make to my ability if I have long hair or not?' As with school, I felt this was an unarguable point.

Gatt, possibly because his own hair lacked the same lustre – time and again I told him to start using Timotei – saw my argument as entirely self-defeating to the point where during a game at Uxbridge he got me in a headlock at lunch and marched me to a barber in the high street. He stood guard while the scissorsmith sheared it all off. Only now did I really see how strongly Gatt felt about it. He didn't miss his lunch for anything. Even now I thank Gatt for forsaking that boiled egg. Had he not made that sacrifice, there's every chance I would not have been picked to go to Australia.

Over the coming years, as one defeat followed another, and the faces of the England cricket team were given away free with every dartboard, my determination to make the most of my time in the sun only deepened, the tour to India being a case in point. As has been mentioned, we won very little on that trip. We beat a couple of makeshift teams, possibly an invitational train drivers' XI, and Uttar Pradesh U-19s Farmers, and that was about it. As unsuccessful tours go, only England's sojourns to the West Indies in the early '80s have been worse.

At the end of the second Test in what was then Madras, which we lost by an innings, we were as ever invited onto the field for the presentation ceremony. I can assure readers that the last thing any cricketer wants after being smashed into submission in a dust cloud of 35° heat is to stand around on an outfield while numerous speeches, interviews and awards ceremonies are delivered. I have often wished that losing a Test match would be marked by being tied to the back of a horse and dragged through the streets for half an hour. It would be quicker and less painful.

With the horse not an option, we put a few odds and sods on and traipsed onto the outfield. A couple of the boys had shirts, another had grabbed a bit of training kit, someone else was in a string vest. We all looked absolutely dreadful.

The organisers did at least provide some ornate wicker chairs, and so there we sat, weary, gaunt and with a few days' itchy stubble, having being advised not to shave during the game because of the dirt and sweat getting into open pores and bringing us out in pustules. Apologies if you're having your dinner.

Through the various categories they went – batsman of the series, bowler of the series, batsman of the match, bowler of the match, groundsman, groundsman's cat, most efficient piece of groundsman's equipment, best roller, best hair, most handsome man on the field, best ball-boy in a supporting role. Flowers would be placed round the neck of each winner, entering the stage as a cricketer, leaving it as Dame Edna Everage. Eventually, the England captain, Alec Stewart, was invited up to say a few words. He kept it short – 'We were outplayed' – and stepped back down.

We were just exiting the wicker when this chap took the microphone. 'Hold on a moment,' he said, 'no one leaves here empty-handed' – a bit like on *Bullseye* when Jim Bowen used to dish out the Bendy Bullys. These blokes then came trotting out with mountain bikes. Decent bits of kit, shock absorbers and everything. There was one for each of us. For some reason, this didn't particularly boost the other boys' mood. They cleared off to sulk in the dressing room. Me on the other hand went 'Oh, great!' and headed off on a circuit of the field. I was pulling wheelies, doing skids, performing bunny hops, and the crowd was on their feet waving and clapping. Brilliant.

Eventually, I jumped off with a flourish and walked into the dressing room. 'Wow, boys, these are great bikes, ten-speed and everything. I've never had one with suspension before.'

I might have misjudged the room. 'Phil,' someone said, 'what the f*** are you doing?'

'What do you mean?'

'We've just got thrashed again and you're out there popping wheelies?'

'I just wanted to try my new bike out.'

'Maybe you'd like to try it wrapped round your neck . . .'

Of course, we couldn't take the bikes round with us. Yes, the planes were on strike but bikes weren't the answer – India is a big country. Nip round to your mother's and it can take three days. Instead, they would be shipped over to our homes.

When I got back my dad asked me how the tour went. 'Well,' I said, 'on the downside we didn't play very well and I got fined again. On the plus-side, I bought a couple of really nice carpets, some stone statues of Indian deities, and a lot of tea. Oh, and they also gave me this really nice bike which I'm expecting any day now.'

At that very moment there was a knock on the door. There before me was a box. I looked inside and found a pyramid of metal. The wheels were buckled and the frame all wonky. I can only think the ship encountered rough seas. 'Dad,' I asked, 'any room in the bin?'

Eighteen months later, Gus Fraser was sat on an exercise bike in the gym at the team hotel in Adelaide. He then did a few pulls on the rowing machine while I sat in the sauna thinking I was working out. We then retired to the outdoor jacuzzi on the roof, trying to keep my fag out of the bubbles.

He turned to me, nipples glistening in the South Australia sun. 'This is the life,' he said. 'Here we are, in Adelaide, in this wonderful hotel, and then we're all going to go out to dinner and get up tomorrow and play cricket for our country.

'Tuffers,' he stated, 'you want to be here for as long as you can.'

And he was right. The alternative was being a county cricketer scratching around for a living. But the flipside of that for me was that you had to be seen to be doing the 'right' things even if the 'right' things weren't for you. The question then is how much of the real you are you willing to deny to earn a few extra quid?

For instance, if/when England lost a game, I wouldn't think twice about going out and having a few drinks; cheering myself up by having a bit of a laugh. People would pull their faces – 'You shouldn't do that – it doesn't look good.' But, honestly, what difference does it make? The game is lost, there's nothing anyone can do about it after the event. Why not go down the pub? To say 'it doesn't look good' is a bullshit reason. On a totally pragmatic level, it makes absolutely no difference. The game's done.

'Yeah, but there are certain things that you just don't do.'

'Okay, so what do you want me to do? Sit in my room whipping myself because we didn't beat Australia?'

'No, but you have to think about the image it presents.'

'Okay. Yeah, yeah.' And out I'd go.

Freddie Flintoff suffered from the same thing. It's okay to have a few drinks when you win. Lose and it's a completely different kettle of fish. When Fred went on his bender after the Ashes victory in 2005, the management didn't bat an eyelid – 'That's Fred! That's just the way he is!' Not too long after when he was having a few drinks after a defeat during a dodgy World Cup, suddenly that same management team was pegging him out on a sand dune for the vultures.

Fred was stripped of the England vice-captaincy and banned for a game after becoming unwisely attracted to a pedalo in St Lucia. The first thing I said to Fred after the incident was 'You shouldn't have got caught' (I did also point out that it could have been quite dangerous). The way Fred was publicly hauled over the coals was disgraceful. On any cricket tour there will be plenty of things like that going on, but Fred's indiscretion seemed to be leapt upon as a chance to position him as a bad person. It felt like the hierarchy were trying to stuff him up. Really? He'd had a few drinks, made his way back to the hotel and done something daft. High jinks. Okay, give him a slap on the wrist but don't hang him out to dry. And whatever you do, keep it in-house.

As I watched that situation unfold I knew exactly how Fred must have felt because I'd been there so many times myself. Every little internal issue played out in public, the result being a none too subtle narrative that you're a bit of a troublemaker. Cheers, boys. Thanks for throwing me under the bus.

Yes, it's a great buzz to win a game of cricket, to go up against another professional side, and do something pretty good like take five wickets. When we went up north to Lancashire, facing a mob who thought they were a bit tasty, and showed them what was what, it was a lovely drive home. But the flipside of that, and what people, in my case sometimes deliberately, misunderstood was my way of dealing with a loss. If myself and a few others, especially for England, went out to drown our sorrows, or just for a bit of a pick-me-up, there was always someone saying, 'You shouldn't be in here. You don't care. You're a disgrace.' That kind of attention can be stifling. It breeds a nagging doubt. 'Am I being happy when I shouldn't be happy? Am I being sad when I shouldn't be sad?' I just wanted to be me but there were always those waiting to judge.

It's funny how me and Fred are the two cricketers to have made the leap from the sport into the mainstream, but I think it's because at heart we're both sociable, fun-loving people. If either of us lost a Test match, you'd see someone who, yes, inside was devastated but equally wasn't going to wear a hair shirt and sleep on a bed of nails. My attitude was: deal with it and move on. I understand that doesn't fit with what some people want to see. They want you to be visibly crushed. But there are too many downs in cricket without letting it infect every other part of your life. You can't beat yourself up every time you lose. I've seen people withdraw into themselves and it's not healthy. That's why, when I had a bad day, I always sought out some mates and went for a beer. I wanted to hear people say, 'Listen, don't worry about it. Tomorrow's another day. Have a drink. It's not the end of the world.' After an hour's moping I was back on the horse and ready to go again. Instead of doom and gloom, I was thinking, 'What a wonderful day to be alive.'

Nobody's perfect. Me and Fred certainly weren't. And again, people relate to that. Getting sucked into the pursuit of perfection is dangerous. Jonathan Trott is a case in point, never switching off, in a constant state of self-analysis, until ultimately it damaged his health. The nature of cricket is you are going to fail. It's a sport where perfection doesn't exist. There is always something – more runs, more wickets, more catches – you could have done better. You really do need to get to grips with those ups and downs quickly.

I never really gave any thought about how I wanted to portray myself. Those who were destined to play sport professionally, like Michael Atherton perhaps, who was always in line to open the batting for England, could pick and choose how they wanted to go about their career. But I think for those like myself who just fell into it, sport moulds you rather than the other way round. Maybe as we grow we tailor our approach a little bit, but at the start it's just get out of bed, have a bit of breakfast and whatever will be will be.

My character, dating right back to my early days in the game, was to be quite aggressive on the field. When I was selected for England that was then seen by the management as being a bit too high-maintenance. I knew, though, that I was a reactive bowler. That's what got the best out of me – a desire to win a battle on the pitch and show people they were wrong. But for them it was all about keeping up appearances. Instead of working with my attributes, they gave me the usual spiel – 'You've got to change or you're out'. The fact that I wouldn't change is why I was made to stand in the corner for the home West Indies series in 1991. Bearing in mind that on my recall for the final Test I ripped through the West Indies batting line-up in the first innings, taking six wickets for four runs in five and a bit overs, people dancing on their seats in the stands, I wondered who exactly that time in the wilderness had benefited.

That night, I found myself in Stringfellows. Next day, I picked up a paper and there I was alongside two scantily clad young women while clutching two bottles of champers. The whole team had been invited up to the club. 'Great, I'll see you in there,' I said to the others, rushing off to brush my teeth and detangle my armpit hair. And then as it turned out there was pretty much only me there. Everyone had stayed for a drink in the hotel. I did think about going back but how often do you get champagne flowing like tap water? I'm surprised a report wasn't immediately commissioned, casting me out into the Arctic wastes for another six months.

Back in the fold, I did actually think to myself, 'Okay, if I want to play for England, I'm going to have to take their advice. They hold all the cards. I'll have to toe the line.' I went out and bowled like a robot. I didn't have the aggression in my approach and I was not as effective. I became stiff, worried, thinking about whether I looked the part they wanted.

Generally speaking, 'Calm down, be more consistent with your behaviour' is pretty good advice. But, depending on what makes a person tick, it's not necessarily helpful. Okay, you can play along and look like you're happy to try a different way, but it will still nag at you inside, and that inevitably will negatively affect your performance.

It doesn't matter what you do, you have to understand your nuts and bolts, what makes you perform, the essence of you. Start trying to be what others want you to be – in my case unaggressive and not prone to the odd sulk – and not only won't you give of your best, you can't give of your best. I'm glad that I stayed true to my own beliefs. I could have taken every bit of advice going but then I'd never have been me. The truth, uncomfortable as it might be to some, is I used to like a fight. I understood that a little bit of conflict could raise my game, even if it was by just 2 per cent. If I was reined in, on the other hand, I was much more likely to just go out and bowl on autopilot. I don't think I'm particularly unusual in that. I've heard it said that sometimes the best way to get Jimmy Anderson going is to pinch him under the armpit. Mike Brearley used to do the psychological version of the underarm pinch to Ian Botham back in the day – 'Oh, I don't suppose you'll be wanting to bowl into that headwind – might be a bit hard for you.' Beefy couldn't wait to snatch the ball off him. Everyone's different; it's just about what makes people tick.

If I'd confined my off-pitch activities to brass-rubbing and prayer sessions, then perhaps people wouldn't have taken it on themselves to mind so much. Of course, the truth is the way I was off the pitch only added to people's ire. My preparation wasn't always what most people would term professional. Even I look back at it sometimes and think, 'What was I doing?' I'd be walking down a beach in Antigua at 3 a.m. pissed out of my head after dancing on a table in a bar and then in a few hours be bowling at Desmond Haynes – and thinking that was acceptable.

But then I also suspect that not thinking in a conventional manner, not having that sort of brain, is what makes some people excel in sport. After all, if you do all your training, eat chicken and rice all your life, don't have a drink and then go out and play and you're still no good, it must be because you're no good. I, on the other hand, consciously or subconsciously was forever putting little obstacles in my way to make myself perform better. I'd be out there with the ball in my hand and be thinking, 'Well, they all know I didn't get in 'til 3 a.m. They all know I'm actually still a little bit pissed. I can't go out there and not perform because otherwise I've really shot myself in the foot.'

It's a strange concept to get your head around, and I'm not sure why I was like that, but I thrived on that worry in a funny sort of way. 'You've f***ed up here. You'd better sort it out – if not, there's a whole world of shit waiting for you.' I needed that in the back of my head. It worked better for me than knowing I had done everything right and so just needed to go out and perform. If I did that, then I'd have no reason not to perform. I didn't operate like that every time, but certainly it existed as a default mechanism.

Alongside that was a permanent capacity to shoot myself in the foot, a self-destruct button, which I've never quite understood. But I'm not alone. A lot of sportspeople have self-destruct buttons. Some of the most talented there have ever been – Maradona, Gazza, George Best. I can't speak for them, but I know in cricket that self-destruct button was made more prominent by there being nothing in place to deal with people as individuals. It was like teachers at school.

'Right, we're all going for a ten-mile run.'

'Why? I don't want to go for a ten-mile run. Can't I go for a two-mile run?'

'Well, a ten-mile run will be good for fitness.'

'But I know I'm fit enough to bowl anyway.'

I'd found out about myself as a person and a sportsperson through playing. There are all sorts of elements – diet, training, sleep – now that people claim can give a team those little extra 1 per cents, but for me, like a lot of people, I felt I'd done my learning coming through school and age-range cricket.

It wasn't just me on the naughty step. Often I had to shove up to make room for Chris Lewis, another who would have benefited from better handling. He needed guidance and support rather than raised eyebrows at the fact he dressed slightly differently and liked going out at 10:30 p.m. Chris actually just wanted to be left alone to get on with his cricket, but he played in an era when you were judged on appearances, when people made instant assumptions about your character. When Chris shaved his head and got sunstroke in Antigua, it was perfect for the doubters – an easy dig at someone who liked to do his own thing – 'Bloody Lewis again.' The papers dubbed him 'the prat without a hat'. One journalist described it as the 'most idiotic cricket injury of all time' (this was before someone left an unattended ball on the grass for Glenn McGrath to trip over before the Edgbaston Ashes Test in 2005).

The same thing happened when he turned up late for a match after a puncture. It was made out like he'd committed the crime of a century, but I've known plenty of people who've turned up 20 minutes late for all sorts of reasons and weren't ridiculed and lambasted from the rafters. I get that posing for a magazine without your clothes on, which Chris also did, isn't in the MCC coaching manual, but so what? You can do what you want, can't you? What's doing a photo spread for a magazine got to do with anything? He can still bat and bowl, can't he? People nowadays do all sorts of things – commercial and media deals – and no one bats an eye. Back then, very different. Knowing that judgemental attitude exists up above creates only one thing – insularity. You don't feel wanted, supported, or valued. And so you withdraw.

Chris Lewis had an immense talent. If it didn't happen, there had to be a reason. It had to be his fault, didn't it? It couldn't possibly be the fault of the people in charge. Instead of trying to help him be better, it was always 'What's wrong with him? Why won't he conform?'

That's what cricket was like. The attitude was simple – 'If he's not delivering, f*** him, we'll find someone else.' That person might not perform either but at least they'd have the right haircut. They simply couldn't understand anyone whose mind worked in a slightly different way.

'Okay, so why haven't you picked him?'

'Well, he wore the wrong trousers and was late for the coach.'

'Hang on, you didn't pick someone because of that? You were happy to miss out on the best years of that person's career because of a T-shirt?' Talk about treating people like children.

I didn't know Ian Botham before he strode into the Oval dressing room when we were both recalled to the England team for the final Test of the series against West Indies in 1991. But the minute I clapped eyes on him and heard him speak it was a breath of fresh air. He had a totally different attitude from what had come before. Until that point, I'd felt slightly smothered by the uncertainty that infested the dressing room. And then Beefy turned up in a cowboy hat with a cigar.

'All right, everybody? How are we all going? West Indies, is it? Don't worry. Give me the ball and I'll bowl 'em out.'

The coaches turned up. 'Come on, let's get out there. Seven laps of the ground.'

'Hang on,' countered Beefy. 'No rush. I'll do my run in a minute. Seven laps of the ground never made me get anyone out.'

I was awestruck. 'At last,' I thought, 'someone's speaking my language.'

Beefy did his bits and pieces of training but didn't do anything just for the sake of it. While some of the boys were always keen to impress the coaches, his attitude was simple. 'I know how to prepare. I've been doing it for years. I'm the best all-rounder there's ever been.'

No one challenged him. The senior players turned a blind eye if he turned up not wearing the right shirt, and that then freed up the youngsters to be their own person, too. Instead of constantly worrying whether they'd got the right training top on, or were clean-shaven to the severest degree, or had a bit of mud on their boots, they felt able to be themselves.

The England dressing room became more like a county one where you could live to your own rhythm rather than being forced into an ice bath every five minutes. If Beefy's attitude was 'I don't need an ice bath', then suddenly you'd think, 'Well, hang on. I actually don't think I need an ice bath either.' Before that, people were fearful that if they didn't conform they'd have a black mark put against them – 'Shouldn't play for England – won't do as he's told.'

Beefy showed that it was important not to lose that sense of being yourself. He played with a huge amount of pride and self-belief, but he also enjoyed the wonderful position we were all in as England cricketers. If someone was nervous or apprehensive, straight away he'd say, 'Forget who's on the opposition. You only live once so go out there and enjoy it. Show them how good you are.'

But Beefy was at the end of his career, and soon enough it was back to business as usual. That 'business' included the tour report, compiled by the management at the end of any trip. A school report for adults – 'Tufnell is disruptive in class. Must try harder. Has a tendency to sulk at the back' – basically, a tour report was a weapon. The management could threaten you with it. A couple of times I was called into meetings and told, 'It's all going on your report.'

'My report? What are you talking about? I thought we were grown men. Why don't you throw a board rubber at me and give me a slippering in the process?'

'It's all going in there about your bad attitude.'

'My bad attitude? It's your attitude to me that's bad!'

Then, waving a sheaf of papers, it would be, 'Look, we've got the files on you.'

The files! What is this? The Test and County Cricket Board or MI5?

I wouldn't have been at all surprised to learn that, like *Line of Duty*, one of the players was an undercover officer from the TCCB.

'He was seen having a rum and Coke in a beach bar at 2 a.m.'

'Mother of God – bring him in for questioning.'

I'd sit there and think, 'Oh shit! What have they written? I'm never going to be paid again. I'm going to be struck off! Struck off the cricket register because I came back at half past ten and had a glass of red wine!'

I've seen the tour reports written about me. After being put together by the England management, they'd be sent on to Middlesex. Unlike a school report, you couldn't intercept it at the letterbox.

So much of what was written centred on that indefinable subject of character. Okay, fine, 'character' – which can cover a million and one things – is part of your make-up as a crick-eter. But if you are going to comment on somebody's character at least do it from a position of knowing what you're talking about. There was an awful lot of very amateur psychology used in putting those things together. People with no experi-ence, no qualifications, nothing, and they judged player after player. Look at the Derbyshire batsman John Morris. The last time he played for England he scored a hundred. Because he went up in that Tiger Moth with David Gower, he got a black mark – naughty boy, bad character – and was never seen again. Crossed out. Gone.

This isn't like going on tour with Middlesex Under-13s. There isn't a teacher flicking off the dormitory light at half past nine. That has to go when people get older. You will never get the best out of people by treating them all the same, but England was one size fits all and I felt so hemmed in by that. 'Everyone's got to be in bed by half past ten.' Why? If I go to bed at half past ten and then lie there wide awake for five hours, what's the point? You have to find a balance that suits a team of individuals. Denis Compton taking off his dickie bow after a night out, slipping into his whites and going out and scoring a hundred probably wasn't the way, but then neither was sending everyone out for a run on the fells. Maybe if I'd played for England ten years earlier it wouldn't have been such a big deal. Back then, if you got the wickets, got the runs, it was all that mattered. Ten years later, meanwhile, England had learnt to accommodate different characters. But in that hinterland of the '90s, time and again I was dropped or not selected for matters not necessarily cricket-related.

'He's a bad tourist.' Wrong – I was a great tourist. Just ask Nasser.

'He brings too much controversy. He's got a bad attitude.' In your view.

Maybe it would have been a better use of everyone's time to try to understand why that perceived 'attitude' was there. What was causing it? How about the managers addressed that rather than me?

It's such an odd set-up where you've got grown men running disciplinary committees and fining other grown men for not doing much else other than being different from themselves.

A hierarchy among equals if you like, which can never be a good idea.

It's easy to talk negatively, I know, but there was a definite undercurrent of forever feeling judged. And it mattered – more than once I'd come back from a tour and find myself sent to Coventry. No phone call to let me know what was going on or talk me through the decision. The best indication I had as to the likelihood of me pulling the England sweater back on in May was whether I got a smile or a grimace from the tour manager as I stepped on the plane home.

Playing for England in the '90s, sometimes it was a miracle that I made it onto the plane home at all ...

CHAPTER 11

How Not to Stay Sane

The knowledge that evidence is being compiled against you generally results in only one kind of behaviour – guardedness. From that moment on you keep your emotions, the way you are actually feeling, to yourself. Add whatever is happening in your private life to the weight of pressure pushing against the dam wall and you don't need to be a genius to know how dangerous that can be.

On that 1993 tour to India, in a three-day match against the Rest of India at Vishakhapatnam, I was fined for kicking my cap along the ground all the way to my fielding position on the boundary after keeper Richard Blakey missed the chance to stump Sachin Tendulkar in what had effectively become a trial for me after I'd been left out for the first Test. When the chance went begging, for 30 seconds I'd basically stood in the middle of the pitch shouting and swearing. This was perceived as me having a go at Richard, but in fact I was raging not at him but at the world.

All manner of things were forming into a swirl of pressure in my head. At that point I was in the grip of some pretty horrendous personal issues back in England and was trying to deal with them miles away from home in a place like nowhere I had ever seen – the India of 30 years ago was very different from now. On top of which, as ever, I was constantly battling for recognition within an England set-up that only ever seemed to tolerate rather than accept me. I was dealing with a whirlwind of emotions that never subsided.

Skipper Graham Gooch spent most of that evening trying to find me in the team hotel. It was exactly what I expected. I'd confirmed myself as the naughty, undisciplined little boy that the management so fervently believed me to be. I knew for sure a disciplinary awaited in the team room and I was in no mental state to face the slap-down, the verbal six-of-the-best, the patronising little speeches, it would entail. Judge, a fantastic friend to me in times of need, provided refuge in his room. Gooch knew we were close and so inevitably came hammering on the door. He suspected Judge was lying when he said I wasn't there, but when he offered to let him search the room, the bluff worked and Gooch walked away. I appreciated that. Judge knew the last thing I needed at that moment in time was to be put through the wringer by a committee of my peers. He was clearly worried for my mental health.

That night I found myself sat on the balcony outside Judge's room overlooking the port city. There was no railing and my legs dangled above a 50-metre drop to the street below. My life felt like it was imploding and I was upset, distraught, crying, as was he to see me in such a state. Judge has since said he feared I might jump. I'm not too sure about that, but who knows? So much had built up in my head at that point. Subconsciously, I was looking for a little bit of help. But actually what was happening was people were after my blood.

When I did eventually feel strong enough to go down to the team room, I knew they'd all be sat there – captain, vice-captain, coach, manager – ready and waiting to give me a bollocking. I knew I had to go in all guns blazing otherwise I'd be steamrollered. I readied myself in the corridor, booted the door open and got my tirade in before they even had time to take a breath.

'What? What's the f***ing matter with you lot. What's your f***ing problem? You've got something to f***ing say?' I wanted to obliterate any chance they had to tell me, 'You're sacked. You're fined. Pull yourself together. Get a shave.' And I did that with an absolute explosion of a message of my own – 'You lot don't know what the f*** you're talking about. You know nothing about me. Who the f*** are you to sit in judgement of me? To send me home.'

Fair to say they were a little taken aback – obvious from the way they were picking each other's jaws up off the floor. My demeanour sparked a realisation that the situation might require a different approach, that actually it was more than a straightforward disciplinary matter – 'Ah, Phil's a little upset with life here' – and so everyone other than tour manager Bob Bennett upped and left the room.

'Come on, Phil,' he said. 'Come and sit down. Calm down. We weren't going to send you home. We were just going to have a little word with you about what happened on the cricket field.'

The bullishness and bluster of my arrival in the room out the way, I had once again collapsed, head in hands, crying and distraught. Bob understood very quickly there was more to this than met the eye. He put his arm round my shoulder and got his best brandy out. 'We'll try and talk through this,' he said and sent out a call for our resident vicar, the Reverend Wingfield Digby, who hurried along for a consoling chat. The reverend, Andrew, who'd played a bit of cricket himself, had become loosely affiliated to the team as the man in whom players could confide. He had that soothing tone that makes a person feel happy to open up. The comfort I felt in talking to him was matched by an easing of the anxiety that was tearing me apart. It had been a terrible day, a traumatic experience, but finally I could feel myself coming out the other side.

The situation in India wasn't dissimilar to what happened in Perth a year later. We had only just arrived in Australia and again I was consumed with issues in my personal life back home. There was no professional support on the tour and so all I could do this time was contact the physio Dave 'Rooster' Roberts; physios, by the nature of the one-to-one work they do, often become sounding boards, confidants, to players. I told Dave how unhappy I was with my life, how bleak everything felt. He listened, was sensitive to my situation and gave me something to calm me down. Sleep, however, wouldn't come. Nothing could slow my racing brain. Everything was bubbling up to an unstoppable eruption. I trashed the room. Lampshades, chairs, bats were hurled around as I careered out of control. At one point, I did actually throw a TV from the window. Not quite the full rock-star treatment – it was a portable.

Poor Phil DeFreitas, unlucky enough to be my roommate, had to take cover in the bathroom while the breakdown – let's call it what it was – ran its course. He didn't know what to do, and when Graham Thorpe came across to my room, he didn't either. I can only imagine what was going through their minds as this desperate scene unfolded before them. Between them they tried as best they could to calm me down, as did Athers and Alec Stewart, but I was barely conscious of their presence, let alone listening to what they were telling me.

Tour manager M. J. K. Smith and Rooster had been alerted, appearing soon after to say they had sorted out some professional help. They took me down to a taxi and next thing I knew I was on a bed at a psychiatric unit with a bloke trying to assess my mental state. That sudden awareness of my surroundings sparked a recovery of sorts. I realised I needed to get to grips with myself and get out of there sharpish before the situation descended out of my control and I lost my career, all I felt I had left.

And so that was it. I upped and offed. Legging it down the street in a hospital gown, a taxi pulled up. Luckily for me the driver liked his cricket. 'Hey, you're that Pommie cricketer Phil Tufnell,' he said. 'Hop in the back, mate. I'll take you wherever you want to go.' Later, I would sort him two tickets for the Perth Test by way of a thank-you. If it wasn't for him I might still be languishing in an Australian mental health institution.

Back at the hotel I grabbed myself a beer and a packet of fags and headed for the team room. I knew I needed to head off at the pass whatever action was being planned. There they all were – Athers, M. J. K. Smith, Rooster and coach Keith Fletcher.

'All right, lads?' I said, taking a swig and tapping some ash into my hand. 'Sorry about that. Things got a bit on top of me. But I'm all right now so let's just get on with the tour, shall we?'

Next day I was back training with the team, having a bowl in the nets, like nothing had happened. Later on, however, I was called back to the team room and fined £1,000 – the price of a mental collapse in the mid-'90s.

The cases of Jonathan Trott and Marcus Trescothick, among others, are confirmation that I'm far from the only one to have found myself mentally floundering on a cricket tour. You might think that after my experiences in India and Australia, and the warning signs they sent out, taking professional help overseas would have been a must from then on. Not a chance. Cricket just blithely carried on with its outdated ways, players shunted from hotel to hotel, game to game, with no one particularly trying to help with what was going on in their heads. Look at the length of tours we went on. Months and months. Everyone said it was necessary – 'You need to play the warm-up games and become acclimatised.' Okay, but what about the disintegration in people's minds?

As ever, the talk from the upper echelons was cricket and nothing else – tactics, bowling better, chipping in with runs. Nothing about the mental side. A listening/talking role is vital in a team and would later be seen as such when sports psychologists came onto the scene. Without such a person, the only outlet for a problem or anxiety is the hierarchy, and experience told you that telling the hierarchy you weren't feeling quite right up top was a 100 per cent guaranteed way to be booted out the team. 'Weak. Can't tour. Fragile. Where would he be in the trenches?' An issue that might actually have been easily sorted with a chat was instead perceived as a character flaw. A player might have taken a five-for against the best batting line-up in the world. No matter. 'Forget it, he's flaky. We're not having him in the side.' Next thing you know your career has gone down the swanny. Occasionally, a player would say, 'Do you think I should go and talk to the management?', and everyone else would say, 'I wouldn't if I were you, mate. Stick it out and you'll soon be home.' And so they disappeared off back to their rooms and, I expect, had a little moment. Sometimes you need to talk to someone in confidence without it going on your record.

Loads of people in professional sport have wobbles. Look at Judgey himself, a big South African, barbecue-eating, beer-drinking legend. From the outside it looked like nothing could touch the Judge, and yet all through his career he, too, was having those moments, and we never knew it. Judge was my hero, a player who could not only stand up to fast bowling but smash it around everywhere. He was my wall, my shield. While Judge was out there those fast bowlers couldn't get me! And yet on the inside, Judge was a very insecure character. Somehow in front of the quicks he managed to divert that side of himself. In fact, that was the environment in which he could be a version of himself he liked and wanted to be. Underneath there was a whole load of torment which resulted in serious difficulties in later life.

Thankfully, the mental health situation has changed a hell of a lot. They've got it pretty much buttoned up. And that's how it had to be. Cricket and mental health issues, suicide even, have an uncomfortable relationship. Something had to be done.

When I started playing, I barely knew a cricketer who hadn't been divorced. The game put too much stress on families and individuals. Forget the cricket field, people's lives were starting to go wrong, and they had nothing to fall back on. Club and national hierarchies were unsympathetic and the Professional Cricketers' Association was non-existent. Family breakdown is a hell of a lot to go through on your own without then having to go out on a cricket pitch in front of thousands of people and try to perform to save your career, which might be all that's holding you together. I don't know how people did it. There are very few walks of life where you're on such public view and expected to behave in a certain manner for so long when actually your head is full of all sorts of stuff. Time and again I saw players missing the births of their children, Christmas, the last days and funerals of family members. All for what? A game of cricket – and the fear they'd be judged negatively if they skipped a match to do something personal.

'You want to visit your grandfather before he dies? Are you nuts? We've got a one-day international in three days.' The more you think about it, the madder it gets.

I really don't know how some of the boys coped. You had to grow a very, very thick skin and hope, if you were struggling, you had a couple of mates who you could go out to dinner with, share a couple of beers and a fag, and just talk about things other than cricket. Basically, our answer to mental pressure was to go out on the piss. People say you'll never find the answer in the bottom of a glass, but when it's not coming from anywhere else, no wonder people keep looking.

On any tour you have low times. When you're away for three months in a completely different environment, and things at home aren't going well, or the tour itself has become a source of anguish, then it can be hard. Easy to feel smothered. Helpless. In the '90s, no one really knew how to deal with any of that. They didn't for a long time. It was only when Tres talked so openly about his problems that the narrative about mental health in cricket truly started to change.

With what happened on that Australia trip and in India, and because it all seemed to be played out so publicly, I was probably one of the first who ever actually brought mental health in cricket to the fore. And because I was throwing TVs out of hotel windows and refusing to open doors, the management had to address it. But it was never done wholeheartedly. The preferred option was always to sweep it under the table. Now there is access to psychologists for those who want it. Especially with the added money in the game, people are really taking mental welfare on board.

I'm sure I've suffered from bouts of depression in my life but, more through luck than judgement, and with the help of mates, close confidants on tour, I always managed to find a way through. I don't think I had depression badly, but I definitely had the opportunity of having it badly. I felt it creeping up on me. I was what felt like a million miles away from home, getting divorced, losing my house, or facing some other crisis, and, yes, there were days when I didn't want to face anyone and not get out of bed.

Instead of talking to a psychologist, my generation of crick-eters talked about their problems down the pub, in a social way, which is maybe why I got a bit lively sometimes. And it helped to level things out in my head. I feel for those guys who haven't got that in their nature. They eat the salad, close the door and beat themselves up. Whatever it is that's happened to cause the upset, the answer will never be found alone in your room. That way you're totally screwed. Go out and talk to someone. Make yourself do it. Often all I wanted to do was shut myself away but I knew I had to get out of those four walls. And I knew it about other people, too.

If we'd had a bad match or a bad day, or people were moping around, I'd say, 'Come on! Let's go and have a game of golf. Or have a few lagers. Or go out for lunch by the beach.' The way I saw it, by putting ourselves in a different headspace, we were, consciously or subconsciously, finding our way through our problems.

On any tour, when you're away for three or four months, there will be periods when you're down, probably not even about performance but about any one of a thousand things going on in your life at any particular moment. Those are the times you need picking up and that's what we tried to do for each other, albeit in a very naive way. Cricketers are pretty good blokes and generally they look out for each other.

In all honesty, there was no alternative. Forget counsellors: we didn't even have a team doctor. When Wayne Larkins had a painful abscess in his mouth down under in 1990, our physio Laurie Brown dealt with it by cutting the roof of his mouth while Ned slugged some whisky. All we had was (sometimes) the reverend and (always) each other. None of us were qualified, but together we always found a way. We had to. The 'none of that in my day' attitude that infected the management quite naturally extended to 'such nonsense' as sports psychology.

Ray Illingworth certainly made his standpoint clear. 'I don't want players who need a shoulder to cry on,' he said. 'I don't think players need that kind of help. I want players strong enough to go out and stuff the Aussies.' Hard to stuff the Aussies when you're already stuffed yourself. That oh-so forward-looking attitude from the top meant that players suffered in silence. Support system? Forget it. 'It's sink or swim, and if you can't swim, f*** off.'

Players deal with pressure, on and off the pitch, in different ways. Having seen close up how full-on Jack Russell was as a player I began to understand why he so enjoyed painting, especially when I retired and began to put up the old easel myself. Painting is very cathartic; it brings on a complete change in mood. With a brush in my hand, my mind is completely blank of any worry, filled instead with an overwhelming sense of calm. And that was Jack's big release. Some guys would play golf. Some, like me, would lie around the pool, but he went off and painted, because to live at match tempo all the time would have meant a heart attack.

Others liked to go fishing, but that one passed me by.

'What time are you leaving?'

'About 6.30 a.m.'

'F*** off!'

On my day off, I liked to get up about eleven. I'd sit in the sun, someone would say, 'Fancy a beer?', and it would soon become one after another. Everyone would be coming back from golf about two in the afternoon and I'd be very merrily sitting by the pool with a bowl of oysters and a bottle of white wine.

Fishing wasn't my bag, but I totally got why a few of the guys would go off, sometimes for a couple of days. I could well imagine that 48 hours listening to the rush and swirl of a river would completely rinse the mind.

It's hard to escape the constant 'cricket, cricket, cricket' on tour. I didn't always want to talk about it, especially if I'd got a pair and gone for one for 170. Even if I'd done well and helped to win the game I didn't particularly want to talk about it for days afterwards.

To talk about one thing endlessly is unhealthy in any environment. I know it sounds strange, because at its most basic cricket is just a game, but if you've just had five days of full-on competition it's exhausting both mentally and physically. It's one of the reasons I used to have a kip in the dressing room. Sit and invest in every ball and you are draining mental energy you'll need yourself. Even if things appear to be going well, there is still the crowd, the atmosphere, the sudden rush of pressure. It's not just cricket. A golfer at the Masters isn't just pootling round having a little game; they are constantly and incredibly switched on.

My way to escape that was to find some normality, which might mean going round to someone's pool, a trip to a winery, or just having a laugh and a beer with people who were experiencing the same thing. That laugh and a beer was basically Cricketers' Anonymous.

'Hi, I'm Phil Tufnell, and I've just played in the second Test against India.'

'Thanks, Phil. Don't worry. You're among friends here. We've all been there. Sit down and grab a beer.'

I'm not a pessimist at heart, far from it – pessimists don't generally sit in a pub for nine hours having a laugh. But then I wouldn't say I'm a huge optimist either. I'm a halfway-house worrier – hope for the best but expect the worst. I can get myself extremely upset at the smallest thing but with other situations I can be quite blasé. Sometimes it pays to just clear your head completely and go 'F*** it. It'll be all right.' And that's what the camaraderie of spending time with similar-minded people can bring, and also why I loved it that my mates away from cricket never treated me any differently when I was playing for England. More than anything their attitude was one of bemusement – 'How the hell have you done that?' – although they could be quite protective on occasion.

We used to play five-a-side football, with me in my favoured position of goalkeeper. One time I went down to make a save at the feet of a player, a bit of a bully, and he slid right in. A couple of my mates steamed straight in there, pushing and shoving him – 'What are you doing? This bloke plays cricket for England! He's bowling against the West Indies tomorrow!' I'm assuming if I'd been a bricklayer or an accountant it would have been fine. For my part, I never gave it the big 'un either. If one of them said, 'Oh, I see you got Viv Richards out yesterday,' I'd be like, 'Oh right, yeah ... what shall we have to drink then?'

I have been to see psychiatrists at various points in my life, but none of them ever gave me any tricks. They just wanted me to speak all the time – 'Tell me about this. Tell me about that.' I'd be sat there thinking, 'Hold on a minute. I thought you were supposed to tell me something.'

At the end of the day, I have always been pretty self-reliant. Right from when my mum died, I have, to some degree or another, looked after myself. It's part of my mindset, part of who I am. I've got a cat tattooed on my left shoulder. Not a big tabby, rather a little one sat there with its head at a jaunty angle. The connection with my nickname is obvious but I wanted it on my left shoulder so when I was getting smashed about I could always put my hand on it and give myself a boost – 'Come on, Cat!' Me, alone – no one else having the faintest idea what I was doing.

I got another tattoo after I met Dawn. As an appreciation of my love, I had her name inked on my arse.

'Oh, that's nice,' she said when I showed her.

'Okay, and ...?' I was waiting for her to say she'd have my name tattooed on herself by way of return. Eventually, she twigged. Her reaction explains why it's never happened – 'Are you mad?'

Hmmmm.

CHAPTER 12

How Not to Be Perfect

In a strange sort of way, I look back on some of those mentally challenging times with fondness and humour. While I know those situations, and the way they made me feel, were all too real, the ridiculousness of them, and the way I was expected to deal with some of the biggest trials and tribulations of my life while trying to establish myself as an England cricketer, make me laugh out loud. On a serious note, I understand also that they exhibit a strength of character. I did after all come out the other side. But, as anyone who has been through rough times will know, it's a hell of a learning curve to have to go through, and I wouldn't wish it on anybody.

For me, it's vital that any cricketer has perspective, that they know the game isn't the be-all and end-all. I look at a lot of players nowadays and they have this face on them, this steely determination, as if a cricket match is by far the biggest thing they could ever be involved in. In my era, Gooch was the same, visibly focused, but a lot of the other boys, while having steeliness in their soul, had a bit more carefreeness about themselves.

David Gower made a couple of fantastic centuries, one at Sydney and one at Melbourne, on my debut Ashes tour, but he didn't walk out there looking like it was a matter of life and death, which in itself caused friction with Gooch, who simply couldn't understand that attitude.

I fear for those with a brick-wall mentality. I hated being hit for a six – as a bowler, the worst feeing in the world – but I could eventually shrug it off. What, though, if you can't take the rough with the smooth? I wonder whether some of the mental issues we have seen are the direct result of the game being built up to be so important, with the pressure that brings. When I first started I didn't particularly feel pressure. I was just out there enjoying moving up the ladder and having a bit of success along the way. Sometimes, having the likes of Botham, Lamb, Gower and Judge messing around was a big positive because it was a reminder that we played cricket for a living and more than anything we should enjoy it. If you didn't do well one day, maybe you would the next.

Pundits often say that the difference between county cricket and the next level is mental – that cricket at the top level is played more in the mind than anywhere else – which perhaps is why those who display visible mental strength are so admired. But I slightly disagree with that. Cricket at the top level is played by the best players. You could have the strongest mind in the world and it wouldn't matter one bit if you didn't know one end of the bat from the other. Janet Street-Porter has a strong mind, but would the England women want her opening the bowling from the Nursery End? I'm not sure. I'm being slightly facetious, but the point remains.

Mental strength is also a very difficult thing to quantify. Nasser said to me recently that I never quite realised how good I was. Is that mental strength or is it confidence? And is confidence just another way of saying 'form'? After all, it's just as fragile; there one minute, gone the next.

What's certain is that in cricket you're put to the test every delivery, and it's hard to do that if you have any doubts in your mind. That's why the Vivs of this world, the likes of Brian Lara, Sachin Tendulkar, Ben Stokes, Joe Root, Kane Williamson, must have an extra confidence chromosome. They can cocoon themselves from their misgivings. They don't go out there with an attitude of 'get to 20 and see how it goes'. They go in there to get a hundred even on a green pitch against the best bowlers in the world. They not only face up to the challenge but go, 'You, mate – I'll be having you today.'

It's an incredible mindset to construct and, I suspect, one that is difficult in the extreme to maintain. I never had a lack of confidence when things were going my way. It's when things don't go your way that the erosion starts. As a batsman you need a very strong mind to play and miss at 20 balls and still think you're going to get a hundred. As a bowler you need the same if you've got nought for 100 and still think you're going to get five for 120. Maybe that's what people mean when they talk about mental strength.

It's been said that my head could drop a little when the other side got on top. I'd dispute that as a statement, but I was someone who perhaps read the race a little bit, as I'm sure anyone who watches a bit of cricket does. With some games it's as if from three balls in you can tell the likely narrative of what's to follow. 'We'll get 180. They'll get a first innings lead. We'll rally a little second time round but the damage will have been done and it won't be enough.' With England's 2021 series in India, after the first over you could pretty much pinpoint within ten minutes when each Test would end.

As a player, I felt there was a limit sometimes to your ability to turn back the tide. If you lost the toss at Brisbane, the sun was out, Australia had got a wonderful batting line-up and the wicket was as flat as a road, I didn't necessarily think we were going to bowl them out for a hundred. Of course, you have to keep thinking that might happen, but when they're 99 for no wicket (again) and the abyss is opening up, it does feel a bit like you're on the edge of the bungee platform with no rope.

There's a time in every sportsperson's career when you've got to understand that you just have to step back and take your medicine; that there's only so much the brain can keep thinking about. That's how it felt in Madras in 1993 when India racked up a massive 560 for six against us. The second new ball usually offers a glimmer of hope. The pacemen will get a new lease of life and make the cherry sing. On this occasion, Devon had the missile in his hand.

'Come on, Devon!' we encouraged him. 'This is it now – game on!' First ball, Kapil Dev ran down the wicket and smacked him back over his head for six. There was no need for anyone to speak. We were all thinking the same thing after all – 'Oh shit. Now what?' Our enthusiasm lasted for precisely one delivery before the long hard slog, in the heat, continued.

Sometimes the game is up. It's done, that's it, and there's nothing anyone can do to change its course. It's not over 'til it's over? Sorry, sometimes it just is. You can hang on to that old adage 'it only takes ten deliveries to win a game' as long as you want. It's true but ultimately it will never happen. It's like when people say if you choose the numbers 1, 2, 3, 4, 5 and 6 you've got just as much chance of winning the lottery as if you choose 27, 8, 14, 19, 33 and 42. It might be true, but inside we all know it's bollocks. When was the last time you saw three hat-tricks back-to-back?

'Keep going, lads, because you never know.'

Well, sorry, I do know. It ain't going to happen. Spike Milligan once said, 'If at first you don't succeed, give up.' He may have been on to something.

Bowling is hard work. On a flat pitch you have to do the hard graft. It's a regret of mine that later in my career I would find myself losing interest in those conditions, a decline born of frustration that could find no release. One of the reasons I decided to retire was when I shocked myself by kicking out at the Essex batsman Darren Robinson in 2002. He'd clipped me off his legs and when he turned for the second, I took a swing. The umpire failed to see it, but he was the only one who didn't, and at the interval the Essex coach Graham Gooch (it's that man again) strode into our dressing room for a more than justified word. All I could do was apologise. I felt ashamed that I'd reached this point and been so disrespectful to a fellow pro. I knew inside my time was up.

For me, feeling disheartened on the pitch came not necessarily through selfish reasons, but because of the thought I was letting people down. You become very tight with your team, your friends, and you want to do well for them, the club and the supporters. When nothing happens, to feel disheartened is not unnatural. At that point who wouldn't have an internal voice asking, 'Where do I go from here? I've only got so many things up my sleeve. I've given it my best shot and my best shot wasn't good enough.' Maybe then a bit of self-doubt creeps in as well – 'I'm not as good as I thought I was' – and at that point I might get a bit down on myself. But then, cricket being cricket, you come back the next day, they slog the ball up in the air and you get a five-for.

Thankfully, I never ever felt like I'd lost the ability to do the one thing I was good at – bowl left-arm spin. I never felt on the edge in that way. While things might not have been going well for me, I always felt in control of what I was doing. Like everyone else, I felt so much for Leicestershire's Scott Boswell, who froze in a Lord's final, bowling a 14-ball over which included six wides in the first eight deliveries, an experience which had mental health repercussions that went way beyond cricket. That's the difference between batters and bowlers. Mess up as a batsman and you're gone. Mess up as a bowler and you're still out there, potentially with plenty more overs to get through. No one ever stops a batsman as they head off to the pavilion and says, 'Come back! We want to get you out five more times and laugh at you.' I was lucky in that I had a nice fluid action that meant I could always land it there or thereabouts. Even if the shit was hitting the fan, I always made batsmen play well to score off me.

At *Test Match Special* we're always very mindful if someone is having a nightmare. That isn't a time to criticise, it's a time to sympathise, because for any professional sportsperson there's an element of 'there but for the grace of God go I'. It's easy sitting up in the commentary box having a cup of tea and a bacon sandwich and we all know it's very different down there if things aren't going your way. Cricket can affect people in ways they never imagined. Middlesex colleague Phil Edmonds completely lost his run-up on a tour of India and in the end was forced to bowl off just one pace. I was never that bad, but another reason that prompted me to retire was that, totally out of the blue, I forgot my run-up – whether I took ten or eleven paces, whether I set off with my left or right foot, the lot. In 18 years of professional bowling, it was the only time I ever got out of rhythm.

People would come up and ask, 'Phil, what the hell are you doing? Why on earth are you hopping and skipping through Strensham services at midnight?'

'Help me! Help me!' I'd cling on to them. 'I'm trying to remember my run-up. Do you know what it is? Is there anyone you could ring to find out?'

So when the decision had to be made – 'Shall I carry on?' – I took the fact I couldn't remember how to move my feet as another prod. It made me wonder if my mind was trying to tell me it was time to move on, to concentrate my thoughts on other things. To escape the pressure of constant competition.

Playing at the top level can be extremely nerve-racking, although I never saw Curtly or Courtney trying to force down an egg and bacon sandwich at breakfast. They were just cruising around. Me? On the morning of a Test I'd be excited while at the same time not straying too far from a toilet. It was like entering the lion's den every time. I suspect most players feel the same. A Test is a great occasion but there's also that nagging feeling you're going to get a first-baller or smashed around the park. I hear people say it's good to be nervous – it shows you care. I don't necessarily think that's the case. I get that the senses are heightened if you're keyed up, but nerves don't necessarily mean positive performance. For a while, you may gain an edge, but nervousness about performance can only be detrimental over a period of time.

Bearing in mind the whirl in my head, I'm surprised I did as well as I did. The best place to be is straight-line calm but I never really got myself into that space. I was a little bit too up and down. I was a little bit too desperate to do well and, as Mark Ramprakash showed, sometimes the harder you try the worse it becomes. Especially if you are too desperate too soon, which you see a lot, a player breaking through and then instantly trying to become better instead of making a natural progression.

Experience is what makes you better, not constant remodelling. Michael Atherton and Alastair Cook achieved longevity not by reworking themselves but by nailing what they were good at. They played within their limitations while making those limitations their strength. How many shots did Alastair Cook actually have as an England player? A flick, a clip, and a cut – three shots. And he's scored more Test runs for England than anyone else in history. Graham Thorpe was another. He didn't have the range of shots of an Allan Lamb or an Ian Bell, but he did know how to score runs and stay in. The fact that he scored a hundred on his debut in an Ashes Test also showed great mental strength, not allowing external issues to get into his brain, unsettle him and apply unnecessary pressure. Like Athers and Cook, he was able to compartmentalise and focus. All three took it ball by ball. Easy to say, hard to do.

Good players don't heap mental pressure on themselves by trying to be perfect. They understand what they're good at and stick with it. I couldn't see how to introduce another distinctive new delivery into my armoury, and so used my experience to be as good a bowler as possible with what I'd got. There is no such thing as perfection, which maybe someone should have explained to Ramps. Play a false shot and you could see it upset him. I never had such worries – my false shots looked better than the ones I meant.

CHAPTER 13

How Not to Be a Batsman

For the one-day internationals in New Zealand in 1997, as another way of modernising the game, players were asked to choose a song to be played on the PA as they walked out to bat. Most of them were fairly nondescript – Darren Gough had 'Walking On Sunshine' by Katrina and the Waves, Andrew Caddick chose 'I Feel Good' by James Brown, and Alec Stewart went for 'Summer of '69' by Bryan Adams, reflecting the time, aged six, he started shaving. Me? I chose Oasis's 'Cigarettes & Alcohol'.

I can still remember the tour manager's face as I relayed my choice to him.

'Really, Phil, do you have to? Couldn't you just have a bit of Abba? Or The New Seekers?'

'I thank you for your advice, manager, but I've made my decision, and it's "Cigarettes and Alcohol".' I walked out with the lyrics booming round the ground.

To be fair, there were one or two other questionable choices. Nasser Hussain had 'Zombie' by The Cranberries, Ronnie Irani had 'Two Tribes' by Frankie Goes To Hollywood, and Jack

Russell, to his great credit, had 'How Much Is That Doggie In The Window'.

'Cigarettes & Alcohol' was not only a belter of a song, but it also epitomised two things I would rather have in front of me than some manic, gurning man-mountain about to hurl a hard lump of leather extremely fast and from a very short distance. Let's be frank here, a cricket ball has the capacity to hurt. Anyone who has taken one hard on the inner thigh will now be nodding in agreement, but believe me they can cause unpleasantness in all sorts of ways. Against South Africa at Port Elizabeth in 1999, for instance, I was in the firing line of paceman Nantie Hayward. Ducking one delivery, it failed to get up. I was huddled in a foetal position, and as it whistled past, the middle of my back felt a terrific pain, like someone slashing me with a red-hot poker. 'Ow! What was that?' Everyone looked at me like I was mad but on my return to the dressing room I looked in a mirror, shocked to find a long red mark stretched across my back where the seam had perfectly sliced the skin as it skimmed across. It was like something out of *The Omen*. Like I'd upset Damien with my bowling performance and he'd tried to have me sliced in two.

I found pace bowling so hard to pick up. I didn't understand how the batsmen did it. How not only did they survive unscathed but even managed occasionally to score runs. Batting against the quicks was for many the ultimate challenge in cricket; the thrill of pitting your batting technique, mental strength, determination and courage against the best in the world. 'That's when you know you're alive,' they said. They might as well have been talking a different language.

Judge would try to put me at ease by telling me, 'It's not as bad as you think.' But I never found waiting to go into bat to be anything other than horrific. Five down, six down, seven down – at which point I'd start getting the gear on, every sinew and nerve in my body anticipating the worst. Never did I sit there thinking, 'I'm going to go out there. I'm going to get back and across. I'm going to see it. And I'm going to hit it.' I sat there thinking, 'Oh my f***ing God. He's going to be bowling at 100 mph straight at my head.' I was in such a fried state of mind, I was barely capable of walking to the crease, let alone taking evasive action when I got there.

That's why I didn't watch. I didn't want to see the ball whizzing around and so would take myself away from that arena, and if that meant having a kip then so be it. If people saw that as being out of order, I didn't care. When the call did finally come – 'Get your teddy, Phil, you're in' (I called my bat my teddy, because like a kid I used to drag it behind me on reluctant expeditions) – every outgoing batsman heard the same question: 'Has he got any wheels?', i.e. 'How quick is he bowling?' No one ever tried to kid me it was fine so in the end I stopped asking.

Instead, later in my England career, when I had established myself as one of the senior players, the management agreed to my request that our physiotherapist 'Rooster' Roberts should sit himself by the gate leading to the field so he could get out to me quickly if my fears of physical damage proved correct. The last thing I wanted was him having to pick his way through the dressing room and pavilion while I was out there looking for an elbow on the floor. Rooster would follow me down to the pitch like a chaperone and sit there with his bag of tricks. Some people thought this was a little over the top. I didn't – if I'd had my way he'd have been stood at square leg.

For me, the whole business of facing pace was utterly baffling. One delivery I'd play back and the ball would whistle past my head. The next, off what appeared the exact same length, I'd go back, wincing at the thought of it hitting me on the helmet or chest, only to hear the wicket shatter behind me.

'Hang on,' I'd think. 'Since when were the stumps six feet tall?' I could never understand that. Perhaps I wasn't a very good picker of length. Some might even suggest it was because I had my eyes closed. Actually, nothing could be further from the truth. Shut your eyes and you can guarantee you'll get hurt. My problems with the bat came more from the brain not particularly liking what the eyes were seeing. A six-foot madman haring in with a rock-like object, fielders urging him on, and a crowd baying for blood – quite literally. 'F***ing kill him!' 'Smash his f***ing teeth in!'

'Steady on,' I'd be thinking. 'You do know it's only a game? Remind me again why I didn't take up badminton.'

That's before the grey matter had to apply its various lobes to the delivery itself. Which way is the wind blowing? Is it a slower ball? Is it going to seam in? Is it going to seam out? I didn't have the right sort of brain to sieve all that out. My brain was much better at, well, requesting a packet of fags and a pint of Foster's. Courtney Walsh once bowled me a bouncer which I played like a turtle. It was a bright sunny day, but I didn't see the ball from his hand, I didn't see it through the air and I didn't see it off the pitch. Luckily for me, instinct took over. My head retracted into my shell and the last thing I remember was a rush of air as the ball passed in front of my nose. It really is time to start panicking when you're not picking up the ball at all. Chris Cairns, too, once came steaming in on a hard, bouncy track and the ball whistled past my ear before I'd even got a shot in. The sound of it hitting the keeper's gloves at least slightly muffled my cry of 'Oh, f***!'

Shaun Pollock was another master of the delivery. His bouncer was virtually unreadable. He could bowl a short one out of nowhere. As a reflex, I defended myself against one such ball and it hit the stickers on the bat in front of my face. Pollock's next delivery, I never actually saw. I was jumping in the air when it pinged off the top of my bat handle and careered away over wicketkeeper Mark Boucher's head for a one-bounce four. I looked at the handle and it was completely red where the ball had deflected. I like to think it was the first ramp shot ever played. As I've always said, ahead of my time. All the fielders thought it was hilarious, as did Shaun. I emitted a little nervous chuckle but, as I took guard again, a sickening feeling filled my stomach. 'I didn't try to bop it on the head with the end of my bat handle on purpose,' I thought, 'which means I didn't actually see the ball at all, and there's another one on the way now, coming right at me.'

Pakistan had the twin threat of Waqar Younis and Wasim Akram. That was fun. When I made my one and only appearance against Pakistan in Test cricket, at The Oval in 1992, I scored nought not out and nought and faced nine deliveries of which I saw precisely none.

In the first innings, my teammates nearly had to carry me off because Waqar hit me on the left foot with one of his trademark 95 mph toe-crushing, reverse-swinging yorkers. It must have been reversing a lot to hit me on the foot because when 95 mph toe-crushing, reverse-swinging yorkers were on the menu I was normally halfway to square leg by the time they arrived at my end. That ball almost broke my foot. I managed to hobble through 30-odd overs but I was in agony. I couldn't get my shoes on. Second innings, when Wasim bowled me for a golden duck, I barely even saw him, let alone the ball. He had a habit of running in behind the umpire and appearing out of thin air like a ghost. A very scary ghost.

Thing was, when I was a kid I could hold a bat quite nicely, but then after I left cricket for two or three years in my mid-teens I came back and everyone had got bigger. Those kids waddling up bowling floaty little away swingers which I could whack around the place were now six-foot-five and bowling at my head. I never quite got to grips with that.

Put simply, I didn't enjoy batting. Unlike a nice cocktail, or an hour's feet-up in front of *The Antiques Roadshow*, it just wasn't enjoyable. For me batting merely provoked a feeling of trepidation. Every time I strapped the mums and dads on it overwhelmed me. It was just so confrontational, and I'm not a particularly confrontational person. I'm a very sort of peace-loving man, really. If I'd been in my twenties in the '60s, there's a very good chance I'd have been a hippie, sat in a henge strumming a guitar.

You know how some people don't like going to the dentist? Well, that was me with batting. The difference being that people who don't like whiny little drills don't have one shoved in their face several times a week.

Dentists, in my experience at least, aren't vindictive either. Very rarely do they hurl hypodermic needles at you when you walk into the surgery. But fast bowlers really don't like you at all. I've always tried to get on with people but every time I put any sort of batting paraphernalia on, some very intimidating people suddenly really hated me. As soon as I arrived, everyone wanted me to leave. No one was going, 'Whoa! Phil! Lovely to see you in your batting gear.' They were too busy going, 'F*** off. Get the f*** out of here.'

It was as though you changed into a different person when

you went out to bat. 'But I'm very nice. What's the matter with you? Can't you see through this batting gear? I'm a nice lad.'

From their point of view I must have seemed unusually accommodating. I didn't hang around very long. I didn't want them all to be shouting at me, calling me horrible names, so I said, 'Okay. I don't want to piss you off. You're bigger than I am and you've got a hard ball in your hands. So I'll try a little bit and then off I'll go.' I didn't possess the necessary will or the conviction with a wand in my hand. I didn't even really have much of a wand. It was always a little bit disheartening sitting in the Middlesex dressing room when the sponsored bats arrived. Ramps and Gatt would be peeling the wrappers off these beautiful bespoke bats, knocking them in 20 at a time. *Donk! Donk! Donk!* 'Oh, that's number one, that's a beauty.' *Dink! Dink! Dink!* 'Not bad – that can be number five.' *Plonk! Plonk! Plonk!* 'I'll shave a bit of wood off that – number sixteen.' It was very atmospheric from that point of view – the scent of these lovely pristine bats combined with the smell of Gatt's bacon sandwich as he sat in his pants knocking them in.

A couple of days after everyone else, my rather slimmer package would turn up. There'd be a couple of bats chucked in there from my sponsor, one without a rubber, and leaves rattling around the bottom of the bag.

'Oh,' I'd announce with a flourish, 'my bats have arrived.' I'd reach for a ball to knock them in. *Dufwh! Dufwh! Dufwh!* The lads all looked outside thinking someone had dropped three bags of cement.

Bat-bartering was rife, like cigarettes in a prison. 'Let us have a little look,' a player would ask a teammate enviously. 'Ooh, that's a beautiful bit of willow. Straight from the top of the tree. Go on, let us have a play. Let us have a feel.' If an agreement was reached, the stickers would be swapped so the sponsor wouldn't be any the wiser. Once or twice, Ramps came over, spying a bat that looked quite good from a distance. 'Let us have a look, Tuffers.' He'd bounce a ball on it. *Dufwh! Dufwh! Dufwh!* 'Actually, mate, you're all right. You keep that one.' You see, that's the real reason I didn't score many runs off the fast men – if I'd hit the ball it would have snapped my bat in two.

The one thing I felt I did have in my favour against fast bowlers was that I was quite good at getting into their mindset and second-guessing them. That was okay at the start of an over – bouncer (yes), yorker (yes), bouncer again (yes) – but by the fifth or sixth delivery I would get a bit confused. 'Right,' I'd think, so what have we had so far? Bouncer, bouncer, yorker, bouncer? Or was it bouncer, yorker, yorker, bouncer?' By that point the bowler would be running in. Being one step ahead of them was my only realistic chance of survival. It was like facing down Clint Eastwood in *Dirty Harry*. 'You're asking yourself one question, punk. "Did he fire five shots or six?" Ask yourself, do you feel lucky? Well, do you, punk?' Which is why on the odd occasion I did a Chris Read and ducked into a yorker – quite tricky to get underneath.

It was during Bumble's reign that the idea of batting buddies was instigated. The premise was that those whose aptitude with the willow was somewhat lacking should be paired with a batting partner who would do a bit of coaching and pass on tips. My buddy was Ramps. When he was told the news he had the look of a man who'd been asked to peel a pile of potatoes with a toothpick. Talk about the short straw. As if he didn't have enough on his plate trying to score runs for England.

Ramps' buddying consisted of arming himself with tennis balls and a racquet and serving at my head. The idea was to teach me how to play fast bowling. If the best way of playing fast bowling is to throw yourself to the floor or to swat manically at the ball as if it were a fly, then Ramps can certainly say he succeeded.

We did that for ten minutes and then went for a Fanta. The batting buddy scheme was, as far as we were concerned, done. I never really warmed to it. A real buddy goes down to the beach and has a piña colada with you.

It was a shame, because 'batting buddies' seemed on the face of it to be the kind of shortcut I liked. Forget practising for years, Ramps' knowledge would be passed on to me in just a few short sessions. But I suppose in batting you can't do that. You've got to get yourself in, get yourself to 20, and then things become a little bit easier. I always felt that was too far off. I was never going to reach that point. That's why bowling appealed. You could do things quickly – bowl out West Indies in an afternoon; bowl two overs and grab three wickets. But you can't bat two overs and get 70. You can't win a Test match from scratch in three hours.

I think like that in other areas of life. When I did a skydive, if someone had told me it would take four and a half hours to get set up beforehand, I'd have been out of there. Truth is I got the kit on, said a quick hello to the bloke who I was strapped to, and that was it. One hit. Done.

Because of how distant batting aptitude was, nets never appealed. They just confirmed what I already knew. Even the ex-England spinner Norman Gifford knocked my poles out of the ground. He was smoking a pipe at the time.

Michael Vaughan, who was a great batsman but terrible at facing left-arm spin, once asked me if anyone had ever offered me any advice. 'Phil,' he said, 'didn't anyone ever tell you that when you're batting, anything outside your right eye you can usually leave?'

'No,' I replied, 'no one told me that in twenty years.'

When I went out to bat, the only thing I heard was someone saying, 'Phil's batting. We'd better get our whites on.' Maybe it would have been better for someone to have said, 'Go on, Phil, get us ten runs.' Maybe it would have been better if someone had made me feel like I could do it.

In 316 first-class matches I managed a remarkable 2,066 runs at an average of 9.69, with one 50, the Worcestershire bowling attack against which that happened retiring immediately. With Vaughany's nugget now revealed to me, I couldn't help but wonder if I might at least have made that average 9.7.

Nobody ever bothered to try to help me improve my technique. Mad really. If I was going to be sent into the nets against endless bumpers, at least show me how to fend them off. Instead, the only batting tip I was ever given was the old MCC manual instruction to go back and across, which in my eyes just got you in line to be hit, so I decided not to bother.

My lack of ability with the willow didn't seem too much of a problem at Middlesex. In the early days especially, the batsmen batted and the bowlers bowled. Those who could do both were rare and highly prized oddities. When it came to us tailenders it was always, 'Right. Nine, ten and Jack, go and have a slog and then we can get on with the game.' I set my sights pretty low and the club never saw the point in trying to help me get any better.

When I did venture into the nets with a bat, it was bumper warfare. 'Let's try to knock the head off Tuffers.' It was like a coconut shy in the fairground. 'Roll up! Roll up! There's a goldfish for anyone who can knock his teeth out!'

My presence in the nets seemed to be a source of great amusement to all the bowlers to the extent they would actually get together at the end of a session and count up how many times they'd hit me, instigating a points system for different parts of the body. They could have been placing bets on the winner for all I know. I'm glad that my own personal wellbeing was so useful in terms of bonding and morale.

In the end, the club and I agreed to call a truce. One day, when Gatt suggested I had another irrelevant net, I said to him, 'Listen, Gatt, not being funny, but this is all a bit pointless, don't you think? I'm hardly going to bat for five hours to save a match or knock off a quick seventy to win one, so let's end this exercise in futility and when the time comes I'll do my best.'

Gatt considered this proposal – 'Deal.'

I faced the same situation when I first started playing for England. The day before the final Ashes Test in Perth, coach Micky Stewart and captain Graham Gooch insisted I bat in the nets.

'Right, Tuffers,' said Micky. 'Your turn. We've got some local bowlers.'

I looked up and saw two blokes wearing knee-length beards who looked like they'd stopped off en route to an audition for ZZ Top. I wondered where they'd parked the Harley-Davidsons. Thing was, in those days the nets at the WACA were as quick and bouncy as the pitch itself. Lightning.

'Micky,' I asked, 'will you have a little word with these guys? They look like they mean business.'

'Yeah, yeah,' he said, 'it'll be fine.'

I received precisely six deliveries – in the chest, past the ear, in the ribs, on the glove, in the balls, whizzing past the eyeballs – before I said, 'F*** this' and walked out.

'Where are you going?' asked Micky.

'I'm not doing this. I've got a Test match tomorrow.'

As I was walked back to the dressing room, I was discarding all my kit. Gloves, pads and guards were flying everywhere.

'Phil! Come back!'

'You might as well have put me in a pit of lions,' I shouted. 'I could have broken my thumb and missed the match.' I considered my actions entirely reasonable. I was better off protecting my fingers so I could try to make a contribution with the ball. Frankly, any runs I scored for England were a bonus.

Whether by accident or design, after the incident in Perth I don't recall ever having a proper batting net when playing for England. On the rare occasions I did venture in there, Jack Russell was usually bowling at me because everyone else had gone. He would offer to round up a few of the local net bowlers to give me a go. 'No, mate,' I'd say. 'You're okay. I'll just have some throwdowns.'

'Now then, Jack,' I'd say as he tossed the ball between his hands, 'nice and slow and up my end because I really do need to nail my technique against the slow full toss' – which actually came in handy on the two occasions I played the shot in my 12-year England career. The only flaw in the approach was that Allan Donald, Merv Hughes and Courtney Walsh would be sending them down at the speed of light around my head and the last person I'd batted against was Jack Russell in his wicketkeeping pads.

Thankfully, umpires rarely needed asking twice before sticking up a friendly finger, especially if they wanted to beat the traffic or fancied an early pint. Initially I did get a bit cross when I was given out leg before wicket to a ball I thought was going down the legside or missing off stump, or when I played and missed at one that went through to the keeper untouched and everyone just walked off.

More than once I'd say, 'Hang on, I never hit that', and the ump would look at me as if to say, 'Look, Phil, I've done you a favour there. This bloke is bowling quick and if you wind him up by actually trying to bat you might get hurt.' It didn't take long to come round to their way of thinking, once actually giving myself out to avoid further unnecessary punishment. A menacing Merv Hughes smacked one into my glove, the ball was safely pouched by Ian Healy, and yet just as I prepared to depart, the umpire, for some reason not sure what the ball had come off, began to express some doubt.

'Ow! I think you've broken my thumb,' I shouted at Merv and marched towards the pavilion.

Generally, I was always more than happy to walk. The only time I didn't, everyone else did anyway. Myself and Graham Thorpe were trying to save a Test in Antigua with an epic last-wicket stand. It was a hopeless cause and everyone was round the bat. Courtney Walsh bowled me one that nipped back, short, round the chest area. I backed away, arms and legs flailing, and felt the ball thud into my chest pad. 'Ow!' I said, as the ball slowly popped up to Clayton Lambert at one of the five short legs. He caught it, at which point the West Indies team grabbed the stumps and ran off to the dressing room shouting and celebrating. Thorpey was following them, the umpires were shoving the bails in their pockets, and I was still standing there telling nobody in particular, 'Well, actually, I don't think I hit that.' When the ground staff came on, I thought to myself, 'Oh well, I suppose I may as well go then.' I tucked my teddy under my arm and sloped off. I'm still not certain anyone actually appealed.

To be fair, those above me in the order didn't always hang around long either. I learnt very quickly that if you wanted to get a snooze in with the England cricket team then it was vital to do so early. I also became very adept at getting my pads and other gear on very, very quickly. Things could snowball. We'd be cruising along at three down when I'd announce, 'I've just got to pop to the toilet, lads.' Surreptitiously, so as not to send out the wrong message, I would then slip thigh pad, inner thigh pad and box into position. No one ever noticed, I'm sure. I always had that cricketer's dream of not being able to get your kit on early enough, and I never wanted it to come true.

I wasn't in the side for the infamous 46 all out at Trinidad in 1994 when Curtly Ambrose ripped through our line-up. If I had I'm sure I could have guided us through to three figures. As it was, I could only watch in shock and awe as Curtly thundered in and repeatedly rearranged our batsmen's furniture. That was the first and only time I have seen the last five batsmen lined up on a bench, helmets on, ready to go. They were sitting there like stormtroopers from *Star Wars*, the coach tapping them on the shoulder and sending them out of the transporter one by one – 'Go! – Go! – Go!'

There's no point anyone saying anything in those circumstances. The eyes say it all. You always know when the batters are shitting themselves. They don't say anything because they know it's their job and there's nothing they can do to avoid it. Bowlers have the same feeling when a batsman is rampant. 'I don't want to bowl at him. Do I really have to?' And you do, because that's your job. But as a team when you look at your top order, real tough guys, and see that they're thinking one thing – 'I'm scared!' – then you know you've had it.

That collapse was widely seen as coming out of the blue.

In fact, the writing was on the wall before anyone had even got their pads on. We'd had the West Indies under the cosh all game but then let it slip in their second innings when they got 50 or 60 more than they should have done, meaning we needed approaching 200 to win rather than something a little more manageable. Those of us not playing thought we had a chance – until we saw the rest of the boys walk in at the end of West Indies' knock. It was complete silence. I could see in their eyes that the lights were going out.

I was thinking to myself, 'Come on! Why doesn't someone get up and say "Look, we can do this. We can knock this off"?' But I could see that wasn't going to happen, and I didn't think it was a speech that would be hugely appreciated from the worst batsman on the tour who wasn't even playing in the match, so, like everyone else, I just sat down and didn't say a word. The aftermath was equally awful. Everyone mutely packed their bags and got on the bus.

In those situations, I sometimes saw it as my job to rally the troops. 'Oh well, boys, f*** it. Let's go and have a beer.' And a couple would agree – 'I suppose you're right. Why not?'

But bowlers and batsmen are different animals. The opposition didn't often rack five or six hundred up, but if they did I'd try to seek a bit of reassurance. 'Devon, it was flat as anything out there, wasn't it? There was nothing we could do. It was like a road.'

'Yes, Phil, you're right. Like a road.' And that would be good enough for me – move on.

Batsmen – they take a little longer to brush things off, aside from Alec Stewart, one of the strongest minds in cricket, who made two incredible hundreds in the next game to help win us the match.

Four years later, at Sabina Park in Jamaica, we were looking at an even lower score before the match was abandoned, the pitch, with more ridges than corrugated iron, deemed unfit after ten overs in which we'd crawled to 17 for three with the physio spending the most time in the middle. That was when my suit of armour, so routinely mocked, suddenly became very popular. Normally it was 'Ah, Tuffers, got your chest pad on? Bit quick for you out there?' Now, all of a sudden, the requests from the top order were never-ending. 'Er, Tuffers, couldn't borrow your chest pad, could I? And your jousting pole.'

I used to go out to bat for England with two arm guards. I was like a north London Wonder Woman, deflecting the bullets. Anything to avoid getting hit on the tip of the elbow. Now that really did hurt. I'd also have thigh guard, inside thigh guard and chest guard. Immobility was my byword. Nowadays, I'd have run one while Jos Buttler ran three. Even so, there remained little areas of weakness. Behind the front leg was one such spot; another was the top of the hip. Then there was the inch and a half between the chest guard and the thigh pad. It was a dead cert that the first ball would home in on that very spot, stinging, pinching, nipping as it hit.

Thankfully, I never batted long enough for my bollocks ever really to be an issue. They were generally as far away from the line of the ball as the rest of me. But that didn't stop me exploring pretty much every other way a shiny red lump of leather can cause pain to the human body. Getting hit on the end of the thumb was never pleasant. Same with the pointy bits on wrists and ankles. I lost count how many times in the field I went down in the long barrier position only for the ball to swerve at the last possible moment and hit me on the side of the knee. Of all the things I carried round in my coffin, the one thing I really needed was never there – an invisibility spray.

Funnily enough, I never really looked the part in my batting gear. Not only was there so much of it, but it never really fitted me. With real batsmen, the gear looks like an extension of their body. Me? I might as well have been out there in a Victorian diving suit, complete with lead boots – I never batted in rubbers in case the ball hit me on the toe.

As the last few wickets fell, I'd be sat there in the dressing room in this stuff – rigid, not only with fear, but because I could barely physically move. Even surrounded by teammates, I felt completely alone.

When the actual time came for me to go out there, every fibre of my being was predicting the worst. Sometimes I wondered if I could make a run for it. Of course, that never happened – I had two armed guards on me at all times – and so down those steps I'd go, knees wobbling, a horrible feeling, as if I didn't have control of my body, carried on to the field by a wave of dread. When I was bowling I enjoyed that arena. But with the bat, it was completely different. Compare that to Viv Richards. When he walked on to the pitch – arms whirling, chin bristling, bareheaded – his body language said just one thing: 'This is my domain.' Even the way he chewed gum was masterful. I just felt tiny.

Blokes like Viv, Alastair Cook, Lara, Sachin and Mark Waugh made the whole enterprise of batting look so natural, whereas even if I did survive a delivery, I never quite knew what to do afterwards. Cooky would take a casual stroll to square leg. I'd just stand there. 'Okay, what do I do now?' I never felt comfortable playing the part of a batsman. Occasionally, I might walk down and tap the pitch like I'd seen proper batters do, but generally such actions would be treated with derision.

'Tuffers, what are you doing?'

'Sorry.'

On the odd occasions I was in long enough to notice the sightscreen wasn't in the right place, I never had the bottle to ask for it to be moved. Imagine me walking out at the MCG and saying, 'Excuse me, could I have the screen moved?' Have you ever heard 80,000 people laugh at once?

I know I should have been more batsman-like. If the sightscreen wasn't right and I had a bat in my hand, then I should have had it moved. But the voice in my head disagreed – 'Ask for the sightscreen to be moved and all you'll do is piss everyone off.' And, of course, the worst thing you can possibly do is get the sightscreen moved and then have your poles knocked out the ground next ball – which was bound to happen, another reason I never dared do it.

There is one thing I would really have liked to do with regards my Test match batting career. Once – just once – I would have loved to have called for a new pair of gloves. That would have been something. Even if it was after two balls.

I can, though, at least say I batted in a cap. Not only that but this exhibition of fearlessness, still no doubt talked about around the dinner tables of Madras, where it happened, led to my highest Test high score, a magnificent 22, outscoring Stewie, Hick and Gatt along the way. These batsmen . . . I don't know.

Okay, so Kapil Dev had done his work for the day and the Indian attack consisted of Anil Kumble's leg spin, Venkatapathy Raju's left-arm spin and Rajesh Chauhan's off-spin. Nonetheless, those runs didn't score themselves and, while Anil Kumble sent six of my colleagues scuttling back to the pavilion, I was glancing it and deflecting and – not that I talk about this much – even hit him back over his head a couple of times for four. Bear in mind, I was also not out. With a little support around me, I really do feel I could have joined Australia's Jason Gillespie as one of the only bowlers to make a double hundred.

I left the field to polite applause from my teammates. Keith Fletcher even came up to me to offer congratulations – 'Really well done, Tuffers. Great stuff.'

I have to admit it went to my head. Usually I'd have been shuddering in a corner, a paler shade of grey, nervously taking my pads off and waiting for a bollocking. Now I was sitting there thinking this must be what it's like to be David Gower, nonchalantly disrobing while someone runs a bath and fixes a cold libation.

'Excuse me, Goochie, old fellow, can you put my gloves in the sun? Blakey, could you pull them off my hands? Gatt, be a good chap would you – hang my jockstrap in the drying room. Robin, is my mint julep ready? Hicky, have you pressed my smoking jacket?

'Oh, and look, chaps, if you want me to explain the vagaries of Anil Kumble, I'm more than happy to do so. I've got him just where I want him.'

I did once also almost get England over the line in a one-day international. In a tri-series match against Australia at the MCG in 1991, set 223 to win, I emerged from the hutch, to a beautiful, 50,000-strong rendition of 'Tufnell Is A Wanker', with 47 runs still needed. At that moment in time most bookies would have given better odds on Kylie Minogue being an alien than they would on an England win, but Gus had somehow got himself set and together we took ourselves to the point of needing a four off the last ball. Unfortunately, it was me facing it.

The trouble with contributing as a tailender is that none of the batsmen speak to you. You have made them look foolish – 'Tuffers has got twenty-two and he can't bat at all. What does that make me?' – and so at best they'll give you a cursory glance and mutter a quick 'well done' through gritted teeth. They know as well that, as a bowler, I'm sitting there thinking, 'Bloody hell, that wasn't hard. What the hell were you lot doing out there?'

Actually, I know only too well what it's like for the boot to be on the other foot; when I've bowled for two days at someone and then Mark Butcher has come on and immediately bowled them round their legs.

I did nearly get in the record books on that Indian tour. In the final Test in Mumbai I was stuck on nought for over after over. The longer it went on, the thought occurred to me that I might actually be on course for recording the longest nought in Test history. With Graeme Hick blasting away at the other end, I would have got there, too, had someone not bowled me a full toss with everyone round the bat. I hit it into a gap at extra cover and realised, 'Oh, bollocks! I can't avoid it. I'm going to have to run. I simply had no choice. In doing so I missed my one and only chance of taking my place in the annals of oddities. I was furious.

In defence of my lethargy, I wasn't a particularly good judge of a run. I was run out twice in Test cricket. The first time, at the MCG, Warney was bowling and the ball hit my pad and ran gently away behind the slips for a single. It was the fourth ball of the over and I didn't particularly fancy starting the next one facing Craig McDermott at the other end and so I thought I'd try to turn it into a two. There was no need for DRS, I can assure you. I was 15 yards short.

Worse was the run-out that sealed our fate when we got beaten by New Zealand at The Oval that fateful day in 1999 which saw us sink to the foot of the Test rankings. I was backing up to Ed Giddins who knocked one back down the pitch where I tried to take evasive action, only for it to hit my pad and ricochet to mid-on. By the time I'd gathered myself, turned round and started to head back to the crease, the stumps were gone. 'Oh,' I said, and that was that.

It was one of those moments when, despite being out on the field, I actually felt like a spectator. 'What's in my sandwiches? Salmon paste? Oh, hang on – what's happening? Shit! Oh no! Too late.'

Far from being a coiled spring, I was more generally in a dreamlike state, perhaps fantasising about Linda Lusardi, maybe my first century. Either way they were way out of reach.

There is one thing I can take from my international meanderings with the willow. The crowd always used to cheer when I came out to bat. Not every England batsman can say the same.

CHAPTER 14

How Not to Be the World's Best Bowler

All that time I spent cowering in front of the fast men, and who should be the only bowler actually to crown me but Muttiah Muralitharan. It was the first time I'd faced the man who would end up the leading wicket-taker in Test cricket, and what struck me was not the dip and turn he put on the ball but the noise it made. It fizzed – 'ZZZZZZZZZ!' – as it came out of his hand. 'What the hell was that?' I thought. 'This bloke bowls balls that talk – literally.'

If my deliveries were to have a noise, which they didn't, it would be a low-level hum, like an old fridge. His sounded like they were alive. I pushed forward on a surface that had been flat as a pancake only for the ball to bounce and hit me on the badge of my helmet. I couldn't believe it.

'What on earth? Has someone changed the pitch and not told me?'

I certainly wasn't hitting people on the head when I bowled.

I was lucky to hit someone on the shin. How did Murali get them to leap up into the face?

That first encounter with Murali came in England's one-off Test against Sri Lanka in Colombo at the end of that memorable-for-all-the-wrong-reasons 1993 tour to India. He had played just three Test matches at the time and we knew almost nothing about him and his skills.

It had been a long, arduous, controversial and unsuccessful trip. Colombo was absolutely sweltering and to be honest all we really wanted to do was go home. Batting first, to cheer ourselves a little, we prepared to face him and his colleagues by sitting in a swimming pool behind the dressing room trying to keep cool. We had a little chain of contact keeping us posted on what was happening out in the middle. If we lost a wicket, the twelfth man would run to the dressing-room window and call out. This was the signal for the batsman two wickets down the line to get out, towel himself down, go across the road and get his gear on.

By the time it was my turn to get padded up, I'd been in the pool for two and a half sessions. I was essentially a walking prune. Even so, I was only facing spin bowlers, so I wasn't overly concerned. Five balls later, Murali got me LBW for one. I thought at the time the ball was definitely going down the legside. Had I not spent the day in the swimming pool, I might have known about the doosra.

I trudged back to the sanctuary of the dressing room where I was greeted by Robin Smith towelling himself down in only his swimming cap. I'd rather have faced Murali. Judge made a hurried shout to the rest of the lads out the back, telling them that the dependable number 11 was out and we were fielding in five minutes.

Shane Warne, too, was emerging onto the scene around that time. In fact, I was watching on the dressing-room TV when he bowled his 'ball of the century' – that beautiful flight from off to leg and then the vicious spin back to clip the top of off stump – to dismiss Mike Gatting at Old Trafford in 1993. Easy to forget that the Gatting ball was not just an incredible delivery but Warne's first in England and first in an Ashes Test.

Warney had great ability, to the extent I don't quite know how batsmen actually played him. Play for the spin and he'd bowl a straight one; play for the straight one and it would turn prodigiously. That's without all the variations of bounce, flight and spin. I think I actually missed a Shane Warne delivery by the largest distance in cricketing history. At Lord's, in the Test after he unveiled his bag of tricks at Old Trafford, I decided, for lack of any other great ideas, to have a slog at one. I thought it was the googly, had a little skip down the wicket, and tried to hit it to the legside. It wasn't the googly. It was the biggest leggie he could bowl. Andy Caddick came down from the other end for a little chat while we did some between-overs gardening. 'Phil,' he said, 'I reckon you missed that by about four feet. I think that actually could be a record.'

'No, Caddy,' I said. 'I was just being careful. I didn't want to nick it.'

I went to Australia in 1994 determined not to be just another notch on Warne's sizeable stump. Before I faced him in the first Test at Brisbane, I sought some advice from our batsmen.

'Listen,' they said, 'when he comes over the wicket, just pad up.'

'Great,' I said, relieved. And then a follow-up question sprang to mind. 'What actually do you mean by "pad up"?' Their reply was processed through the sausage machine of my mind and duly came out the other end as 'get yourself in the way of everything'. Thus, the first legside ball he bowled I smothered in the manner of a marine saving his fellow troopers from a grenade. I then fell on my arse. I got up and brushed myself down, taking note how, very decently actually, the Aussies had turned their backs on me so I couldn't see them laughing, although the shoulders going up and down were a bit of a giveaway.

'All right, all right,' I said to David Boon. 'But I'm still not out. I could be here for the next two hours doing this. You won't be laughing then, will you?' He didn't think that a likely scenario.

Next up was a waist-high full toss outside leg stump. For this ball I believe the best batting coaches recommend a karate kick, which I duly performed. Then came a similar delivery which I actually got a bat on – while walking sideways to square leg. You can laugh, but 11 balls I lasted for that nought. Those who gave me the benefit of their great batting knowhow didn't do much better. Warney pocketed not just my wicket, but ten others in the match.

At Melbourne, meanwhile, I sat in the hutch feeling increasingly nauseous as Warney got a hat-trick of Daffy, Gough and Devon. I was next man in. As I headed out of the door, I couldn't help mentioning to the other boys that not only was I on a pair – I'd been run out for nought in the first innings – but now I was also on a quadruple. Unluckily for Warney, his hat-trick had come off the fourth, fifth and sixth balls of the over. He never got to bowl at me. Craig McDermott was operating from the other end and had me caught behind off his fourth delivery. The pair happened, but I swerved the quadruple. In fact, even if Warney did have a ball at me, I'm confident I'd have survived. I was set to be his hat-trick victim in the previous game at Brisbane after

Daffy and Martin McCague had fallen to the cheese-toastie-loving maestro. After no small degree of consideration – Warney loved a bit of theatre – he bowled me a googly which I mistook for a leg-spinning half-volley. I played a huge expansive waft outside off stump, at which point it turned back and went over the top of middle and leg by about an inch. For the record, that day I saw him off with aplomb during my not out innings of two.

Eight years after first facing him, in what would turn out to be my last Test, I hit Warney over mid-off for a one-bounce four at The Oval. Have that, Shane!

Adam Gilchrist couldn't believe what he was seeing. 'Tuffers, mate, that's a great shot.'

'Thanks, Andrew,' I replied. 'I've been working on that one.' Of course, the truth was I'd got my timing wrong – I'd meant to hit it on the floor.

I looked at Warney. 'Have another go!' I told him. 'Let's see what you've got.' Well, you have to seize the moment – it may never happen again.

It didn't.

Let's face it, getting done over by Murali and Warney was no disgrace if you were a number 11. The damage those two did to me was more off the pitch. Until the arrival of the blond bombshell that was Warney, I was considered the best spinner in the world. Then, Warney began ragging it, bowling doosras, zooters, balls with names that sounded like own-brand crisps from Asda. When Murali then turned up, too, it was as if the entire game had been reinvented. Prior to that, everyone was saying spin bowling is dead, that the likes of me were a dying breed. Now everyone was asking why England didn't have a mystery spinner. No mystery there – we had nothing in place to improve our orthodox spinners, let alone develop a mystery one. Mention a desire to bowl the one that goes the other way and there would be blank looks all round. I feel quite jealous about the help and knowhow that's in the England set-up now. I would have loved to have learnt new tricks. I see all these different kinds of deliveries, bowlers messing about with seam and wrist positions, low arms and high arms, release points, 'superskills'. My superskill was my arm ball. That was it. I did try different seam and wrist positions but not from any place of knowledge. That's why I hated nets, because I ended up just practising the same old stuff. I wanted to do something different. I once started talking about how I'd like to develop a left-handed doosra. Everyone looked at me like I was mad.

It got to such a point that I had a chat with Robin Peterson, a young left-arm spinner from South Africa. He would go on to play a few Tests but at this point he was just a kid. I saw him trying something new at a net session and he told me he was working on the one that goes the other way. I was getting advice from someone who was at that point bowling in a second XI.

For English spinners, it seemed, too much relied on the pitch and how the batsman played. It was much more difficult to force anything, make something happen. And that's what I was looking for. I wanted to be more proactive, to do something a little bit more than just contain and try to take a few wickets. But the answer was always the same – 'Phil, that's what you've got to do' – which was a little bit unfulfilling. I think Monty Panesar felt the same.

At the start of 1992, the year Murali and Warne made their Test debuts, I'd played seven Tests and taken 32 wickets, including a five-for against Australia and Sri Lanka (the latter of which earned me a place on the Lord's honours board), a six against West Indies, and a seven against New Zealand.

Perhaps after that I tried too hard to repeat those efforts, to find that magic feeling. At the same time, there is a freshness to a player's early career. You are coming up against players you have never encountered and who have never encountered you. Over time, that relationship changes. Inevitably, batter and bowler counteract one another, at which point the game can feel harder, less of freshness, more of attrition. Added to that, the pressure of expectation is increased. Instead of just turning up and having a crack, you become an essential player in the side. You've got to perform. What was freedom becomes a job. Once you've done that first lap, people work you out. They find a way to put you under pressure.

That was the change I was going through when Murali and Warne really started making their mark. The conversation among the management turned very quickly to 'Oh f***, they've got Shane Warne and Murali – and we've got Phil.' What they could do and I couldn't. That kind of negativity just wasn't conducive to getting the best out of anyone – 'Thanks for bigging me up.'

By way of comparison, you only have to look at how Ashley Giles thrived under Michael Vaughan. He was never expected to match Shane Warne. Instead, he was backed every inch of the way for the job he could do for his team – 'All we ask of you is that you're as good as you can be.'

It's amazing how a conversation can change. Prior to my appearance on the scene, England had become reliant on playing four seamers. Occasionally, they'd chuck in Phil Edmonds, Embers, or Eddie Hemmings, but generally it was four seamers and that was that. I like to think I helped reignite spin bowling in Test cricket. Martin Crowe and Sunil Gavaskar both said I was the best in the world and there was a view that I was leading the way in the spin renaissance, that I was its torchbearer.

But even in those early days I was a torchbearer in a losing team. Don't forget England rarely played well. I hardly ever had any runs to play with. You can only work with what you've got. You can't be expected to bowl people out for 160 all the time. Spinning wickets, too, were at a premium. On flat pitches batsman could sit on me.

Umpires didn't exactly help. The worst decision I ever got was the one which should have given me my first Test wicket. On my debut at the MCG, David Boon almost took the cover off the ball so blatantly did he nick it through to Jack Russell. I don't blame Boon for not walking, but I do blame Peter McConnell, the Aussie umpire who looked at me, smiled, and said, 'Not out.' It was an absolute disgrace. Even in the MCG with 60,000 screaming Australians, you can still hear an edge. McConnell must have been the only person in a hundred-yard radius whose hearing was off.

'You f***ing bastard,' I said to him. I made sure he heard that okay.

To me, McConnell was using the game to get back at me for an earlier incident when I had asked him how many balls were left in the over.

'Count 'em yourself, you Pommie c***,' McConnell replied. I couldn't believe what I was hearing. 'Sorry? You what?'

McConnell said nothing. 'Look,' I told him. 'All I did was ask you how many balls there were to go in the over – I'm not having that.'

By now Graham Gooch was marching in my direction, something which rarely foresaw anything good happening in my universe. Except this time Gooch was as irate as I was.

'You can't talk to my players like that,' he told McConnell. The official didn't apologise but clearly wasn't expecting Gooch to have heard the abuse he gave me. He looked a little unsettled until he reimposed himself by refusing to give the Boon decision which could have been the turning point in the game. Australia were chasing around 200 to win, and Boon would go on to get 94 of them.

McConnell was back for the third Test at the Sydney Cricket Ground, objections to his decisions this time round earning rebukes for Alec Stewart and Eddie Hemmings. Thankfully, when my first wicket did finally come – Greg Matthews skying one to mid-off – there was nothing McConnell, stood at square leg, could do about it. However, considering the earlier injustice, I couldn't let the moment go unnoted.

'I suppose that's not f***ing out either,' I told his white-coated compatriot Tony Crafter – who then went on to refuse my endless LBW appeals against Carl Rackemann as the Aussie paceman took root for the best part of two hours in an attempt to stymie our chances of winning the match. Rackemann was a great big lump with great big pads and an even bigger stride who just plonked his front foot down the pitch and let the ball hit his leg. In order to play for England, you've got to be a reasonable bowler. As a professional England spinner, I could hit the stumps six times out of six. We were appealing virtually every ball, to which Crafter eventually said, 'Right, I'm not even going to look at LBW.'

'Hang on,' I said, 'so LBW's out of the equation? You're actually telling me I can't get him out LBW?'

Crafter looked at me and sniggered. This was my first tour.

'So I've either got to get him caught or bowled?'

Caught? What was I thinking? When Stewie picked up a sharp chance at short leg, that wasn't given out either. His disgust was obvious – 'This is a joke.'

Crafter wasn't alone in his reluctance to give LBWs. The reluctance was widespread across the board. If the batsman went forward, officials didn't give them out. They said they were guessing the trajectory of the ball. But then they'd give that same batsman out if they came forward to play the sweep. What was the difference? The batsman was playing across the line, but the leg was in exactly the same position. It was as ridiculous as it was illogical. It was a major reason I didn't get on with umpires at the beginning of my career.

'Phil,' they'd ask, 'will you just stop appealing?'

And I'd say, 'Why? It's pitched middle and off, it's gone straight, and he's misjudged the line. What the f*** is that missing?' So many boys who couldn't play spin just tucked the bat behind the pad and pushed forward. It drove me mad.

'They can't be allowed to do this,' I'd tell the umpires, but they never did anything. I'd get more angry, they'd get more fed up with me and that would turn into a blunt refusal to give me anything.

The knock-on effect was massive. Jacques Kallis gets away with pushing forward with his pad on ten and a day and a half later he's on 180. Give him out and the next person in knows they have to use their bat, which then brings bat-pads and out-side edges into play. For a while, it was nearly the end of flight bowling. Deception isn't a workable tool if the batsman can rock forward with the full confidence that even if they've misread the flight they can let the ball hit them on the knee roll.

Umpires would say to me, 'I can't give that out. I'd be guessing.'

'Well,' I'd reply, 'have a guess, because otherwise I may as well not be bowling. The game is effectively not even happen-ing. He can't get out, he's not trying to score, and I can't get him out. We might as well not be here. We're at an absolute standstill. I may as well stand here and bowl underarm.'

In Guyana in 1998, Shivnarine Chanderpaul and Jimmy Adams were constantly padding myself and Robert Croft away. The final session of the first day was the most ridiculous in which I ever bowled. They didn't play a shot, just let the ball hit their pad – again and again and again. At the end of the day, Bumble went up to Darrell Hair, one of the umpires.

'Hold on a minute,' he said, 'this is a farce. These two boys can bowl straight deliveries, you know? You can't just have people putting their foot forward and letting it hit them on the pad.'

Next morning, Adams began doing exactly the same – and within no time Hair gave him out LBW. I'd like to think it heralded a new era. Sadly not.

Sometimes umpires would actually say, 'Phil, will you stop appealing?' I was as annoyed as I was astonished. 'No. How can you ask that? It's my job to appeal and it's your job to make a decision.'

But they would literally turn their backs. I'd have bowled an absolute banker, hitting the middle of middle, only to turn round to appeal and find the umpire shuffling one of his six stones from one pocket to another, looking at someone in the crowd. Luckily, mobile technology was in its infancy, otherwise I reckon they'd have been playing Candy Crush, ordering a Chinese for dinner.

I'd look at them. 'Come on. The one job you've got to do is have a look down that end, at least for my sake. It's my career. I've put a lot of effort into this and you're not even watching my delivery.'

Good job they never went into the medical profession.

'Doctor, will you pronounce the patient dead?'

'Blimey, another one? I can't be faffed. *Hollyoaks* is just start-ing on the telly. He's a bit pale. Just stick him in the morgue.'

As a bowler it's demoralising not to see wickets on the scorecard. That's your bread and butter. Go a couple of games without a wicket and the pressure is on. If the captain leaves you out for the next match it's no use saying, 'Hold on a minute, I had seven LBWs that weren't given and three of those sixes were off the inside edge.' I tried that and they looked at me like I was mad.

'Hold on, Phil. You got none for 120.'

'No, I didn't. Fake news! It was actually eight for 60. They just didn't give the LBWs. Oh, and their bats were too big. Don't you know what a good bowler I am? It's just no one gave them out. Can't you see? Why can nobody see?' I was like that bloke in *The Fugitive*. Constantly trying to make people believe.

A good job that other innovation, the umpire's head-cam, wasn't around at the time. No one wants to see an irate spin bowler turning puce while spewing deeply offensive expletives.

I got most of my wickets through mistimed drives or edges, or the batsman going for a big shot and hitting the ball up in the air. Out of 121 Test wickets, I got nine LBWs. That's 7 per cent. Compare that to 25 per cent for Monty Panesar and 27 per cent for Graeme Swann, the difference being the introduction of the Decision Review System (DRS) in 2008. With DRS on my side, I can't help feeling my international career would have been a different story. I'm not bitter, but FFS! Give me a seasonal adjustment! I want my past deliveries taken into account!

That stagnation in LBW decisions is why everyone wanted the mystery spinner, because the batsman had negated the deliv-ery from the finger spinner. We couldn't get them out LBW. If we had, it would have changed entire matches, series even.

1990–2001 would have been a golden period for England. We'd have won every match. Well, a man can dream. But it did effectively mean the batsman had arbitrarily been given one less way of getting out. Imagine the outcry if they had equally arbitrarily been given a new way to be dismissed? 'From now on, play the hook shot and you're out.' Those boys would have gone on strike. They'd have marched on Lord's.

When DRS came in, every time I saw another umpire forced to give a decision, I'd be punching the air – 'I bloody told you! Twenty years I was banging on about this and you never listened.' Once umpires saw it was possible, they almost went the other way. Hit on the pads by a spinner? 'Go on, off you go!'

Even now when I call them in the commentary box, I'm often ridiculed by my colleagues. 'He can't give that, Phil. Not with the stride the batsman's got in.' What has DRS shown? It would have hit middle stick halfway up.

Umpires hold a bowler's fortunes in their hands, something it took me a while to understand. At the outset of my career with Middlesex, I actually thought that all umpires were going to be very nice, very honest and all know their jobs. Assessing a decision would mean ticking a few boxes and then the finger would go up. When that wasn't the case, I tended not to be entirely happy.

I can thank Gatt and Embers for calming me down, Embers especially because he knew from experience the frustration I was going through. 'Listen, Phil,' he said, 'I get why you behave the way you do, but you've got to stop swearing at the umpires and threatening physical violence, at least in the first over, because if you do they are not going to warm to you. We're here for the next three days and perhaps you haven't got off on the right foot by already calling him a c***. Think about it, if you tell an umpire you're going to key their car, remove its wheels and set it on fire, are they really going to look at you in a favourable light? So can you please shut up because not only is it affecting your chances, it's affecting the team.'

I could see where Embers was coming from. My view was that I could be an absolute diva, strut about and call the umpires names, and they would still give batsmen out if it was warranted. But that, of course, is not human nature. Problem was, even when I reined it in, I still had to spend the next 15 years trying to drag the relationship back. They've got long memories, umpires, sort of grudge-holding elephants.

Then again, I like to believe that some umpires look back and think they quite liked umpiring when I was on because it woke them up. It was never dull. Forget standing there counting the six stones and having a ham sandwich at lunch. I offered a bit of spice. Some of them actually said that – or was that another dream?

Occasionally, if it was felt I'd gone over the top, I'd be called in at the end of the day to be disciplined by the match officials. I wasn't one for hanging around. 'Okay, come on then. Let's hear it – how much?' As far as I was concerned once the fine had been announced that was it – done. Except they always then felt the need to admonish me with a little speech, tell me what a bad thing it was I'd done, how I needed to change my behaviour if I wasn't to end up in the same position again.

'Look,' I'd say, 'I'll take the fine. But don't then make me stand here like I'm in a court of law. You're not a judge. You're not a policeman. Just because you played thirty-eight Test matches for New Zealand twenty-five years ago, you cannot make me stand here like a naughty schoolboy. You can't arrest me. You can't wave to the court official and say, "Take him down!"'

I never gave Dickie Bird any trouble. There was no point. He exhibited a mild exasperation that you'd even asked. 'Tuffers,' he'd say, pulling at his cuffs in that slightly fidgety way of his, 'it wasn't out. It was not out.'

Anyone else I might have had a bit of a shout and swear, but not with Dickie. He was just too nice. Have a go at Dickie and you'd just end up looking a fool. He had a hold over gobby blokes like me that no other umpire could match. Merv Hughes was giving Graeme Hick a load of stick once, frustrated by him continually playing and missing. Even at the best of times, Merv's language was rarely of the sort heard at a vicarage, and eventually Dickie felt compelled to have a word. 'Mervyn,' he told the paceman, basically a wardrobe with a moustache, 'I want you to be a good boy. Don't swear any more.'

He stared at Dickie for a moment. 'Dickie Bird,' he said, 'you're a legend. I won't swear again.'

Okay, the pledge lasted only one ball – Hick played and missed again at the next one – and Merv went off like an expletive volcano.

Ultimately in cricket you just have to accept the umpire's decision and get on with it. Rather than sling the aluminium bat of disdain onto the square of despair, it's down to you to progress your own career in your own way and hopefully find some high spots along the route.

The most exciting match I played in was our win in the first Test against New Zealand at Christchurch in 1992. At tea on the last day, with seven wickets still needed, and their stalwart opener John Wright having taken root, batting more than six hours for 99, our cases were packed. But I'd successfully pinned him down to the point where he'd virtually stopped scoring. At one point, he actually said to me, 'Jesus, Tuffers, I've had enough of you. Even when I go to sleep all I see is your boots running in and bowling at me.' I bowled 85 overs in that match so I can see where he was coming from. It was as if he could literally stand the sight of me no longer, to the point where after tea, one away from a 400-minute century, Wright had a rush of blood and charged down the pitch – Jack Russell doesn't miss those kinds of stumpings.

Next over, I got rid of middle-order batsmen Mark Greatbatch and Shane Johnson. Suddenly, from nowhere, it was game on, confirmed when I soon had Dipak Patel and Chris Cairns back in the hutch. New Zealand's mindset had been disrupted because they were following on and only needed a few runs to make us bat again. The change of innings would use up enough time for the match to be declared a draw. Martin Crowe was eventually left to see out roughly an hour with last man Chris Pringle. He'd negotiated his way to within four of the target, not a massive ask for a batsman of his class, when we started trying to get into his head. 'Just one hit to save the game. Go on! Have a go! Smash him over his head.' And that's exactly what he did to me. I swear that ball went so high it almost reached outer space. Derek Pringle was circling underneath. We were all shouting – 'Catch it! Catch it! Catch it!' And into those big bucket hands it went. We all went nuts.

That game is memorable for me in another way. It was the only time in my career I felt like Curtly Ambrose. Every time I walked back to my fielding position at fine leg, by the New Zealanders' dressing room, I could see the fear in their eyes. Except it wasn't so much that they were scared of me; they were scared by the situation. The thought that they were going to mess up, lose seven wickets in the last session of the last day, was too much to bear. I kept making funny faces at them because

I knew the fact they were being hustled out by a slow bowler would be killing them. 'This little twat can't bowl us out!' It felt like a moment of real power.

'Don't let Tufnell get me!' I could imagine them saying. 'I'm petrified of his slower one. Don't make me go out there. Send someone else! I can't face him bowling at fifty-two miles an hour.'

That feeling of having power on the field is also part of 'the zone'. Sometimes that happens because you are bowling beautifully – in my case with flight, guile and a change of pace – sometimes it happens because other people's brains, without them even noticing, have gone haywire. Whatever the cause, in the zone things happen in slow motion. You have great clarity of thought. 'I'm going to bowl this one two inches shorter and three inches wider.' And then you do exactly that. Everything slots into place. It's a beautiful feeling. I've had it four or five times. The only trouble is that you spend the rest of your life trying to find it again. That's the difference between good players and great players – the latter find it again and again.

CHAPTER 15

How Not to Give Up

Good times such as Christchurch make up for those times when bowling was utterly, maddeningly, dispiriting in the extreme. I'm sure I was bowling cricket balls at Brian Lara when he made his 375 in Antigua, but for all the impact they made I might as well have been tossing pebbles into the sea. After two days in the field that felt like a slow death, I thought for sure it was a good time for the part-time bowlers in the batting line-up to come on. Of course, none of them did. Which then allowed me to make a point – 'You know you're always asking me to get ten runs at number eleven? Well, I don't see you sticking your hand up to help me out now.'

Maybe pre-match we should have listened to Andy Caddick. He announced he had a plan to get Lara out. He reckoned it was possible for him to hit the pitch with an upright seam and intentionally make the ball nip back, but all he received was ridicule.

'Don't be stupid. If the seam hits the pitch no one knows which way it's going to go. Who do you think you are? Even Curtly Ambrose can't do that.' A couple of players even asked

Curtly, who confirmed that particular delivery wasn't in his repertoire. I watched that happen with nothing but sympathy for Andy. He'd come up with an idea and for his trouble been totally humiliated. And, actually, the more I thought about it the more I thought he had a point. Richard Hadlee always seemed able to bowl the nip-backer from the upright seam, maybe not at will, but fairly routinely. Caddy had a similar action; maybe he could do the same.

I shared Caddy's penchant for plans, mixing things up a bit. I was never a bowler who just liked to hit one spot and keep ploughing away. I was a bit of a fiddler – bit wider, bit slower, drop it back a bit, try and take him wide. You need good control to be able to do that. If a player liked playing across the line and whipping me through midwicket, I'd bowl a couple of quicker, straighter balls and then take midwicket out, encourage him to hit through there, and then follow the same line but with a little more flight and a little bit slower to try to get a leading edge. I needed the control to put it in the right spot to create that plan. No use bowling three good balls and then hanging a full toss outside off stump. It's like fly-fishing. If you want to catch the trout you need to cast in exactly the right place, just upstream, down his nose. But there's no point having a plan if you then cast your line and it gets stuck in the trees.

I actually worked on an over-the-head delivery to Dean Jones. The Aussie had a habit of haring down the wicket to my first delivery. My plan was to nip it over his floundering form before Jack Russell pounced in for the stumping. We practised it a couple of times, with a few balls whizzing off over the back of the net and Jack leaping around trying to get a glove on the others before diving on the stumps, but never actually tried it in a match.

Dean was obvious in his approach, but I found other batsmen would come down the wicket by numbers – balls one, three and five, for example, or two, four and six. They'd block the first one and you'd know next ball the big shot was coming. I'd even say it out loud, 'He's coming down the wicket here!' and they'd still do it. Of course, a bowler can only counter the numbers approach if they can count – which wasn't my forte. I was forever asking the umpire how many balls left in the over. 'If it's number five, I need to bowl it legside so he can't hit it. If it's number four, I'll try something a bit more orthodox. Or maybe this is the time for the one over the head ... maybe not.' With tailenders it didn't matter so much as they tended to telegraph a rush down the wicket. Better players, however, are able to disguise their intent.

Nowadays, the overhead floater would be called a no-ball, something I bowled an embarrassing amount of in Test cricket – although I suspect few of them were actually illegal deliveries. My action meant that while I used occasionally to land over the line, my foot would then screw back, so at the point of delivery I still had something on it. Umpires, of course, would only see half the proceedings before they had to turn their gaze on the batsman. It would wind me up and often end up with an altercation – 'Listen, umpire, I'm not sure whether you know the rules ...'

The worst wicket I lost because of a no-ball was at Durban when, with South Africa following on, I had Gary Kirsten stone-cold LBW with just a few on the board. Nasser, captain at the time, tried to build me back up. 'Not to worry, you'll get him next ball.'

I wasn't convinced. 'No, Nasser,' I thought, 'that was my chance and now it's gone. He'll go on to get a ridiculous score, save the game and they'll win the series.' He went on to score 275, South Africa saved the game and won the series. Again, Tufnell the soothsayer.

The match finished on 30 December. I felt I'd ruined everyone's New Year. It had been my job to bowl South Africa out, I'd had all the time in the world and I hadn't done it. Next night it was Millennium Eve and, as I saw Nasser and Athers sat with a few of the boys, I started apologising.

'I'm really sorry. I've ruined New Year's Eve. I've let everyone down.'

'Listen,' they were saying, 'it's not all your fault.'

But I knew on the inside what they wanted to say. 'You're right. You have f***ed up New Year's Eve. If you'd just not bowled that no-ball – if you'd done what you were meant to do, and paid to do, in that fourth innings, our New Year would have been great. Now it's shit.'

Sometimes the disappointment is the team's; sometimes it's personal. I could have had a hat-trick at Sydney on my first Ashes tour. First, I had Allan Border caught on the sweep by Gooch, then Dean Jones came down the wicket and clipped it back to me, at which point I got very excited, to the extent that Tony Greig on commentary advised that someone lock the gate to the ground fearing if it was open I'd run straight through. As it was, I was still in the ground when Steve Waugh came in. We packed men round the bat, he pushed forward and the ball flew hard and down towards David Gower at second silly point. He got a little finger on it, not quite enough. Border, Jones, Steve Waugh – I still count that as the best hat-trick that never was.

Had it been Mark Waugh, I might have had some luck. I didn't know it then, but he was my bunny. I got him out seven times, including for 99 at Lord's, not a bad tally since he was one of the best players of spin I've ever seen. I seemed to get under Mark's skin. Before my recall for the Oval Test in 1997 he had a bit of a pop at me in the papers, saying he was going to smash me everywhere. As it turned out I got him out for 19 in the first innings and one in the second. I was tempted to whistle the theme to *Watership Down* as he departed a second time.

Modern players are more overtly destructive than the majority of those I bowled at. Whereas batsmen used to play traditionally – if they tried a cover drive they'd do so with a high elbow – now it's a slap, as perfected by Jos Buttler. Before, they said only the Indians could play like that, as if it was a physical difference. 'Wristy', they were always called. That was clearly never the case and now batsmen around the world have cottoned on to a style of play that must be a nightmare for a player who is effectively left bowling at a hockey player. That batsman is also getting greater rewards. Attacking intent in T20 means hitting the ball for six not four. High elbow is a four shot. Flapping, flicking, or skimming delivers leverage.

That's not to say there weren't players who would mangle you. South African all-rounder Lance Klusener was one I rarely enjoyed the sight of, a man capable of such destruction that I'm surprised he went into coaching and didn't hire himself out as a wrecking ball. He had a horrible habit of blocking my first four balls and then smashing the last two for four and six. It's at such times that teammates say, 'Don't worry, that's what we want him to do. He'll slog one up in the air in a moment.' A question: what happens if he doesn't? I do it myself now on commentary for *TMS*. I see a spinner punted into the stand and say, 'He won't be too disappointed with that.' Lies. Pure lies. Of course he'll be disappointed – someone's just smacked him into the crowd.

Oblivious to health and safety legislation, captains would occasionally ask a slow bowler to entice a batsman down the track in the hope they'd make a mistake. Thing is, generally, when a batsman ventures down the pitch, it isn't to half-heartedly ease one through extra cover. More than a few whizzed past the old noggin. New Zealand all-rounder Chris Cairns once parted my hair with one he clubbed back towards me in a Test. An issue of *The Cricketer* from his heyday chose for its front cover a picture of me in my follow-through as this great bear of a man heads down the wicket. I'm not looking up. Not looking forward. Just countering. I imagine like a hedgehog does when it sees a 44-ton truck approaching. Keep your eye on the ball? No thanks. Nowadays, with big bats, I'd be coming in to bowl on horseback in shining medieval armour. 'And here comes Tufnell,' Rob Key would commentate. 'Look at that lovely bay mare.'

I learnt very early on that cricket is a batsman's game, and so as a bowler took it upon myself to seize any chance to even up the balance. If that meant Mankad-ing the odd batsman – running them out at the non-striker's end as they backed up too far – then so be it. After all, if the ball slips out of my hand, lands at mid-wicket and the batsman wanders out and smacks it to the boundary – as did happen – then they're not hugely interested in the spirit of the game, are they?

But if I'm honest, there was also a part of me that Mankaded people just for the sheer bloody-mindedness of it. I did it many times, especially when I got the arse-ache with people. They'd look at me like I'd smeared myself in dogshit, but I'd stand my ground.

'Look,' I'd say, 'I don't need to warn you. That's actually not in the rules and I would like you out.'

The umpire would be having kittens. 'Oh no, Phil. Don't put me in this position.'

'But, umpire,' I'd say, 'there is no position. I'm asking "How is that?" All you need to do is your job.'

The way I saw it, it was a simple line call. The batsman needs to be warned? Why? If I bowl a no-ball, it's called a no-ball. I don't get warned. The rule was there so I was going to use it. I welcomed someone – teammate, batsman, umpire – telling me I should have given the batsman a warning just so I could go, 'No, actually, that's wrong. I know the rules and you don't have to.'

'Okay,' a captain might say, 'you've made your point. Now will you please shut up and get on with the game?'

'No – no I won't. I know my rights.' It drove me mad that there was a valid dismissal in the rules of cricket that was treated as if it was an oddity, something to be ignored. If a batsman is two inches out of their crease at the end of a run, they are run out. What's the difference between that and being two inches outside when you set off? It's a straightforward line decision. It's not 'Ask the Umpire' on *TMS*. It's not someone enquiring if a batsman can be caught out if the ball passes through the rotor blades of a helicopter while it's in the air and the bloke at fine leg bags one of the 75 resultant pieces.

As a professional sportsperson you are forever looking for loopholes. Maybe sometimes I was a bit too clever for my own good, but if someone is going to tell me I'm wrong when I'm not, then I'll fight back. It's like that thing of people thinking I was always late, when actually the truth was far from it. I had no problem in telling people they were massively mistaken. In fact, I used to enjoy sitting anonymously at the back of a room so that when the inevitable assumption was made that I wasn't there, I could put my hand up – 'No, actually, here I am.' Same as when in New Zealand I was accused of smoking marijuana in the toilets of a bar. I wasn't going to roll over and just let someone say I had when I hadn't. In the end, it was shown that the bar was just after some publicity and that was that.

Flat wickets, benefit of the doubt, short boundaries – after the batsmen had enjoyed their feast, if there were any scraps left for the bowlers I was going to have them. That meant if a catch went to slip and I knew the fielder hadn't got his fingers under it, I'd go up for it anyway.

But then captains, who are generally batsmen themselves, would sometimes intervene. 'No, no, no. It didn't carry.'

'Will you please shut the f*** up? The umpire's given him out. He's there to do a job. Let him do it.'

I had captains call batsmen back. I'd be livid, absolutely fuming. I'd look at them and think, 'You absolute turncoat. I hope he gets 180 and then you can sit there patting yourself on the back for upholding your spirit of the game – and then when you bat I hope they Mankad you.'

Not all batsmen were called back. Chanderpaul was like a limpet for the West Indies, so when an edge was caught by second slip on the half-volley, and given out, not many of the England boys were keen on giving him a reprieve. Athers felt we should do the right thing, at which point we readied to smother him, wind him, or render him speechless with a swift knee in the bollocks.

It was as if once a year a skipper would get that Christmassy feeling – generosity of spirit, goodwill to all men. More often than not, though, it would be a tailender called back, an individual who carried no threat. Allowing them to continue meant we could show the umpires we were good sports who would always intervene if a miscarriage of justice occurred. Then, when a better player was caught on the half-volley, the officials would be more likely to believe our appeal.

Thankfully, I was never called back. 'Heh, Tuffers! No, we got it wrong. Come back. Don't worry about Curtly. I'm sure he'll be fine with it.'

'No, no. I'm fine. The umpire's decision is final. In fact, I think it's rather rude of you to even question it. Carry on, everyone.'

Worth remembering also that while bowlers will rant and rave if an opposition batsman doesn't walk, they'd be just as disgusted if a batsman from their own team didn't wait for the finger.

I honestly don't know why people still make such a song and dance about it. If everyone walks for our side and we're bowled out for 78, and then the opposition gets 500 while resolutely staying put, who's the idiot? We can sit there and pat ourselves on the back as much as we want – 'Aren't we brilliant? That's the way to play the game' – but while everyone else is allowing the umpire to make the decision, we are actually just mugs. Batsmen walking? The biggest load of bollocks I've ever heard, and yet they still claim the moral high ground today. I hear countless players say they were a walker and I know full well the whole lot of them would have more than happily nicked it and stayed put without compunction.

Also, while we're at it, can we lay another myth to rest? This idea that batsmen sometimes don't know if they've hit the ball. Every batsmen I've ever spoken to says they always feel something. To try to claim otherwise is plain nonsense.

As a bowler, there's nothing worse than a batsman who knows they've got away with it. The good players will say nothing to you for a couple of overs. They're too busy buttering up the ump, 'Good decision, mate. I don't know what they're on about. You've got that spot on.' But 25 minutes later you catch their eye, and that's when they get you.

'I hit the cover off that, Tuffers, you absolute twat. Thanks for that. What a bit of luck. I was only on twenty. Now I'm on fifty seeing it really well. I'll buy you a beer for that, mate.' Where's the heavy roller when you need it?

On occasions, I didn't help myself. I mean, if you want to get someone out you do really need to appeal. At Port Elizabeth, on about 30, Lance Klusener edged me behind to Alec Stewart and neither me, him, nor anyone else appealed. The ball had skimmed soundlessly off the face. Klusener went on to get 174. The last thing you need to hear when you've just been smashed all over the place is that you had a player served up on a plate and failed to bite, but that's exactly what happened when Duncan Fletcher sidled up later.

'Tuffers! Oh, my God! I can't believe you didn't appeal.'

'What? I didn't know! I didn't even hear!'

I'm not saying gamesmanship is great, to be encouraged. Like everything, there's a limit. When Australia's Greg Chappell ordered his brother Trevor to bowl underarm to Brian McKechnie whose New Zealand team required a six off the last ball to draw a one-day match in 1981, his actions were so far over the limit as to almost cause an international incident. Broadcasting legend Richie Benaud could barely contain his ire as he wrapped up his broadcast for Channel Nine, describing it as 'one of the worst things I have ever seen done on a cricket field'. Even the Australian prime minister,

Malcolm Fraser, called the act 'contrary to the traditions of the game'.

You might have hoped that would be the end of Australian prime ministers expressing dismay at the antics of the national team. But then 37 years later, with Sandpapergate, when it was revealed the Aussies were shopping at DIY stores for matchday equipment, another PM, Malcolm Turnbull, stated how it had been a 'shocking disappointment' to find Australian captain Steve Smith and sidekick David Warner involved in such subterfuge. Once people were putting glue on their hands and dipping them in sand, or wearing finger bandages liberally covered in the grainy stuff, then something was bound to give.

Beforehand, any messing about with the ball was generally within the bounds of what was legal, like throwing it into the ground when returning it to the keeper. On an older, bashed-about ball, I used to pick the mud out the seam, which would make it stand out a little more. Other times the ball would be thrown to me at the start of an over and the stitches would be sticking out like sharks' teeth. I could hardly grip and spin it because it would cut my fingers and draw blood. A couple of times the umpires would see what was going on – 'Come on, boys, stop messing about.' They were never overly bothered. A lot of them had been bowlers themselves and had done exactly the same thing in their time. But then people started going too far. A win–at–all–costs mentality created a brain fog which meant people became blind to what they were doing to win a game of cricket.

I was as shocked as anyone at Sandpapergate. I was also shocked at the vitriol unleashed on the players – all these sup-posedly righteous people shouting, 'What a disgrace!' Yes, it was a disgrace, and something needed to be done – a line drawn in the sand (sorry!) – but everyone makes mistakes and everyone deserves a second chance. The punishment, the level of public humiliation, didn't fit the crime. Glass houses and cricket balls were never a good mix.

CHAPTER 16

How Not to Be a Fielder

'TUFNELL IS A WANKER' was the first banner I saw in an Australian cricket ground with my name on it. The Aussie crowds seemed to enjoy giving me grief from the stands. I did try to engage with them to keep things nice and friendly but that could occasionally backfire as well. Someone once asked for my autograph and when I went across to oblige they squashed a minced beef and onion pie on my head.

It was all a bit of a minefield for a lad from Hertfordshire whose world up to that point had not extended much further than a packet of peanuts, a pint and a fag.

'Give us a wave, Tuffers,' someone would call out. Which I did. Then someone else would ask and I'd give another wave so as not to upset anyone. But you can't keep waving forever. You're a cricketer not a royal. And so in the end you stop, at which point you hear a small voice crying, 'Dad, he didn't give me a wave,' and a rather larger voice bellow out, 'You Pommie bastard! Give my son a wave!' To wave or not to wave, that was always the question.

I was listening to Rob Key and Nasser ahead of the Ashes series in Australia in 2021–22 talking about how it wouldn't be a great idea to give a player a debut in such a big series. I was sat there enjoying the debate when suddenly it occurred to me – 'Hang on! That's exactly what happened to me!' And not just any debut – the MCG, a vast and boiling cauldron of bloodthirsty Aussies, the biggest arena in world cricket, on one of its greatest occasions – the Boxing Day Test.

I was just getting aerated at this unforgiveable and potentially career-crushing situation that had been forced on me, mulling over various conspiracy theories – it was a way of killing me off before I'd even started; it was a punishment for taking the piss out of Graham Gooch at the Christmas lunch – when it occurred to me that actually I hadn't minded one bit.

What struck me most about my Test debut wasn't the size of the occasion; what really resonated was the colour. The sky was so blue, the grass so green. Everyone in the crowd seemed to have been painted in the most vivid of ways. Go to Lord's on a chilly spring day and everything's a bit grey. There'll be the odd blue shirt in the stands and that's about it. Walk out at the MCG, and everyone is in yellow and orange. Everywhere, colour, made even more stark by the sheer brightness of the sun – a really hot sun. I loved that. I can see it even now in my mind's eye – astonishing.

The vast majority of those people had come to witness the slaughter of the England side. I did my best to stop that happening by going wicketless in both Australia innings and not scoring a run in either of ours. Four big round noughts – an Audi as it's known. Not that I went unnoticed. The Aussie crowd soon realised they'd found someone who they could get a bit of a rise out of. I didn't know how to react when I first trotted down to third man to find several thousand Australians bellowing abuse. What do you do? Ignore them? Give them a wave? I actually pulled a few faces and gave them a little thumbs-up, which maybe wasn't the best idea, because immediately I could see what they were thinking – 'Brilliant! We've got one that we can take the piece of piss out of all day and he's going to react.'

That actually was the start of a fun relationship with Australian crowds. I enjoyed the theatre of the set-up, as obviously did they, and soon found, aside from scooping the occasional lump of pie filling from my hair, I had quite a good rapport with them, possibly because I wasn't the sort of stiff-upper-lip Pom who traditionally got their backs up. Instead, they saw someone who was a bit of a 'larrikin', such a great word and one which should possibly have been the job description on my passport.

I kept telling myself one thing – 'They're calling you a wanker, Phil, because they like you.'

There has always been the odd Pom who the Aussies have taken to, notably Fred and Beefy, and I think it's because they see a bit of themselves in them. I think they looked at me, turned to their mate, and said, 'How the f*** is he playing? I mean, Christ, if he can get a game of cricket at the MCG maybe I've got a chance!'

The second banner – 30 foot long and bright yellow – I saw in an Australian cricket ground with my name on it was 'The Tufnell Fielding Academy', an organisation formed after I massively ballsed up a run-out in front of 40,000 during a day/night ODI at Sydney. We'd got them 82 for four, with me snaring Geoff Marsh and Dean Jones, when Steve Waugh came out to bat with his twin brother Mark. The latter proceeded to push a single off me to Eddie Hemmings. Steve called for the run and Mark tried to send him back. But it was too late and the pair found themselves stood side by side at the striker's end, at which point Steve gave up – he was in a hopeless position – and started to take his gloves off.

What should have happened next was this: Eddie throws the ball to me, I break the stumps, job's a good 'un. What actually happened was this: Eddie throws the ball to me, I take my eye off it for a split second and it cannons off my hands like I've hit it with a frying pan. Steve sees this and now does try to get back, even though he knows he still has practically zero chance as all I have to do is collect the ball, walk back and nick off a bail. Instead, for a reason that will never be satisfactorily explained, I take a massive shy at the stumps from fully one yard and miss them completely. There's a split second of silence and then one of the biggest roars of jeers and jubilation in sporting history. Steve jogs back, puts his bat in, smiles, and says 'In!', like we used to do in the playground.

I look at the faces of the Waugh boys. They can't believe what's happened. I look at the faces of my teammates, of Alec Stewart behind the stumps and Eddie Hemmings. They can't believe it either. Then finally I look at the face of Graham Gooch, which tells me he can believe it only too well.

He just looks at me open-mouthed. 'F*** me,' he says, and walks on.

I feel such a fool. As I wander down to fine leg, the entire stadium is pissing itself with laughter. I know these things look funny, but when you're the person that everyone's laughing at, it's horrible. At that point I wasn't experienced or grown up enough to say 'Shit happens' and get on with the game. So, instead of doffing the cap to the crowd and smiling at the joke, I pull it down over my eyes and try not to burst into tears.

Thankfully, I did manage to get Steve caught behind in the next over. But the incident would always follow me round Australia from both crowd and commentators. Ian Chappell, the former Australian skipper, advised Gooch to keep me bowling for as long as possible because at least that way I would spend less time in the field. But that's slightly problematic, because there might be the occasional time when there's a caught and bowled. You need to factor that into the equation, Mr Chappell.

When the Tufnell Fielding Academy banner appeared at our next game, some saw it as something by which I would feel humiliated. But to me it was just a bit of fun. There was no viciousness attached. In fact, right now I'm thinking back on it with nothing but affection. I've always been pretty good at laughing at myself, quite self-deprecating, and that was the attitude I had at the time. Gooch, however, wrote in his autobiography that he was disappointed at my reaction to the banner, that he felt I enjoyed it too much. He says that I 'took this notoriety as a sort of fan-club hero worship'. He's mistaken there – I just took it in the spirit it was intended, a bit of harmless fun. What would have been the 'correct' reaction? Go up to them and remonstrate? 'I say, chaps, please could you take that down? It's rather putting me off my game.' I certainly didn't set out to court that kind of attention, but I knew also that if I made a big deal out of it I would get it a thousand times worse.

Thing is, in the field there's no escape. You're out there for hour after hour – well we were! – and I found my own way of dealing with it. If you don't do that, a cricket field can be a very lonely place, like when you see a player misfield the ball and from that point on the crowd goes 'Whoaaaaaa!', a sort of crescendo of noise, every time it comes their way. It's horrible to be on the end of that. It's a confirmation that every pair of eyes in the place is on you. Different players deal with the microscope in different ways. I'd rather be myself than pretend to be someone I'm not six hours a day.

Crowds can be quite original in their interaction. The most famous comment thrown in my direction, and one which always appears in any list of great boundary sledges, was the one I received again on that Melbourne debut – 'Oi, Tufnell! Lend me your brain, I'm building an idiot!' I rather preferred patrolling the boundary in the West Indies. Instead of abuse, they used to chuck big spliffs and lighters at me. I used to gather them all up and give them to the umpire. 'Excuse me, could you look after these? Perhaps bring them to the dressing room at the end of play?'

I was hit on the back of the head with a lump of fruit in New Zealand. Even a Pot Noodle once. The worst were those big cardboard fours and sixes that sponsors used to give out. People would make them into aeroplanes, quite heavy and aerodynamic. Get the pointy end of one of those pinging into the back of your neck and you really did know about it. At least they weren't real flying objects, vicious, and with big ugly beaks. When England players fielded in front of the old Bay 13, a particularly lively area of the MCG, fans had a habit of throwing chunks of bread onto the grass. Initially, the player would be bemused – 'Why on earth are they doing that?' And then all of a sudden the sky would darken as hundreds of seagulls swooped down like a scene from that Hitchcock film *The Birds*.

Bay 13 was notorious, but pretty much all of those bays at any ground were the same. They could erupt at any time. At Brisbane, the sun disappeared for another reason. Down in one corner they used to have a daily beer-can fight. Since they'd all been drinking for six hours they had plenty of ammunition to go at. Cans would fill the air, hopefully not above your head. This was the same part of the ground where some jokers had once sent a pig scuttling onto the pitch with 'Beefy' written on one side and 'Eddie' (Hemmings) on the other. When Gatt went to field down there he was greeted with a chorus of 'Who the f*** is Father Christmas?'

I played a one-day game at Melbourne where someone doubled up their corporate box as a driving range. I was just getting ready to bowl when a golf ball came flying on. I'd say, from the distance it was struck, possibly a four-iron. To be fair, I'm sure if the Tiger Woods wannabe in question felt he was going to crown anyone he'd have shouted 'Four!' Had I been able to identify the culprit, I'd have asked to borrow his club. The MCG was a par three throwback. A decent iron could only have helped.

If the golf ball wasn't startling enough, not long after a huge roar went up. It's an automatic reaction to look when that happens and I did a classic comedy double-take as I turned to see this naked bloke absolutely pegging it – Usain Bolt-esque – out to the middle. As ever in these situations, while the stewards hared round after him, the crowd was massively on his side, as, in all honesty, was I. The chap, possibly fearing catching himself on a bail, didn't go for the old-school hurdle of the stumps; he just leapt across the pitch, and as he did so he caught my eye.

'All right, Tuffers!' he gasped as he started for the other side of the ground.

'Go on, my son!' I urged him. 'You can make it.' And then he was gone. It was a while ago so I'm not sure I'd recognise him now. Not by his face anyway.

Back in Blighty, Dad, bless him, was keeping an eye on my progress on my first tour. He got the Betamax out, videoed every session, and filled scrapbooks, too, as he did throughout my career, although all too often the headlines were more to do with matters off the pitch – 'TUFNELL FINED!', 'TUFNELL BREAKS CURFEW – AGAIN', that kind of thing.

Dad had a well-established and ingrained habit of writing to all and sundry to let them know his opinions. But who do you write to in Australia to say you're unimpressed with the traditional antagonism being aimed at the English tourists? Why, Richie Benaud of course. Off flew a missive to the broadcasting legend. Richie, exceptional bloke that he was, wrote straight back. 'Dear Mr Tufnell,' he inked, 'I think your son has done very well over here. Perhaps he needs to brush up on his fielding and his batting a little bit, but I think he's bowled very, very well – and as a fellow spinner I can say that.' Dad was very, very chuffed with that. And so, still, am I.

Times change and remarkably, four years later, on the Ashes tour of 1994–95, I pulled off two contenders for the Kentucky Fried Chicken classic catch of the series. Bizarrely, both were taken to dismiss Michael Slater. But he shouldn't be too hard on himself because they were, if I say so myself, a pair of minor miracles.

The first, at Sydney, involved physical freakery of which Michael Jordan would have been proud. I was actually facing the wrong way when the ball hit my paws. At that point Slater and Mark Taylor had put on 208 for the first wicket and whatever plans we had didn't seem to be working terribly well. We all met up in the middle of the pitch for a huddle. 'Right,' said Athers, 'we've tried pretty much everything else, so how about we bounce him?'

The idea was not without merit because, while Slater was an

aggressive and skilful hooker, sometimes he could get under the ball and still go through with the shot.

'Great plan,' I said, turning to wander back to my fielding position at mid-on.

'OK, Tuffers,' said Athers, 'down you go.'

'Oh, what, *I've* got to go down there for the hook?'

Even though every fibre of my being was telling me it was going to be a disaster, and that everyone present would end up either being angry or laughing at me again, I had no choice but to head off down to fine leg.

And then it happened. Gus sent down a nice perky bouncer, Slater got a solid connection, more top edge than middle of the bat, and suddenly I was on. Now, it didn't matter how much I concentrated, how much I anticipated, the sight of a catch coming my way always slightly startled me. It was always a 'Shit!' instead of a 'Yes!'

My thought process on this occasion went as follows: 'Oh f***, it's coming this way. I can't hear anyone else shouting "Mine!" There's no one else in the vicinity. I've got to run for it. Bloody hell, I've caught it!' My teammates all came running towards me but instead of congratulating me they all looked at me open-mouthed. Someone even said, 'F***! You caught it!'

'Of course I did. Would you mind not looking so shocked?'

The second catch happened in the next Test in Adelaide, part of a crazy win against the odds. Injuries had left us depleted. Gatt had struggled for runs but had to play and dug deep to score a gritty hundred in what turned out to be his penultimate Test. By the time Australia batted last they needed 263 to win. Devon fired it down at the speed of light that day. One delivery to bowl Steve Waugh first ball was about the quickest I've ever seen.

I played an early part in Australia's downfall when I held onto another high one at deep fine leg. I got the flight of that one wrong, too. I ran towards it so fast that I nearly went straight past it. Turning around with the ball in my hand as the Barmy Army came running down the grass bank, kicking over their beers, hanging over the fence, swinging their tops round their heads, was one of the greatest sights of my career. As was Gatt catching Mark Waugh in his tummy off my bowling a little later in the game.

I can't recall which of those two catches earned me the ultimate fast-food prize – a KFC Colonel's Privilege Card which meant I could eat free wherever I went – but I made full use of it. I'd walk up to the counter, open my jacket, and show them my secret ID. 'Hello. My name is Tufnell, Phil Tufnell. I'd like a bargain bucket. Shaken not stirred.'

'Of course, Mr Tufnell. I hope we haven't kept you waiting.'

'Quite all right. But I wonder if you could make sure there's a couple of extra breasts in that bucket. I don't want none of your legs and wings.'

Mind you, true to Aussie form, the first time I used it I got stick from one of the employees.

'There you go, you Pommie bastard,' he said as he handed me my food. 'There's your free chicken, now f*** off out of here – oh, and have a nice day.'

With or without a bucket of fried chicken on board, I was never the quickest to the ball. I was fielding at midwicket once when Dean Jones knocked one off his hip just past my right hand. I sprinted, picked it up, turned on a sixpence and threw it back. As Dean was at the non-striker's end I silently congratulated myself for managing to restrict him to a single. At the end of the over I was half-expecting a pat on the back from Gooch.

Instead he gave me yet another dark look. It took a couple of seconds and a glance at the scoreboard to work out that in the time it had taken me to execute this fine bit of fielding, the Aussie batsmen had not run one, but three.

Another lesson learnt the hard way was that batsmen didn't always call for a run. If players batted a lot together, they might just drop it, nod and go. I'd be walking in to pick it up and my teammates would be shouting, 'Phil, they're running!'

'But nobody called! How am I supposed to know they're running if they don't call? They're supposed to call. That's not fair.'

For me, there was very rarely a smooth transition to the ball, effortless underarm pick-up and lightning quick flick at the stumps. Coaches now say to watch the ball from the bat, but I always watched it from the bowler's hand. I felt to have it just ping at me unannounced would be even more of a surprise. In fact, to be honest, in my signature position of third man I spent most of my time watching the crowd, so I didn't really get the benefit of all the little nuances that the pros spoke about.

Very occasionally I found myself at slip. I didn't like it in there. The ball came so fast that I would actually try to push it way – once a goalkeeper, always a goalkeeper. There was so little time for depth perception. I never mastered the technique – all I could see was broken fingers. I quite fancied keeping hold of my head and my bollocks, too. I still consider every slip catch a minor miracle, though I have to admit I had a rather different perspective on anyone in the cordon who dropped a catch off me.

You'd think that when the ball goes up in the air for a high catch it would be easier. No crowd, no background. But it can be very hard to judge speed and trajectory, especially out of a clear blue sky. Many times I've walked in too far and the ball has gone whizzing over my head. And equally many times I've stood back and the thing has just dropped in front of me. Perhaps the worst catches are the ones where you're at third man and the ball skims off a top edge. A top edge that goes up in the air is all right, but those that travel fast on a flat parabola are horrible. I was regularly hit on the knees or in the nuts. In the field I would like to have been clad in the get-up of the Michelin Man. Actually, I wasn't far off that look when I took my first catch for Middlesex – Clive Lloyd off Simon Hughes at Old Trafford. It was freezing that day and I was lucky enough to have three jumpers on when Clive whacked one down to me at mid-off. I wrapped my arms around it, rolled around on the floor and when I stood up there it was tucked in among the folds.

Later, I would hear Jonty Rhodes and Paul Collingwood, two real experts in the art, say that fielding aptitude all comes from your legs, delivering a strong core and a strong base. No one ever said that to me. All I heard was, 'You've got to have good hands.' But what are good hands? I've got hands, which is good, but it didn't necessarily mean I could field. So often it seemed that tips for improving your fielding had precisely nothing to do with picking up the ball or catching it. 'Walk in as the bowler runs up.' Why? When Rafa Nadal receives serves he isn't walking in; he's more like a goalkeeper poised to go this way or that.

I also found it odd that despite the thousand catches you take as a professional cricketer in warm-ups, when the pressure of a match situation was on, a totally different ball game was taking place. I'd catch the ones that didn't matter 99 times out of a hundred, but then, when it did matter, my success rate dipped to about 50/50. The same balls I'd pouch with casual proficiency in training always seemed to come at me a lot harder and faster in a game. High catches would start off the size of a pea and then get bigger and bigger until suddenly they were on you, ready or not. If you performed a mathematical equation of everything you have to take into consideration in order to pull off a catch of that kind – flight, depth, pace, distance to travel, light, background, match situation, etc. – it would, I'm sure, be beyond the capabilities of the average human mind. It was often beyond mine.

Fingers pointing up or down? No time to consult the manual. You're on your own and everyone is looking right at you, in my case probably expecting the worst. More than once I went fingers up, the Aussie way, for a ball coming flat towards me only for it to dip in flight, taking me down and down and down and down until I ended up face-planting the pitch. Tough to style that one out. If you caught the ball fingers down, meanwhile, the English way, you were supposed to catch it like an egg in a pair of mink gloves. I lost count of how many times my mink gloves were ruined.

When I did manage to hang on to one, we usually won the game. And no funny comments about that's probably why we won so few in those days. At the Kensington Oval in Barbados in 1994, I took a really tough over-the-shoulder catch to dismiss Brian Lara off Andy Caddick. The pressure was on. Lara was cruising along on 64 at the time. If I hadn't made that catch, there was every chance he'd carry the West Indies to a successful run chase. As it was we won by 208 runs. Chris Lewis came sprinting over and picked me up – 'You beauty!' – because the bowlers wanted more than anything in the world to see the back of Lara. Drop Lara and they wouldn't speak to you for the rest of the day. 'Never drop Brian Lara' – that's the golden rule. Just ask the Durham wicketkeeper Chris Scott, who, after dropping him on 18 in a championship match, noted, 'I bet he'll go on and get a hundred now.' Lara did just that: five of them plus a single to be precise.

The pitch invasion that followed that Barbados win was brilliant. I was fielding on the boundary and, with Curtly and Courtney at the crease, the England supporters, many of whom had suffered the ignominy of watching their team capitulate in the previous Test, had gathered by the rope in readiness for the moment of unexpected victory. There were thousands of people behind me, some so close that they were actually patting me on the back. Chris Lewis knocked Curtly's stumps out of the ground and that was it. Everyone – crowd, fielders, batsmen, umpires – just ran. It was absolute bedlam. I legged it in the general direction of the pavilion but so thick was the throng that I had no actual idea where I was going. Even now, I can see the faces of blokes running alongside – big red sunburnt faces, showing sheer delight – as they overtook me. It was both fantastic and a bit of a shock – 'Christ, even a big lad with fifteen pints of lager on board is quicker than me.'

They stayed outside the dressing room for what must have been an hour, chanting and calling for individual players to come out. Every few minutes, someone would head to the balcony and shake a load of beers over them. One of my all-time favourite days as an England cricketer.

Some of those sprints back to the pavilion could be pretty hairy. On occasion, I arrived back in the dressing room with no sunglasses, shirt hanging off and one shoe. It was nuts. People were getting injured, players bouncing into fans, accidentally nutting each other. Forget cricket skills; the one thing every professional needed to master was the body swerve. It reached the point where a fielding side doomed to defeat would position everyone on the pavilion side in advance of the winning hit. Before the batsman even struck the ball they were gone. Utterly mad, but somehow part of what made it all so brilliant.

Over time, I did make myself into a pretty consistent fielder. I even ran people out. At Christchurch, I positively swooped in at mid-on to throw the stumps down and run out New Zealand's Simon Doull. Actually, I think that's it for run-out anecdotes.

Even the finest fielders of my era would be left drop-jawed by the skill and athleticism of those in the field today. Imagine me and Angus haring round the boundary, leaping over the rope and palming the ball back into the other's hands before landing. Chances are we wouldn't even know we were near the rope. We'd end up chucking it into the crowd for six or back towards the field with no fielder within 30 yards, all the time wondering why no one was cheering.

What's that banner I can see in the crowd?

CHAPTER 17

How Not to Make Friends

'I haven't cleaned my teeth for three months,' Jack Russell once told me, 'because when I'm standing up I want to breathe all over you.'

'Please', I thought as I prepared to bat against Gloucestershire, 'let that be a wind-up and not true.' If it was, Jack could effectively sledge without even saying a word.

It's an odd game, cricket. At one end of the spectrum you have the village green, leather on willow, old Sid in the third XI guiding it down to fine leg where Wilf, temporarily diverted from unwrapping a Werther's Original, scuttles across to field in front of a whitewashed cottage on the boundary. And then at the other, there's a bunch of puce-faced blokes swearing like dockers and threatening to cause grievous bodily harm to one another.

As a young player, I was under the impression you had to sledge; that there was an expectation or responsibility to do it whether you wanted to or not. If you didn't, it could be perceived that you weren't aggressive or willing enough to impose yourself on the opposition. So I did get a bit carried away when I first started. Possibly because I'd also heard so many legendary stories about great putdowns and cutting replies. Not that I was part of that club. I was somewhat lacking in flashes of rapier wit. When I first started, I just told everyone either to f*** off or that I'd shagged their auntie.

Chances are this spindly Londoner with the gob came as a bit of a shock to some of our posher opponents. Hampshire had the likes of David Gower and Mark Nicholas, a lot of well-to-do public-school chaps, and there I'd be shouting, 'Oi! What are you looking at?' and telling everyone I'd got their mum up the duff. Crazy really. I was a left-arm spinner. It wasn't like I could back it up with bouncers or come in later and smash them out of the park.

When a few batters started coming back at me I found it quite unnerving and decided it might be wise to ease off a bit with the verbals. Same when I was batting. The first time I took guard in a first-class match, Worcestershire's David Smith asked, 'Who's this f***ing muppet?' I didn't see that particularly as a sledge. I thought he was saying hello. But nevertheless it was slightly intimidating.

Justin Langer and Matthew Hayden switched the whole narrative of sledging in my last Test at The Oval. Instead of the 11 sledging the two, they turned it the other way round. Coming out to bat, and with the series, as usual, in the bag, they proceeded to tell the England team, 'Come on, you bunch of bastards. Bowl the ball if you f***ing dare.'

This was the time when the Aussies were absolute giants, careering along at four or five an over in Test cricket with a top seven who would walk into any global 11. Throwing the ball in hard occasionally was hardly going to unsettle them.

As I turned to bowl my first delivery to Hayden, I'd barely got into the initial skip of my run-up when he started walking down the pitch at me. Quite naturally I stopped. 'Hang on!' I said. 'You're not meant to do that.'

'I'll do what I want when I want,' he replied, somewhat undiplomatically.

'But I haven't bowled the ball yet.'

'Doesn't matter where or when you bowl it. I can stand where the f*** I want.'

It was like bowling to a Viking. I don't know why he didn't come out in a wolfskin with his face smeared in sacred oils and carrying a double-headed axe. Hayden and his ilk carried themselves in a way that said one thing and one thing only: 'I'm going to make you look like a child and ruin your career. And when I've done that, I'm going to rip off your testicles and feed them to you in an omelette. If you're lucky.'

In all honesty, I didn't like the cut of Hayden and Langer's jib. 'I don't want to bowl. Can someone else bowl? They're being horrible to me.'

Langer got 102 that day and his confidence was such that, later in the innings, as I ran up to bowl, halfway through my core position, he shouted, 'Arm ball or slower ball?' It was the most unexpected thing. I'd never seen a batsman do that. 'What do I do now?' I panicked. 'Do I carry on bowling the delivery I had in mind? Do I try to do something completely different, a little cutter perhaps?' I ended up in a bit of a pickle, which was exactly what Langer had intended, knowing a last-second brain freeze could lead to a nice juicy full toss which he could smack to the boundary. In the end, I stayed with my original plan and managed to get it down the other end unscathed.

I shouldn't have been surprised at Langer's approach. When he was with us at Middlesex, he played an epic innings to win us a game on the last day and the whole time was verbally kicking the bowlers in the teeth.

'F***ing come on! You can't do anything. Wherever you f***ing bowl it, I'm going to f***ing crunch it. You can't get me out. You're not fast enough. You're not good enough. I'm going to hit you so f***ing far.'

He hit the winning runs and actually came off the field laughing. 'I knew I had them when I was on fifty,' he said. 'They were running in with terror in their eyes. They knew that they were going to get smashed all over the place and there was nothing they could do about it.'

'Right, er, great, Langs, well done.'

Sachin was a little more reserved. The first time I bowled against him he was at least polite in telling me he was going to annihilate me. 'Thank you very much, Mr Tufnell,' he told me as I sent down a couple of deliveries which I'd held back a little, 'I'm going to spank you everywhere.'

Brian Lara was so superior, so brilliant, that he didn't need to say a word. He'd just give a little laugh every now and again, especially during that record-breaking 375 in Antigua. He didn't have to explain – I knew exactly what it meant: 'Oh, Phil, you've come back on. Isn't it a lovely day? Perhaps a bit hot. Is that why you look a bit tired? Now, are you going to bowl another one of those slightly slower balls outside the off stump which I'm going to come down and hit back over your head for six? Because if you are, thank you very much.'

I had actually tried to unsettle Brian a little bit until he got to a hundred, trying to get on top of him, to make him feel awkward and uncomfortable at the crease, to assert my will and create drama and points of conflict. But never did I resort to verbals. That could come back and make you look very silly indeed. The other problem with Brian was that he was just a really nice bloke. I always quite liked having a friendly chat with him.

In fact, after his 375, Brian showed how nice he was by spending a penny or two on a little tribute to me. Off the back of that innings, the Trinidad government gave him a beautiful plot of land on which to build his dream home. This place had it all, including a cricket bat-shaped swimming pool. As a thank-you for our part – all 538 balls and 766 minutes of it – in his remarkable feat, next time we were on the island he invited the England team round for a barbecue. We had a few drinks, bit of a dance to a steel band and then he pulled me to one side – 'Tuffers,' he said, 'let me show you round the house.'

He took me on a little tour, and blow me, there it was above the khazi door, a little plaque: 'The Tufnell Toilet'. Thank you, Brian, so much.

It wasn't just Brian; rarely was it a good idea to have a dig at the West Indies. Brian's fellow great, Viv Richards, intimidated not with words but sheer presence. 'Is that it, Phil?' his body language blared. 'Hardly worth me coming out here, really.'

I'd have still had a shout of 'I've shagged your auntie', but the others were adamant. 'Phil, I really don't think that's going to work against Viv.'

And yet on the one occasion where I did confront Viv, he was on his bike in no time. We were playing Glamorgan at Sophia Gardens in a match that looked to be heading for a draw after both sides had posted first innings scores in excess of 500, Glamorgan's 562 for three including a brilliant 224 not out from the man himself. In their second innings, though, I got on a roll, and had seen off the Glamorgan top three before Viv appeared, nonchalant and intimidating as ever. As I skipped in to bowl, he stood back from the wicket, waving his arm as if to say he wasn't ready.

Now I'm not sure quite what possessed me, but I decided, Viv or no Viv, I wasn't having it.

'What? We've all got to wait for you?' I asked him. 'We've all got to play your game?'

The look he gave me could have turned me to ice. I checked I could still move, returned to my mark and came in again. Only this time I stopped.

'Gus,' I shouted, 'would you mind just moving a little bit to your right?'

Viv was staring me straight in the eye. I glared back. Well, in for a penny in for a pound and all that.

As I returned to my mark, Dessie urged me to reconsider my approach. It was, he suggested, the only way I might escape Cardiff with my head still attached to my shoulders. 'He'll punch you,' he kept saying. 'He'll punch you.'

'Right, are we all ready now?' I asked with a flourish. 'Okay, good.'

I ran in, the ball bounced higher than Viv expected, and he gloved a chance to short leg. A golden duck. I resisted giving Viv a send-off but did end up taking eight for 29 as Glamorgan subsided and we won by ten wickets. I was celebrating in the dressing room with the rest of the boys when Dessie tapped me on the shoulder.

'You might have messed up there,' he said.

'How do you mean?' I asked. 'I've just got my best bowling figures ever.'

'Viv wants a word.'

If ever there were four words to send dread into a cricketer's heart, those were the ones.

'What???'

'He's coming to see you.'

I was just scouting round for the nearest drainpipe when in he walked. He gestured to sit down with him.

'Well bowled,' he told me, 'but be careful.'

I didn't know what to say. 'Er, right, okay, Viv. Thanks. I will.'

He got up and left. And as he did so I picked my heart and several other bodily organs off the floor.

Dessie himself once sledged me and Gus three months before a game even started. All three of us were just packing up after the last county match of the season when Dessie, anticipating our reunion for the imminent Test series in the Caribbean, told us, 'Oh, by the way I'll be telling our quicks not to bother bowling at the stumps for the first three overs but to aim at your head or, failing that, to try and break your arm.' That was a sledge when not only weren't we actually playing the game, we weren't even in the appointed country. And those quicks did it, too. I was running away to square leg, showing all three stumps for them to hit and get it over with. But still they kept following me.

'Will you please just bowl at the stumps? Look, there they are. Just hit them, will you?'

When Curtly and Courtney played for Northamptonshire or Gloucestershire, they just ran in and got you out. When you were playing for England, they tried to intimidate you first. Rarely was their aggression accompanied by sledging. They didn't need to bother. They let the ball do all the talking. That little red thing was basically telling you to f*** off every time it whizzed past your nose. Occasionally, though, you'd hear

Courtney tell Curtly to 'perform the operation'. Now that truly was terrifying.

The Aussies weren't quite so selective. They were always aggressive, always sledged – it was as natural as breathing to them. Although with me it was more piss-taking.

'Oh, f***ing hell, Tuffers. For f***'s sake, just get out, let everyone else get on with it.'

I was reassured to find I got the same treatment as everyone else when Warne bowled. The ball would zip past the outside edge. 'Warney,' the close-in fielders would say, 'can you tell him which way it's going to turn before you bowl it?' Less abuse, more, 'The bloke doesn't know what he's doing. He simply doesn't know what he's doing.'

Those fielders would try to shatter confidence and build confusion. 'Oh, that was the other one,' they'd say as the ball popped into Ian Healy's gloves. 'He couldn't pick that either.' And I'd be thinking, "Hold on a minute, was that the other one? I thought the one before was the other one."

One time I was batting, they told Warney, 'Give him the zooter!'

'Zooter?' I thought. 'What's the zooter?'

He bowled what I thought was just a normal leg spinner and they all applauded. 'Great zooter, Warney!' In the end I'd just lunge forward with my eyes closed and hope for the best.

All teams would get the men round the bat chirping if there was a newcomer on the other side. It was natural to zoom in and try to get in their faces. 'Oh, you're looking a bit worried. Is it your first time?'

Or, if it was someone enjoying a recall – 'Hang on! You're in the side again? When will they learn?' Sometimes it's more effective to remind a bloke of his average than shout and swear at him.

Another tactic is to talk about the batsman rather than to him. 'Blimey, I can't believe how lucky this bloke is still to be in the team. If he messes up this time, that'll surely be the end of him.'

If we were playing India or Sri Lanka and I was batting, I didn't particularly know what the close fielders were talking about, but then I'd pick up the odd word – 'average', 'rubbish', 'worse than Devon Malcolm' – amidst the chatter. Also, while I might not have had a great knowledge of the world's languages, I always knew all the swear words in the jar.

Occasionally, the Aussies would try to up the ante. 'Let's keep him out here for a couple of overs and smash him up a bit. Let's break a rib.' I always found that a little more intimidating than somebody calling me a wanker and saying that I can't bat very well. A threat of harm felt slightly more real. It could actually happen. Everything else was just nonsense.

'I shagged your sister.'

'You didn't, though, did you?'

'Come on, let's sort it out, here and now.'

'Shut up, mate – you're not going to have a fight in front of ninety thousand people at the MCG any more than I am.'

A lot of it was laughable, about as real as the wrestling they used to have on *World of Sport*.

'Come on! Come on!'

'What, shall we have a roll around on the grass at Lord's in front of the members? I don't really think that's likely to happen.' If it had been, Kent Walton would have been up in the commentary box rather than Richie Benaud.

After a while, it all becomes a bit tired and predictable. Same lines, same put-downs, same sneers. It becomes less cricket match and more Prime Minister's Questions. That's why I always found the best sledges to be the ones nobody saw coming. One time in a county game, for example, we kept saying how this one batsman's jumper really smelt.

'Can't you smell that?' we kept asking him. 'Honestly, can't you smell that?'

'It's not me. It's not me,' he kept saying, sniffing at it.

'Are you sure? I really do think it's your jumper.' It drove the poor bloke round the bend.

Worth remembering, too, that not everyone is good at sledging, or it might simply not be part of your personality. In that case, doing it because you think you should is wrong. Angus Fraser could be grumpy, but his actions were always better than his chat. Andy Caddick, too, would say a few words but it just never came across as being authentic. Sometimes it's better just to have a rant and rave at nobody in particular, get it out of your system, than feel like you have to come up with the wittiest repartee ever. More than anything, you have to do what's needed to keep yourself in the right mental space – that has to come before mouthing off at the batsman.

I found myself mentally strengthened by getting into a fight. It focused me, made me scrap every inch to get the batsman out. Same as when Dean Jones smacked the ball back at me and hit me on the ankle with the third ball of my first over in Test cricket. Suddenly, after being in a daze from the magnitude of the experience, I was wide, wide awake. A bit of pain on a cricket pitch isn't a bad thing sometimes. It's something you can bite on, the fastest way to get into your work, and a bit of confrontation is the same.

They say the only thing worse than being talked out is not being talked about. As a bowler, the cricketing version of that is when it all goes quiet and you have a horrible feeling that the batsman, rather than seeing you off, is trying to keep you on.

Maybe he's played inside the line of one outside off stump, so it looks like you've got him in trouble, when actually he just wants you to keep bowling and knock you around for four an over.

'Is he milking me here?' is not a question any bowler wants to ask himself, but it's something you have to keep at the back of your mind.

'Why did he hit that ball for four and not the exact same delivery I bowled in the last over?' That's slightly disconcerting, but on the other hand a batsman underestimating you will always be in your favour. The power is in your hands because you can use their arrogance to draw them into a false shot.

Nevertheless, actions that constituted a personal attack on my performance could sting. Once or twice when I was fielding against Australia the batsman would play it in my direction and then call 'Tuffers!' to his partner to indicate there was a single where perhaps there might not otherwise have been. That doesn't make you feel great, and obviously in a case like that you are being humiliated in front of your team.

Like most sports, there is a delineation between what happens on the pitch and off it. But the intensity of Test cricket would sometimes stay with me to the extent that I found it difficult to socialise with the opposition. Players would head off into the other team's dressing room but quite often I'd hang back.

'Hang on,' I'd think, 'your batsmen have been trying to smash me out of the ground and your bowlers have been trying to knock my head off while calling me every name under the sun. Pardon me if I find it a little difficult to warm to you over half a lager.'

I've never got my head round the rugby boys. The other team knock seven bells out of them, stamp all over their face, rake them in the scrum, give them a right-hander when no one's looking, rip their testicles off, and then as soon as they're back in the clubhouse it's 'Hello, mate, fancy a beer?' If that was me, I know what my reaction would be – 'You're joking, right?'

For me, Test cricket meant putting yourself in a bubble for five days, during which time you bit, scratched and kicked to try to win the game. Once that game was done, the last thing I wanted to do was spend some more time with Mark and Steve Waugh. 'Where are you, boys? Come on, I really want to see you!' I wanted to go away, chill out and be with my crowd.

When I started out in the England team, the old guard all knew the opposition as mates. Players on both sides would be giving each other slaps on the back and asking, 'How's it going, mate?' I didn't feel so comfortable raising a glass to someone out to destroy my fledgling career. Not only that, but they were all such pals it never felt like us versus them. If someone got a hundred, everyone had a beer afterwards and said, 'Well played!' Same if someone got a five-for. I wanted it a little bit less friendly. I needed an edge to perform to my potential. When Nasser, one of my generation, came in as skipper, he agreed – 'We don't speak to them.'

Nasser would never have time anyway. He was too busy fighting fires. I looked at him as captain and thought how glad I was just to be the humble spinner. Although sometimes, which took even me by surprise, there'd be the occasional twinge of envy.

CHAPTER 18

How Not to Be a Captain

Towards the end of my playing career I put myself forward as a candidate to take over the captaincy of Middlesex.

I'll just give you a moment to get back on your chair.

I understand your surprise – possibly the most fined cricketer in the history of world sport being put in charge of a cricket team. But, yes, I did fancy a go and I did apply, and not just because the skipper earned more money and got a better sponsored car and a nicer hotel room when we were on the road. Not that it had escaped my attention that the skipper earned more money and got a better sponsored car and a nicer hotel room when we were on the road.

I was quite serious about it. People always need new challenges and while, for most of my career, challenges, mostly of my own making, weren't something I was lacking, I had a desire to test myself in a more legitimate way.

At the turn of the century, Middlesex was going through a period of change. The club needed a new captain and a few of the chaps had thrown their hats in the ring. At that point I'd been playing county cricket for more than a decade, almost deserving of that awful word 'stalwart', and did actually know a fair bit about the game, certainly more than most people gave me credit for.

I approached Don Bennett, now on the committee. 'Don,' I told him, 'I've given this a lot of thought and I'd like to put my name forward for consideration for the captain's job.' When he'd finished spitting out his coffee, he said, 'Okay, Phil. Thank you very much for your application.'

He looked at me in a strange way, as if he'd been possessed. Having watched *24 Hours in A&E*, I now know this to be a consequence of shock.

The full horror of what I had proposed dawned on him about half an hour later. Still sweating slightly, he took me to one side. 'Phil,' he said, 'I've given it some thought and I reckon captaincy might not be for you.'

He tried his best to word the rejection nicely. 'I'm very pleased that you want to further your role, but I think you've got enough on your plate as a senior player. It's very hard for a bowler to be a captain. Best if you concentrate on taking wickets.'

Sadly, I was oblivious to Don's subtlety. 'Well, Don,' I carried on, 'I appreciate all that, but I still fancy having a go.'

It was time for simple brutality.

'Phil,' he said, 'no.'

The job went to the bowler Angus Fraser.

While my application may have seemed like madness, in fairness to myself I wasn't the only one who believed I might possess leadership qualities. We'd had a team-bonding week-end at a manor house in the Buckinghamshire countryside. Thankfully, this was more cerebral than the team-bonding exercises that soon became all the rage – freezing your nuts off in the middle of a Bavarian forest, donning full combat gear to run up a mountain, or beating the living crap out of one another in boxing gloves before skinning a hog.

Will Carling, not long retired from his brilliant triple Grand Slam-winning rugby career, was in charge of the operation which involved us being shown videos of various desperate scenarios – stranded on a sinking ship, coming face to face with an angry bear, arriving too late for the hotel bar – and asked to come up with solutions. We then went outside for a practical test. Those who have been on corporate events like this will know the kind of thing – build a raft out of the items provided: a toothpick, a packet of digestives and a dog. I think in our case it was a barrel and three planks, all different sizes. The point of all this, apparently, was to discover which of us was the natural leader of the group, the one who possessed all the necessary qualities to take us into battle on the field. I got myself involved. Who knew when raft-building skills might come in handy? Global warming was already very much a thing and Lord's was only a mile or so from the Thames.

I enjoyed the weekend a lot more than I thought I would – initially I had tried to get out of it by booking a dental appointment – but thought no more about it until years later when Will was a guest on *A Question of Sport*. We got chatting and the subject of the bonding event cropped up. I asked him what he thought of my effort.

'Did they not tell you?' Will replied. 'You came out very well. In fact, I recommended to Middlesex that they should make you captain.'

I had been the victim of a cover-up. The bastards. Think of what might have been.

Actually, Don was probably right. When you're in the ranks,

captaincy looks so straightforward. Everyone knows where to go, who should be doing what – how hard can it be? But then comes the day when someone shoves the Duckworth Lewis calculation sheets in your hand. Even thinking about that I can feel a sharp migraine coming on.

Actually, it wasn't just Will who looked at me and thought 'Leader'. Nasser once said that had I not been 'such a lunatic' (thanks, Nass) I'd have made a good vice-captain because I'd accrued such immense knowledge of people and the game. I thought that was a good call. I have always been a good people reader. As a spin bowler, especially on a flat pitch, you have to work players out a little bit. It's pretty much all you've got. I could also have bridged the gap between the older players, the hierarchy, and the younger ones coming through.

I was the 547th cricketer to be capped by England. By the time I finished at The Oval in 2001, that number had risen to 609. We shouldn't have been sponsored by Tetley Bitter, but by a revolving door manufacturer. Number 591 was Andrew Flintoff, coming into the England set-up three years before the end of my international career. It was interesting to see how he fared early on in that England dressing room. Like so many others before him, he didn't really know how to act. He was a naturally larger-than-life character but didn't know where he fitted in. Thankfully, by the time Fred arrived there were people, like myself, who understood exactly how he felt and would try to welcome a new arrival, even if it wasn't exactly subtle – 'Come on, let's go out for a beer.' The fact that in the past I'd seen people in the England dressing room not make others feel welcome always amazed me. Surely the first question anyone should ask themselves in a situation of that kind is 'How would I feel?' Fred was actually quite shy, and his way out of that was to do something a bit daft. He didn't know how else to feel comfortable in that environment. Should it really have been like that? Should players feel the need to wear a mask?

I would have liked to have got my teeth into that intermediary role, to try to get the best out of myself as well as others, be it for club or country, but I was never encouraged. Past misdemeanours, I expect, weighed heavily.

The good news was that, as England skipper, Nasser brought in a culture change where, instead of someone standing over us with a big stick, we were slowly coaxed into wanting to be part of something. He made us hard to beat, a little more feisty. His attitude to a setback was not a wholesale clear-out. It was regroup and push forward with the plan. Nasser had come into the England set-up around the same time as me, part of a new intake of England batsmen such as Thorpe, Ramps and one or two others. I tended to gravitate towards them as we were the up-and-coming youngsters and had progressed through the age groups together. Because of that closeness, Nasser knew how to handle me a bit when he became captain and could see things from my viewpoint. He tried to fight my cause when Duncan Fletcher, who saw me as coming from the dark side, came in as coach.

I always got on well with Nasser, and Athers, too. Our counties – Middlesex, Essex and Lancashire – were a force and so we had lots of tussles. On and off the field we respected each other, although I still apologise to them every time I see them for the litany of issues I caused them as captains.

'Look, lads, just before we start – sorry.'

It wasn't just them. I've had cause to say sorry to all my captains and most of my coaches at one time or another. No matter what they thought deep down, none of them went so far as to refuse to accept my apology. Generally, with the odd notable exception, they would say things like, 'Oh, Tuffers, don't worry about it. We love you for what you are, never a dull moment.' And then they'd wander off and you'd hear them mutter to themselves – 'Twat.'

Nass and Athers always say, 'There's no need to apologise,' but I know that for sure I caused them a headache a few times. And yet they never caused me one back. They were captains who tried to work out how to get the best out of players, to treat them as individuals, and give them a bit of a run in the side to make them feel more comfortable.

Having known them so long, I saw what the England captaincy did to them, taking them from good lads and great cricketers who loved playing and enjoyed life to people whose features became awash with stresses and strains. It was as if they were carrying a sackful of bricks on their back. Watching that happen in front of me made me realise there was a lot more to the job than anyone on the outside could ever possibly understand. I tried, in my own little way, to help. Perhaps explaining Nasser's vice-captaincy comment, he credits me with being open, honest and helpful around the younger players while with Athers I'd discuss tactics and try not to keep him awake too many nights on tour, certainly no more than 75 per cent. Whatever happened, I never went out of my way to be awkward.

For their part, they went through that strange and instant transition of going from everybody's mate to captain, with the distance needed to make it work. If you want to command respect, expect people to follow your lead, then you can't be swinging from the chandelier at 3 a.m. Whereas nowadays that transition is not so marked – players are less wedded to the social side of the game – back then it was a noticeable shift. In those days it was, 'Hold on a minute. Yesterday you were with us in the pub having a beer and a laugh, and now you're telling us to pack that in and go and have a net? You've changed!'

Sometimes a captain would have to lay down a marker. There was an incident with Nasser in Port Elizabeth where I'd exited the nets a little earlier than perhaps I should – about an hour and 50 minutes earlier to be precise.

'Where the f*** is Tufnell?'

'He's gone, skip. Picked up his stuff and went.'

'What? Get him back here now!'

I duly returned and was given a dressing-down in front of the lads. That was definitely a case of letting everyone know that the relationship between himself and the team had changed. Privately, he'd have said it differently – 'Look, Phil, I've let you off the last five times, but this time you're going to have to come back and do a bit more. You are not paid to sit in the dressing room drinking Fanta.'

The bigger picture was that Athers and Nass were trying to build bridges between management and players. In the old days it was all about issuing fines and bollockings and making people feel about an inch tall. They saw that a better way was man-management, to encourage inclusiveness in targets and goals. With me that meant reiterating how the time could come when the two or three extra runs I made because of improving my batting would win us a Test. Okay, nets could be a pain in the arse but they were also a chance to help out the team.

Of course, the bigger picture tends to be obscured by results. When we lost against New Zealand in 1999 and dropped to the bottom of the Test rankings, we were booed off the pitch. There was even talk of the stumps being burned to mark a low point comparable only to the first loss to Australia on English soil in

1882. A little bit harsh, and, anyway, who was to judge? As far as I know, only Geoffrey Boycott was present at both games.

As I walked off the Oval pitch that day after another horrific collapse, and sat in a silent dressing room taking off my pads, I felt genuinely upset, especially for Nasser, who I knew behind the scenes was working so hard to turn the situation around. At that point an official from the ECB, slightly dishevelled, possibly after being pelted with tomatoes, appeared and invited Nasser to accompany him to the presentation ceremony. The condemned man – 'Take him down!'

'Oh, f***,' muttered Nasser and staggered out of the door. Thirty seconds later, we heard an avalanche of boos. And then Nasser came back, really quite shaken. England had been knocked out of that summer's home World Cup before the official song had been released and had now been beaten in a four-Test series by New Zealand. Nasser would soon be joined by new England coach Duncan Fletcher. At that point, however, he was trying to turn the drifting oil tanker of English cricket around on his own.

Few series better epitomised how the England team was viewed by the public at that time. We had basically become a Class A drug. People wanted us barred from society but at the same time couldn't leave us alone. They would come in their droves, from miles around, when England were playing because it was like mainlining hallucinogenic substances. Spectators never knew whether they'd be up, down, or in an entirely different universe. It was worth the ticket price to save on the pills.

There were never any calm waters playing for England. I'd kick the ball to mid-on and be run out backing up; Thorpe would drop a catch and kick the ball for four; the ball would hit the spare helmet and the five penalty runs win the match for the opposition. There was always something happening, never a nice easy few days where everything rattled along smoothly. It was either magnificent and the whole crowd were up and celebrating, or it was a disaster and that same crowd was hurling small items of Tupperware from the boundary. I compare it to playing golf with your mates. You might hit the odd good shot, but then there's those other ones – the tee-shot that ricochets into someone's garden and kills their chicken, the missed putt from two inches, the one that lodges in the club secretary's wig. That was exactly what playing cricket for England was like. We had all the gear, all the right equipment, we'd play a couple of good shots, and then someone would fall flat on their arse. Laugh or cry? It's up to you.

Even if, against the odds, we did win a Test, chances are there'd be no opportunity to celebrate. At home, we'd have a Benson & Hedges Cup zonal game or some such the next day. On tour, the schedule meant we were out of the ground and straight onto a plane.

Nasser, for one, felt it was important to sit back and celebrate an achievement, which is exactly what happened when we won the fifth Test against South Africa at Centurion in 2000, a game which would become notorious when it was discovered that Proteas captain Hansie Cronje had taken a £5,000 bribe in exchange for ensuring a result. Afterwards, we all had a drink and were chatting, congratulating one another, when our Welsh contingent, Dean Conway and Robert Croft, appeared holding a silver platter with a big cloth over the top. We were all sitting there wondering what the hell was going on when they lifted the gingham and revealed to all a sheep's head, beautifully coiffured, as if it had spent some time in a salon and been blow-dried before it met its maker. Even the little tongue that was hanging out of its mouth was spotless. No two ways about it: what we had here was a very attractive sheep. Not a bit of hay on it. As reward for having won the match, we were informed, we all had to kiss the sheep. Some boys gave it a peck, others gave it a lingering kiss, and one or two had to be dragged off.

I couldn't help but think it was a bit weird. Fair enough, give someone the bumps on their birthday, but don't ask me to French-kiss a sheep. I didn't know where this sudden development in victory celebrations might lead. This was one match; what if we'd won the series? Were we expected to sacrifice goats out the back of the pavilion?

There's another thing I remember about that match – Nasser's trouble with mathematics. I was charged with running Crone's offer out to the skipper in the field.

'They're offering us 250 in seventy-six overs,' I told him.

Nasser looked a little shocked. 'No,' he said, 'tell him I'm not accepting anything more than 270 in fifty.' Now numbers aren't my forte – I'm happy to watch an episode of *Countdown* but the numbers round leaves me cold – but even I could see Nasser had got the bartering the wrong way round. I don't know how his house is for rugs, but he'd have been awful in a souk.

'No,' I told him. 'Look, you've actually just asked for more runs in less overs.'

Eventually – possibly an abacus was brought out – he agreed.

Athers knew more than anyone how Nasser must have felt as he stepped out in front of that unforgiving crowd at The Oval. He'd been in that position more than a few times himself. Sandwiched between the players on one side and outdated administrators on the other, Athers was wheeled out in front of the press for every conceivable reason. Win, lose or draw, everything was down to him to explain – team selections, preparation, sandwich fillings, whether we drank PG Tips or Typhoo.

In football, there were always people to dissipate that pressure. In cricket, if the coach to the ground was late turning up, chances are it would be down to Athers to sort out. England failed again and again to take the pressure off the captain, which then restricted their ability to be as proactive and close to the players as they'd surely have liked.

Being a decent sort of chap, I was always keen to provide a momentary diversion from the weight Athers carried in the captain's role. On one particular occasion in New Zealand, a few of us, Athers not included, hired a fishing boat. I didn't fish but it sounded a laugh. It was turning into a great day out – we'd caught nothing, stank of diesel, were a bit pissed and felt sick – when out of nowhere Alan Mullally snag-hooked quite a serious shark, six foot long, slim, with a proper big fin on it. If I'd been a shark I'd have definitely fancied it. Somehow we got the beast in the boat. It was slapping around, careering all over the place, not having any of it. Instantly I was reminded of Dennis Wise.

Initially we were going to throw it back, but Mullally had other ideas. 'Tell you what,' he said, cogs well lubricated by Castlemaine XXXX, 'why don't we take it back to the hotel and put it in Athers' bed?'

Well, the rest of us thought this was an absolute genius idea. We got back to shore, wrapped the shark in an old bit of tarpaulin and hauled it to the boot of the motor. We parked by the back door of the hotel and nervously heaved our quarry from the car. One of us then secured Athers' room key from reception while the rest shuffled into the laundry lift and took our guest up three floors.

Carefully we pulled back Athers' duvet, placing his copy of *The Complete Works of Jane Austen* on the bedside table, deposited his new bedmate, and then arranged everything so that it looked as if nothing had happened.

Not long after, we bumped into Athers in the downstairs bar. A keen fisherman himself, he was interested to know if we'd landed anything.

'Oh no, Athers. Nothing. Absolutely useless, the lot of us.'

We were all then sitting there tapping our fingers waiting for Athers to retire for the night. Eventually, the moment came – 'Right, lads, I'm calling it a day.'

He headed for his room with us following behind, tiptoeing, peeping round walls, desperate not to miss the big moment.

He shut his door. There followed 30 seconds of quiet. Then all of a sudden, 'F********k!'

We appeared at the door. 'Blimey, Ath – you all right? What on earth's the matter?'

'There's a shark in my bed!'

'Don't be silly. A shark? Have you gone mad?'

'No. There's a six-foot shark in my bed.'

'Come on, Ath, calm down. Let's have a look. What is it, a spider or something?'

While for some captains a shark in the bed would have been a hanging offence, Athers was more than able to take a joke. He was an open-minded chap, with caring, compassion and under-standing. He knew not everyone was Cambridge-educated, not everyone preferred *University Challenge* to *Going for Gold*. While there would always be some who looked at me and said, 'He's got an earring – he should never play for England,' Athers could see the short-sightedness of such a point of view. His attitude was, 'Well, hang on – it's hardly the end of the world.'

The captain with whom there was an unbridgeable distance was Graham Gooch. The complete opposite of Gatt, who taught me a lot, liked to laugh as much as anyone, and was great company, full of funny stories, Gooch never seemed to want to get to know me. It was as if he was on one wavelength and I was on another, which always amazed me because Embers, a big mate of Gooch's, always said he was a great laugh. This is a man, after all, who used to turn up at Essex on his Lambretta in the early days.

As he got older, though, it seemed as if he never really wanted to let anyone know what he was like under the skin. He was either running, batting, or in his room. I don't know whether it was a generational thing, but he never sat down with me and had that fatherly captaincy chat that happens in cricket. The result was that all too often around him I felt awkward, shy and stupid. Myself and Graham get on fine now, but back then there was a chasm between us. He only ever really spoke to me to fine me. Even when I got six for 25 on my home debut against West Indies, there was no 'Well done, mate'. I'm sure inside he was happy, but sometimes it doesn't hurt to show a bit of emotion.

Thankfully, Beefy made up for it. 'Well bowled, Tuffers. That's the first time I've ever drawn a series with these.' It was lovely and meant a lot. Beefy, too, is a hard man, traditional in the way he handles his emotions, but he always knew the value of a positive word and a pat on the back.

To be fair, certainly in Australia in 1990–91 I suspect the captaincy wore Gooch out a little. He was dealing with a number of big players coming to the end of their careers and instead of being able to concentrate on putting his pads on and going into the fray against some of the greatest bowlers of all time, he must have felt the burden of fighting so many little battles.

Gooch was especially resentful of Gower's perceived inability to be a shining example for the younger players in the group. But it wasn't all Gower. There were some proper mischief-makers on that tour – 'Can you just give me a bit of an easier ride, lads?' I, of course, got up to a few tricks myself. But I was at the start of my career not the end.

The conundrum Gooch faced, as did many other captains, managers, selectors and coaches down the years, was that I could be a matchwinner, change a game. While I might have seemed high-maintenance, no one could ever accuse me of not bowling for them.

I look at later captains – Andrew Strauss, Alastair Cook, Joe Root, Eoin Morgan – and see a different relationship with players that comes with the lifting of responsibilities elsewhere. Such captains were allowed to be themselves, exhibiting a kind of reassuring level-headedness that I've always liked to be around. Sounds mad, but my fellow team captain Matt Dawson used to be like that on *A Question of Sport*. I could get a little anxious sat in the green room waiting for the recording to start, panicking that I was feeling a bit rough and hadn't done any preparation, at which point Daws would say, 'Look, that's absolutely fine. It doesn't matter. We're just having a bit of fun. It always works out great.' And suddenly I'd feel a whole lot better about the whole thing. I'd instantly relax. I love people like that. I can get twitchy about little things, like not having my keys to hand. Dawn's another who can instantly put my mind at rest, show me that a train being five minutes late is hardly life or death.

I am grateful that Athers and Nasser somehow found time amidst the endless storms that peppered their captaincies to work with me and give me at least some of what I needed. Once again, guys, for those occasional forks of lightning I provided, I really am very sorry.

CHAPTER 19

How Not to Be a Celebrity

'Come on, you miserable bastards – what's wrong with you?'

I'd been invited to a huge celebration at the Grosvenor House Hotel in London to mark Ian Botham's knighthood. It was a bit like *This Is Your Life*, as the great and good of sport, entertainment and industry were invited on stage in twos and threes to talk about the cricketing behemoth and the times they'd shared. Alongside Ryder Cup-winning golfer Sam Torrance, I was one of the last ones up. I was feeling unusually nervous, a definite case of 'What the f*** am I doing here?', and in an attempt to calm myself had been going pretty heavily at the wine on our table. Standing backstage, though, I was still panicking inside, made even worse when I saw Eric Clapton hanging around. It was a perfect storm of drunkenness, fear and being totally starstruck. All I wanted to do was go and have a little sit down but instead I had the same few words in my head going round and round.

'I don't want to mess it up. I really mustn't mess it up.'

I messed it up.

My time came, I walked out in front of this throng of incredible people – and froze. Sam said his little bit and I just sat there staring into space with my tongue hanging out.

'Phil, anything to say?' asked Sam. He looked over to me and saw immediately that even if I could speak what might come out of my mouth was unlikely to make sense. I had just about managed to slur, 'He's a good lad', when a hand alighted on my shoulder and I was escorted off stage and back to my table. I was mortified by what had happened. 'Dawn,' I said, 'give us a glass of red wine. I've just made a right twat of myself up there.' No sooner had I drained the third glass than I heard the unmistakeable strains of 'Layla', perhaps Clapton's greatest ever song. He was only up there performing on stage. Well, suddenly I'd never felt more alive.

'That's Eric Clapton!' I told everyone on our table, which happened to include Athers. 'That's Eric f***ing Clapton!'

I looked around the faces at the dinner tables, all sitting there shovelling in the prawn cocktails. I couldn't believe it. The most excitement I could see was a bit of light clapping. Why was no one getting up and dancing? I staggered to my feet. 'Come on, everyone!' I beckoned to the rest of my table. 'It's f***ing Eric Clapton.' I swerved elegantly onto the dance floor and right up to the front, where I spotted a microphone on the stage. If there was one thing I didn't need to be at that particular moment, it was amplified. I grabbed it, and beating Eric, one of the biggest superstars in global music, to it, started screeching, 'Layla!' while doing the 'dow – dow, dow – dow, dow, dow!' riff on an air guitar.

Still no one joined me. I can't imagine why. And so I issued an invite. 'Come on, what's wrong with you? It's Eric Clapton! It's Eric f***ing Clapton!' Think Delia Smith's infamous half-time encouragement to the crowd at Norwich – 'Come on! Let's be having you! Where are you?' – only a million times worse.

It was as I tried to claw myself onto the stage – I'm sure in itself an unedifying sight – that I was hauled back to my seat where, not without justification, Dawn gave me the biggest bollocking of my life, which in itself is saying something. We left soon afterwards. I can only guess what Athers was thinking – 'Ah, Tuffers! Nothing ever changes.'

Beefy didn't speak to me for about a month. Even now the embarrassment sends chills down my spine.

I'm not a great musician myself, although I am an accomplished trianglist, once called upon to display my skills at the Royal Albert Hall for the Professional Cricketers' Association dinner. There were some high-profile faces on stage, including my old England colleague Mark Butcher, a really talented songwriter and guitarist. I was confused to see some bloke with a fez among this lot. I was just thinking, 'Who the bloody hell is that?' when someone explained it was the best percussion player on the planet. He would be overseeing my stint on the steel.

So there I was, ready to play my one note, while the fella in the fez was running all over the place, banging things and sweating. Eventually, my big moment came, sadly at a point where I had allowed my attention to wander for a second. I was only brought back to the matter in hand by him frantically nodding at me and whispering – 'Phil! Now!' Too late. The rest of the band was poised for a final frantic crescendo and not even the man in the fez could hold back the tide. When finally I delivered my much-anticipated 'Ding!', it was lost in the roar of numerous guitars and drums. I had one job. I so wanted to put my signature on this great musical event. I wanted to own the moment. I failed. Utterly.

I don't know what it is about music royalty that makes me behave in an odd and unpredictable manner. I even encountered the Bee Gees once. Not all of them, just the big hairy one, Barry. It was before a game for Bunbury's, the charity cricket team. I was having a quick kip in the dressing room when in he walked. Sitting bolt upright in shock, my immediate reaction was to give him a quick rendition of 'Stayin' Alive'. Something about his facial expression told me he would have preferred a quick hello. He left and I went back to sleep.

When you become quite well known, like after I won *I'm a Celebrity*, you get invited to all sorts of weird and wonderful things. At first, the temptation is to go to everything. It's a night out and free drink. Over time, though, you realise that not everything is for you. I was, for instance, invited to the opera, but then I couldn't understand what they were singing. And they only did champagne in the bar. Not a pint of lager in sight. The Royal Ballet was the same. I've seen too many blokes in their Y-fronts to want to look at even more in tights.

You tend to then limit yourself a little bit and go to things that matter, like the charity do for the Children's Trust I attended at the Roundhouse in Chalk Farm. I was just sitting down when I heard 'Hello, Tuffers!' from behind. I didn't need even a nano-second to recognise the voice. Prince William had come along to deliver a speech. I wasn't sure of the correct way to address the second in line to the throne so after giving it some brief thought I settled for the old standby – 'Hello, mate.'

What was I thinking? Hello, mate? Hello, mate? This bloke was two heartbeats away from being the king. *Hello, mate?* I'm not sure that's how former England left-arm spinners addressed Queen Victoria. I was just thinking I'd done for my chances the next time the gongs were handed out, and wondering why he wasn't making the 'Kill!' sign to his security guard, when he continued. 'Just wanted to say I love *A Question of Sport.*'

I've met his grandma, too, introduced on the outfield at Lord's a couple of times.

'What do you do?' she asked me.

'Non-turning left-arm spinner, ma'am. And I don't bat very well. Not a particularly good fielder either, now I think about it. Not very keen on the hard ball, Your Majesty. Have you ever played with a tennis ball? Anyway, nice to meet you.'

Thinking back, she didn't say much. She didn't really get a chance.

I met Prince Philip when Middlesex won the county championship. Everyone in the team had got dressed up – blazers, ties, freshly buffed brogues, trousers de-fluffed and ironed, for the do at the Palace. And then there was me, with all the above apart from my long hair, earring and pair of Pierre Cardin white powder cut-out slippers.

'Very nice shoes,' the duke commented. 'Can you tell me where you got them?' He didn't do that with anyone else's shoes, so what does that tell you? I expect he had a footman order a pair immediately. It was a lovely do. Butlers, food on trays, Wagon Wheels. I tried to nick an ashtray, but they told me to put it back.

Linda Lusardi was my teenage pin-up. I always used to pick up a paper on my way to Dad's factory and there she'd be – in the paper, not at Dad's factory. Eventually our worlds collided at a masquerade ball. I let it be known that I'd had the odd poster of her on my wall as a teenager. I was tactful. I didn't just blurt it out.

Perhaps the most famous bedroom wall poster at that time was the blonde tennis player scratching her left buttock, possibly a midge bite. I must admit I always thought the woman in the photo was Sue Barker – you couldn't see her face as she was facing the net. The first time I went on *A Question of Sport* as a contestant I took the opportunity to ask Sue, the programme's host, whether it really was her. She responded that I was far from the first person to have made that assumption and were she to have received a pound for every time she'd been asked she'd be a very rich woman indeed.

She wasn't my only point of confusion across 13 years as a captain on the series. We would film several episodes a day, and all the coming and going of contestants could leave my head spinning. I expect I'm one of the few people who, while I was sat in make-up, greeted a multi-Olympic medal-winning rower with the words, 'Excuse me, mate, couldn't get me a cup of tea, could you?' As he walked off, an ashen Dawn said, 'You do know who that was, don't you?' I thought he was one of the staff on the show. I could just imagine him chuntering in the green room – 'All those years of graft and when I finally get on *A Question of Sport* Phil asks me to go and get a cup of tea and a packet of fags.'

Maybe I wouldn't have got the *A Question of Sport* gig had I not won *I'm a Celebrity*, a show which probably came my way because I was a bit of an unorthodox cricketer. People think being on *I'm a Celebrity* can be unpleasant. Actually, it's a breeze – basically a fortnight sat on a log with your legs out. Even so, when I was asked to be a Covid reserve for the 2020 show, decamped from Australia's Gold Coast to a castle in Wales, I thought being shacked up in an empty house in the Principality for a couple of weeks in December on the off chance of appearing might be a bit odd. Actually, I couldn't have been more wrong. It was bloody lovely. In fact, the longer it went on, the more I was hoping I wouldn't be needed. Me and Dawn were put in this lovely gaff with its own gym, while the production team made sure we had regular food deliveries. They'd ask for our list of stuff. Dawn would be going, 'Well, we need low-fat yoghurt, blueberry juice, lean chicken breasts, fruit and vegetables,' and I'd be chipping in, 'Twelve bottles of Sauvignon Blanc, one of vodka, and four hundred Benson & Hedges.'

We had a security detail outside the house. I'd look out of the window occasionally and there he'd be doing his check of the perimeter. Inevitably, Dawn started feeling sorry for him and would make him bacon sandwiches and run the coffees in and out. I was worried about where this might end up.

'Look, it's not the way it works,' I said. 'He's got his own stuff. He's quite happy.'

Sure enough, one night it was really blowing a gale. We were there in this massive five-bedroom house while he was sat in his car. 'Right,' she said, 'I'm not having this. Go and get him. He can sleep in the spare room.'

I couldn't believe what I was hearing. 'He's the security man. It's his job. He's meant to be outside. I mean, fine, leave him a cup of tea on the wall. But he can't be in here topping and tailing with us.'

He stayed in his car. Possibly the showrunners dropped an ostrich anus round. That's the thing with *I'm a Celebrity* – the food never quite matched *Test Match Special*.

CHAPTER 20

How Not to Ruin *TMS*

Summer 2019, and it's a beautiful sunny Sunday at Tufnell Towers. I haven't gone to Headingley with *TMS* for the third Ashes Test – not for the first time in my life I haven't been selected to perform at the white rose citadel – so me and Dawn have decided to have a barbecue and listen to *TMS*. I'm in the outdoor kitchen, pottering about with the radio on, while various guests are wandering in and out of the French doors keeping an eye on events on the telly. Still needing another 73 to win, Ben Stokes is being joined by England's last man – the bespectacled Jack Leach.

'That's it,' I say. 'It's done.'

But then, as the afternoon progresses, things start getting interesting. In fact, they get more than interesting, to the point where those mad old cricketing superstitions start to rear their heads. As Stokes bears down on a very unlikely target, everyone packs into the living room and is told to stay exactly where they are.

'But I want to play on the trampoline.'

'It'll have to wait, poppet, this is serious.'

Through the sound of crying, the throng, laden with burgers, salad and lagers, watch excitedly while listening to the *TMS* commentary. Aggers is there, naturally, as are Alastair Cook and Glenn McGrath. There is something very special about radio commentary, the way it captures an atmosphere and the build-up of tension, and this is no different. People keep asking, 'Phil, can he do it?', and I keep saying, 'No, no, of course not. It can't happen. It won't happen. It's all going to be an anti-climax.' And remember this is coming from someone who played for 20 years and who's a pretty shrewd judge of the game. In the next few balls, Stokes is dropped, survives a close LBW call and Leach is nearly run out – so my judgement isn't that far out. Now we're at that stage – as every Australian must have been with Edgbaston 2005 – when the finishing line is so near that not to get across will be an almost unimaginable kick in the guts. And then Stokes does it – smacks the ball for the winning boundary through extra cover. And at that moment two dozen pints of lager, burgers and several gallons of tomato sauce are thrown up in the air.

'You bastards! You've ruined my front-room carpet!'

There's ketchup all over the Axminster, mayo on the ceiling, red wine up the walls. It feels like the floor's going to go through with everyone jumping about. The springs on the sofa are ruined. And the weird thing is even now I get goosebumps when I think about it. Every penny of that redecorating bill was worth it.

To have one exhibition like that in a summer was great; to get two was simply unbelievable. Just weeks before I had actually been present at the World Cup final. As a former player, one of the great privileges of commentating is that you can allow yourself to get really excited. In the middle, you can't do that. Get too caught up in the moment and the emotion will be too much. Pressure and nerves will take over. You have to keep a cool head. Up in the commentary box, though, it's a totally different mindset. Think about it – as a commentator I can look forward to any number of things that would have totally terrified me as a player. Nowadays, I can't wait to watch Mitchell Starc and Pat Cummins bowl. If I'd been facing them I'd have felt sick. Same as watching someone bowling to David Warner – bring it on, can't wait. If he'd been snarling down the other end from me I'm not sure I'd have felt quite the same.

For sure, commentating is the second-best thing to playing. You get all the buzz and are present for the big glory moments without having to put yourself through the wringer to get there. As a commentator, I wake up early excited at the day ahead. I'm ready for the off. If I was playing, I'd have been shitting myself, praying for rain, or heading for a kip under a bench.

To see that last half-hour of the World Cup unfold was incredible. And again, Aggers was truly brilliant. My stint took me up to the last 30 minutes and so then I could sit and watch that intense drama unfold. Sit? Sorry, I mean run around like a headless chicken going, 'Run! Run! What are you doing? Jesus Christ!' That was the thing with that game: everyone, in the ground, at home, in the car, down at the Scrubs, was going through it as much as the players were.

Amid all that drama, the weight of what that victory would mean to the country, England having never won the competition before, let alone the craziness of the Super Over, Aggers somehow managed to describe with absolute precision exactly what was unfolding on the pitch. While everyone else was screaming, he found exactly the right mix of excitement and description, from the gut, from the soul, which is an art in itself. Me? I spent those final few balls in a corner of the box, looking over people's shoulders, spluttering, 'Vaughany! Vaughany! We can do this, can't we? Tell me we can do this.' I was like a child.

When Jos Buttler whipped the bails off and England won, there was a split second before the place erupted. I've never seen Lord's rock like that. The place was jumping. All the old boys usually asleep in their *Daily Telegraph* crosswords were there in their eggs and bacon ties singing 'Sweet Caroline'. In the commentary box, people were leaping around; pens, headphones, iPads and notepads were flying everywhere. I know we're meant to be impartial on *TMS*, but surely no one would have begrudged us a few seconds off.

After everyone had calmed down, I did find it in me to make a contribution. 'You will never see another game like that in your life. We have witnessed something unique.' I'm glad I was wrong and a month later Ben Stokes was back at it at Headingley.

After the elation, I just slumped in a corner. There's a picture of me and it looks like I've run a marathon – sweating, ripped shirt, exhausted with a huge smile on my face. It just shows, the crowd is everything in sport. The passion, the energy, is truly amazing.

In terms of sheer adrenaline and excitement, my most exciting on-mic moment came during the Trent Bridge Ashes Test of 2015 when Stuart Broad took a ridiculous eight for 15 as the Aussies were skittled for 60 in 111 balls – the shortest Test match first innings in history. I was commentating with Henry Blofeld, a man who likes to settle into a Test match. His usual routine is to say hello to the listeners – 'My dear old things, welcome to Trent Bridge on this beautiful sunny morning' – and then deliver any relevant bus and pigeon news. He never even got a chance to mention an errant wasp. At one point, Broad took five wickets in 19 balls. 'He comes in again. He's got him! He's got him.' Blowers' face was getting redder and redder. 'No scriptwriters – not even Sam Mendes in all those James Bond films – could have written this,' he wheezed. Blowers should know. Blofeld is after all one of 007's most infamous enemies – named after Henry's father Thomas who was a schoolboy pal of Bond creator Ian Fleming. By the end of Blowers' stint it was like sitting next to a slightly delirious lobster. I'd never seen the bloke so excited. He didn't so much leave the microphone as wobble away with steam coming out of his ears, in so doing perfectly capturing the atmosphere in the stadium. I wasn't in a much better state myself. It really wouldn't surprise me to receive a letter from someone saying they gave birth to twins while listening that morning. Little Phil and little Henry, or Philippa and Henrietta, will be out there somewhere.

You always know when something big is happening at a cricket match because suddenly there's no one walking round the ground. No one is up and down the stairs with pints or cheese sandwiches. The corridors at the back of the stands are clear. Forget the pork pies, the jugs of Pimm's. People are totally gripped by what's happening in front of them. Broad, a streaky bowler, had done something similar at The Oval six years earlier, during which I actually started singing 'Ashes coming home!' mid-broadcast, not the done thing when we're supposed to sit on the fence. 'Oh sorry,' I apologised, not altogether convincingly, 'am I on air?'

You do have to try to keep your emotions in check, but sometimes what's happening on the other side of the glass overwhelms you. I've been involved in a couple of those spells with the ball in my hand and it really does feel like there's something in the air. Added to that, we have the best seat in the house and when that drama unfolds right in front of your eyes it really is spine-tingling. I get very enthusiastic about it. People sometimes don't realise how much I actually enjoy cricket. Okay, not every session is going to see a flurry of wickets, a shedload of runs, and on *TMS* we can fill those gaps in the action by unveiling a couple of cakes or talking about Henry's trousers, but when those spells are afoot, that commentary box is something special.

Thankfully, however feverish the atmosphere, I've never actually sworn on air, which for someone who's spent his life around dressing rooms and, before that, my dad's silversmithing factory, I think is pretty good going. It helps that to go on air you have to put a headset on which also flicks a switch in your head – you go into broadcast mode, a different zone.

Of course, there can occasionally be issues with names. Myself and Aggers were called upon to commentate on the ICC Trophy Final between India and Pakistan, one of the biggest rivalries in world sport, at The Oval in 2017 – a truly remarkable occasion, one of amazing colour and noise. In fact, I'm reminded that when these sides met two years later at Old Trafford in the World Cup, one Pakistan fan arrived at the stadium on a horse.

It was a privilege to be part of and actually, as a commentator, easier to enjoy because there was none of the tension of England being involved. Me and Aggers were doing a bit of prep, looking down the list of players when our eyes alighted on the Pakistan opener Fakhar Zaman. We both looked at each other.

'Well, that's going to be a bit tricky, Jon,' I noted, 'I might leave that one to you. You're the boss after all.'

Pakistan batted first. 'Hello, everyone,' declared Aggers.

'Welcome to The Oval for India versus Pakistan. India have won the toss and elected to field first – and here come the Pakistan batsmen Azhar Ali and and Fakhaaarrr Zaman.' He really was doing his best to be polite, myself also joining in the vocal gymnastics.

After about ten minutes, Aggers turned to me off-mic. 'This is crazy,' he said. 'His name is Fakhar – so I'm just going to call him Fakhar.'

I gave him a look of, 'Well, okay, if you're sure.'

And then it happened. 'In goes Bumrah, over the wicket, bowls to Zaman, and he's flashed outside the off stump at that one, and he's caught behind.'

I chipped in with a few sage words before it became apparent there was an issue.

'He's hanging on for a moment,' explained Aggers. 'They're checking the no-ball.'

'Oooooohhhh!' (incisive remark from me).

'And let's have a look ... it is a no-ball. It's a reprieve for Fakhar. He'll come back, and it's going to be a free hit as well. What a lucky ...'

Aggers had developed an evil glint in his eye – and suddenly I realised what he was going to say. My mind raced. All I could think of was BBC inquiries, suspensions, a squalid end to both our broadcasting careers.

'What do I do?' I thought. 'Do I grab the mic out of his hand? Have a coughing fit? Knock his coffee in his lap? Faint? All of the above?'

It was as if I was in a film where they slow the frame speed as someone desperately tries to prevent a major incident – 'Nooooo ...'

'... chap,' said Aggers.

In that instant, I nearly fell off my stool, but somehow managed to retain my composure long enough to mutter unconvincingly, 'Well, it's the first one that he's gone after.' But I was gone and Aggers knew it. I couldn't speak for about five minutes.

That's the thing with *TMS*. The more comfortable you get, the more you start thinking about maybe adding a bit of your own character and humour. One time there was a discussion going on about heroes – who everyone had pictures of on their bedroom wall when they were growing up. Someone said David Gower, someone else said Ian Botham, and another said Wally Hammond.

'And what about you, Phil?'

'Linda Lusardi.'

I'm not totally sure Christopher Martin-Jenkins got the reference. I loved Christopher and we both seemed to enjoy the fact we were a bit of a strange coupling on commentary. CMJ had very clipped pronunciation and wrote for *The Times*. My way of talking is – how shall I put this? – a little bit more earthy, and I had always left the *Times* crossword for Gatt and Embers. Where translation was most needed was with my sense of humour. On one occasion I described someone being bowled as them having been 'Feng shui-ed'. I could see straight away he had no idea what I was talking about. They say you should never explain your jokes, but actually it was a great laugh illuminating CMJ because he was so lost.

'Feng shui,' I explained. 'Had his furniture rearranged.'

'Oh, the Chinese custom of moving the furniture around. Oh, I get it. I get it.'

Next day, again someone was bowled while we were on commentary.

'Feng shui-ed, Tuffers?'

'Feng shiu-ed, CMJ!'

'See, I remembered.' From that point on, everyone who was bowled in that match was feng shui-ed.

CMJ was a very educated chap. We'd chat, and talk some lovely cricket stuff, but then occasionally I'd try to lead him outside of his natural environment to places he was less likely to dwell. CMJ wasn't averse to such expeditions, but I always felt a little uneasy about starting the journey. It's like Christmas. You sit there, read out the silly joke from your cracker, and then maybe someone suggests charades. You've got a slightly older relative there who doesn't really do this sort of thing but, as its Christmas Day, rather surprisingly wants to join in. On one occasion we were watching a player who, with a curly mullet and thin moustache, looked every inch the classic '70s porn star. Well, not *every* inch, but you know what I mean.

I decided the time had come to try CMJ out with the porn star name game. For those who don't know it – and where have you been all your life? – your porn star name is the name of your first pet followed by your mother's maiden name. However, because we were on the BBC, and thinking CMJ might not be too keen to go along with that one, I altered the porn star name game to the rock star name game. 'Don't say porn star! Don't say porn star!' I was telling myself over and over to make sure I didn't embarrass CMJ.

Casually, I eased the conversation into the relevant domain. 'That player could easily be mistaken for a rock star,' I mused, 'I wonder what his rock star name would be?'

'His rock star name, Tuffers?'

'Yes, CMJ. Haven't you heard? There's a very simple way of

sort of coming up with your ('Don't say porn star! Don't say porn star!') rock star name. The name of your first pet followed by your mother's maiden name.'

He had a little think and eventually said, 'Well, when I was very young I did have a cocker spaniel called Rambler.'

Rambler! I could hardy breathe. Just add any maiden name you like for instant porn star.

Mine, for the record, is Trooper Mason – star of X-rated military-based films.

CMJ was one of those voices who represented cricket on the radio. When you heard CMJ you knew you were in good hands; the world was a safe and settled place. It was desperately sad when he passed away.

Sometimes, the funniest stuff happens off-air. At Lord's, when England hosted Bangladesh in 2010, we discovered from the running order that Aggers had been asked to ring the famous pavilion bell signalling the start of the fourth day's play. With him momentarily out of the studio, we decided to tease him a bit – we'd say we'd already been asked but had been unable to fulfil the commitment.

When he returned, Aggers was very excited and actually a little bit nervous – to ring the bell is an honour bestowed on only a select few.

'I can't believe I've been asked,' he told us.

'What?' we all went. 'Day four against Bangladesh in front of twenty people?'

Immediately, his bubble was pricked. 'Oh, yes,' he said, deflating rapidly, 'but it's still a great honour.'

One by one we started to pipe up. 'Well, they did ask me,' said Vaughany, 'but I've got to nip off to do something on telly.'

'Oh, I see,' said Aggers, his voice a little flatter than before.

'They asked me, too,' I revealed, 'but I've got to quickly present a prize at the back of the media centre.'

Poor Aggers. He was crestfallen, to the extent it would have been cruel to keep up the pretence any longer.

'You bastards!' he said, as he set off down to the pavilion.

Four years later, my own experience of ringing the bell was skewed slightly by myself. England had played Italy in the World Cup the night before and I might have got to bed slightly late. I was a little bit nervous as well. How many rings do you do? Do you hit it hard? Really go for it? Or just give it a little tap? All these things were going through a mind already befuzzled by a massive headache. Every chime felt like a reverberation through my soul.

TMS has been a part of my life now for almost 20 years. In all that time, nothing ever was, and I hope nothing ever will be, quite as challenging as Covid. The pandemic took its toll on everyone and like so many others I was grateful that cricket did its best to provide an element of escape. When West Indies came over to play three Test matches it was such a relief to have cricket to wallow in for a few weeks. As the touring team their players sacrificed a lot to make that work and we were duly grateful.

There were times during that series where I was stopped in my tracks by the underlying oddness of the situation, especially bearing in mind that cricket is a sport so overwhelmingly social. Working for *TMS* could be especially weird. Sat in the commentary box with a mask on, separated by screens, was strange enough, and that was before you looked out of the window and saw some of the world's best players and no crowd. Jimmy Anderson took his 600th Test wicket at Manchester and the only person applauding was a cameraman.

Like the players, the media had their own bubble at Old Trafford. Beforehand, we had a briefing from a police chief, at the end of which he asked if we had any questions. People were asking about PPE, where we could go and where we couldn't. Can we do this? Do we have to do that?

'Phil,' asked the officer, 'anything from your point of view?'

I mulled this over for a few seconds – 'Is there anywhere we can have a fag?'

It seemed like, for want of anything else to do, everyone took up an instrument. Charles Dagnall would be strumming on his bass, Aggers on his banjo. It was like living in the middle of a band practice. Me and Vaughany were doing our Tuffers & Vaughan radio show live from one of our rooms and next door Aggers kept coming out onto the balcony plucking his strings.

'Aggers! Shut up!' But still he kept on plucking. To this day I still feel he should count himself lucky he didn't end up wearing that thing.

At the end of the day we'd all go down to dinner, sit at little tables spaced out like in an exam hall, and have shouted conversations with one another.

'England batted well today I thought.'

'Sorry? Didn't quite catch that.'

'I SAID, ENGLAND BATTED WELL TODAY I THOUGHT.'

'Okay. Jesus! No need to shout.'

To be honest, because we were all brought together in these bizarre circumstances we had a great laugh, and spending a few days cut off from home wasn't so strange because we'd all done it before on tours, but there were definitely a couple of moments where all of us would just stop and think, 'Hang on, what exactly is happening here?' – generally when the pie and peas arrived, served in a box, with a plastic knife and fork. To counteract that, I'd usually bring along a case of wine.

TMS even managed to cover the winter series in Sri Lanka, albeit in conditions rather chillier than those in Galle or Colombo. Again, having cricket in my life really buoyed me, so much so that when the car arrived to pick me up and take me to the *TMS* studio at The Oval at three in the morning I almost sprang out of bed. Almost.

The original plan had been for the entire *TMS* team to form a bubble at the BBC's MediaCity base in Salford. However, when serious lockdown restrictions were enforced due to a second Covid wave, the producers had to be a little more imaginative. The result was a number of different branches. Myself and Dan Norcross were the Oval branch, Simon Mann and Michael Vaughan were the MediaCity branch, while Aggers formed a branch in the Belvoir, broadcasting from his attic in pyjamas. Thankfully, very few pictures exist of him in this get-up.

Commentating from a TV feed rather than from the actual match was something we all had to get used to. Not only were we denied the ability to bring the colour and atmosphere of the occasion to the listeners, but there was scope for a little confusion, including a classic moment in the first Test when Aggers watched what he thought was two wickets falling to consecutive balls.

'Has Root caught him again?' he wondered. 'It's spun out of the rough. Another brilliant catch – like an action replay.'

Back at The Oval I couldn't believe my luck.

'Aggers,' I pointed out, 'it *is* an action replay.'

It was the oddest feeling commentating on a Test being played in the heat and humidity of Sri Lanka while looking out on an Oval covered in snow. But, again, somehow it worked. What we couldn't see in Sri Lanka was replaced by what we could see as dawn slowly broke in London. Every day we'd watch the same little family of foxes pad across the outfield, no doubt heading back home after a night of urban bin-rummaging. And then there would be these glorious sunrises. For a bloke not known for being an early riser, it all came as a terrific surprise.

In the end, the oddness of the situation became part of its appeal. Stadiums are strange places when they're empty, a bit like the seaside in winter, and yet I love the seaside in winter and it wasn't long before I began to feel the same about that big empty frosty Oval. Meanwhile, people – technicians, production staff – would bring in cake (it's *TMS*, it's the law) and before I knew it I couldn't wait to get there every morning. Every day I went home with a smile on my face. I just hope we weren't too good at otherwise we'll never get sent abroad with *TMS* again.

Some of the letters we received at that time were truly humbling. What really touched me was the number of people who wanted to thank us for bringing some normality into their lives. 'I'm sitting here in Wigan. It's snowing. It's Tuesday. It's four o'clock in the morning. And I feel better than I have in months.' The message was always the same – 'everything seems all right again'.

Then there were the really heartrending ones. 'My dad's in hospital with Covid and I'm not allowed to see him. But I know he's listening to *TMS* and he knows I'm listening to it, too. For these few hours every day we can feel like we're together.' Wow. Until Covid I don't think I ever quite realised what *TMS* means to people. I always understood people loved it, but those human stories really did hammer it home. At a time when people felt they had nothing, *TMS* really did give them something good; something they couldn't get from the doctors or from going for a walk. Us just sitting, chatting away, gave them a release. And them letting us know gave us so much back.

CONCLUSION

I can thank my dad for those coffins in the shed. It was him who kept all my stuff and packed it away. I'm not a big one for mementoes. Some cricketers, you go in their houses and there's a little shrine to their career, but I'm not one of them. I had always kept my first England cap, but even that I gave to my brother's boy. He's probably doing the gardening in it right now. Better that than it be stuck in a cupboard for however many years. I also have the ball that I bowled the Aussies out with at The Oval in 1997, and the one I knocked the West Indies over with at the same venue six years earlier. But they're just rattling around in a drawer somewhere. I'd be up to my eyes in old pens, curtain hooks and staplers before I found them.

So while it has been incredible to sift through all my old stuff, chances are I won't keep much of it, certainly not the England blazers that have been chewed by rats, although I was pleased to find a few old England jumpers, the proper ones with the three lions and the crown raised slightly from the wool, plus the MCC versions, long-sleeve and short. Trouble was, after so long in a coffin they were all a bit mouldy and smelly. I shoved them in the washing machine and they came out in miniature.

The ECB never saw the commercial advantage of making a doll of me so they're destined for the bin.

What I really need to do is organise a bring-and-buy sale, but I don't think anyone has had one of those since 1985, so a lot of it will either go in a skip or to the charity shop. I'm looking forward to seeing people wandering around Sutton in old Middlesex sweaters from the '80s and '90s.

Wow, the '80s and '90s! It seems a lifetime ago and yet at the same time it feels like yesterday, like when a song comes on the radio and you realise it's 40 years old – 'How the hell did that actually happen?'

Just the other day, Athers rang. 'Tuffers,' he said, 'guess what?' With Athers, a question like that can lead anywhere. There was every chance he was about to impart some deeply technical information about the Large Hadron Collider or the diet of a rare moth in the Amazonian jungle.

'What?' I asked nervously.

'They've found some old cinecamera footage of the India tour we went on. Remember?'

'Hardly likely to forget, Athers. That was the one where we won nothing and every plane we went on nearly crashed.'

'That's it. Well, you remember Dermot Reeve had that little handheld camera? They've found the footage. We all look about 12 years old.

'But you look so big as well,' he added, which was a surprise, as we'd been there for about a month at that point and this footage had clearly been filmed on one of the rare moments when I wasn't on the toilet.

There was another clip showing me and Judge on exercise bikes which looked like they dated back to around 1940, possibly originally used as punishment in prisons.

Seeing yourself as you used to be is something that every sportsperson has to get used to – cricket's rain-sodden broadcasts are often filled with footage of old games – but this was somehow different. The unseen everydayness of playing for England brought to life in flickering detail. The fun, the togetherness, the absolute uniqueness of our position.

Watching the film made me realise just what a lucky boy I'd been, and it reassured me I'd always done the right thing in forever trying to be true to myself, on and off the pitch. Even with a bat in my hand, people knew I was either going to trip over or smack one for four. I'm not sure that's something you can wholly and deliberately set out to do; I think it's more in your character. Maybe it's no coincidence that I went on to do a lot of stuff on TV and stage. That side of me was always lurking in my make-up.

People still come up to me today and say they remember where they were when I did this, that, or the other. They might have been sitting at work with one eye on a television, at school doing double maths with a radio under the desk, or prosecuting a criminal trial while listening on an earpiece. It's a bit like everyone knowing where they were when JFK was shot, only not quite as dramatic. Okay, it's a bit weird when people tell me they enjoyed my antics so much they've named their dog after me – just think, right now there'll be someone picking up Tuffers' mess in the park – but I always feel massively privileged, quite emotional actually, when people come up and say those things.

It reminds me of being a kid, watching Alan Sunderland score Arsenal's last-minute winner against Manchester United in the 1979 FA Cup final when the Gunners had lost a two-goal lead towards the end of the game. Some things make you so happy they stay with you all your life. If I was going to play sport, I wanted to experience moments like that, create memories for myself and others. I just never quite appreciated how many of those memories would surround me stirring things up a little.

Sport can be a lonely place; it can be a tough place. But never should it be life and death. I was someone who always gravitated to a scrape – was, as stated, always 'in the vicinity' – but did so, most of the time, with a smile on my face. *How Not to Be a Cricketer*, at any level, is to take yourself too seriously. Soak up the good moments, learn from those that are more difficult, and you, too, will store up a shedful of memories. If among them isn't a spat with a bunch of line-dancing Australians, a flight from menacing Herefordshire farmers, or a trouser-dropping incident involving several dozen gloating New Zealanders, then I've got bad news – you really haven't lived.